The Politics of
Media Policy

The Politics of Media Policy

DES FREEDMAN

polity

First published in 2008 by Polity Press

Polity Press
65 Bridge Street
Cambridge CB2 1UR, UK.

Polity Press
350 Main Street
Malden, MA 02148, USA

ISBN-13: 978-07456-2841-7
ISBN-13: 978-07456-2842-4 (pb)

A catalogue record for this book is available from the British Library.

Typeset in 11.25 on 13 pt Dante
by SNP Best-set Typesetter Ltd., Hong Kong
Printed and bound in Great Britain by MPG Books Ltd, Bodmin, Cornwall

The publisher has used its best endeavours to ensure that the URLs for external websites referred to in this book are correct and active at the time of going to press. However, the publisher has no responsibility for the websites and can make no guarantee that a site will remain live or that the content is or will remain appropriate.

Every effort has been made to trace all copyright holders, but if any have been inadvertently overlooked the publishers will be pleased to include any necessary credits in any subsequent reprint or edition.

For further information on Polity, visit our website: www.polity.co.uk

Contents

Preface

This book aims to go beyond the often procedural and technical accounts of media policy to offer a broader picture of the voices, arguments, actors, arenas and controversies that dominate contemporary media policymaking in the USA and the UK. It offers an analysis of key policy topics in relation to two ways of thinking about politics – liberal pluralism and neoliberalism – and is meant to provide both a critical perspective on the dynamics of media policy and a guide to some of the major points of debate in the media today.

It is based, in part, on a series of interviews carried out mainly in London and Washington, DC, between October 2004 and January 2005, for research funded by the Economic and Social Research Council that investigated the balance of power in British and American media policy environments. Over forty interviews were conducted with a range of participants in the policymaking process, including politicians, special advisers, congressional aides, journalists, broadcasters, lobbyists, activists, academics and think-tank members. In order to ensure their full and frank participation, the interviews were carried out anonymously and their comments remain unattributed in the many references to these interviews used throughout this text. This book was completed thanks to a research leave scheme award provided by the Arts and Humanities Research Council.

I owe a great deal of thanks to all my colleagues in the Department of Media and Communications at Goldsmiths, although Natalie Fenton, James Curran and Aeron Davis in particular have listened patiently and responded critically on many occasions to my ideas. I would also like to thank Gholam Khiabany, David Hesmondhalgh, Chris Nineham, Colin Sparks and Toby Miller for their comments on my work. I have sorely tested the patience of Andrea Drugan at Polity, and her continuing support and calmness has been greatly appreciated. Finally, the book was completed despite the interventions of Stanley, Dexter and Kirstie. After six months of my being in a shed, I owe them everything.

1

Introducing Media Policy

Is policy political?

Media systems do not emerge spontaneously from the logic of communication technologies, or from the business plans of media corporations, or from the imaginations of creative individuals. The thesis of this book is that media systems are instead purposefully created, their characters shaped by competing political interests that seek to inscribe their own values and objectives on the possibilities facilitated by a complex combination of technological, economic and social factors. There is, therefore, little that is inevitable about the 'shape' of the media in a particular country or region – whether it is largely commercial or state-controlled; whether it is open or resistant to technological change; whether it is critical or complacent in terms of its social role. In other words, there is nothing predetermined about the personality of the media systems to which we are exposed. While the form a media system assumes at any one time is by no means the direct expression of a state's political priorities, it makes little sense to ignore the impact of political actors and political values on the character of the wider media environment. Media policy, the systematic attempt to foster certain types of media structure and behaviour and to suppress alternative modes of structure and behaviour, is a deeply political phemonenon.

This is not a widely accepted assertion. For many participants and commentators, media policy – like many other areas of public policy – refers to a *disinterested* process where problems are solved in the interest of the public through the impartial application of specific mechanisms to changing situations. Policymaking, in this view, is a rather technical procedure where policy changes emerge in response to, for example, technological developments that *necessitate* a re-formulation of current approaches and a new way of 'doing things'. Consider the introduction by the former British Secretary of State for Culture, Tessa Jowell, to what became the 2003 Communications Act: 'The infrastructure of the future *needs* fast, efficient and affordable communications – telecommunications, the internet and broadcasting. It *requires* the best competitive environment, effective regulation and continued public and private investment in the technologies of the future' (HoC Debates, 3 December 2002: col. 782 – emphasis added). Policy is therefore developed in a situation in which, because of irrepressible external forces, there is no alternative *but* to introduce new legislation or forms of regulation if desirable social or economic objectives are to be pursued.

This mechanical notion of policy creation often marginalizes politics and political agency in favour of administrative technique and scientific principles. This was most famously expressed by Harold Lasswell's conception of a 'policy science' where ' "policy" is free of many of the undesirable connotations clustered around the word *political*, which is often implied to mean *partisanship* or *corruption*' (Lasswell 2003 [1951]: 88). Policy development and implementation work best when they are executed in an informed but impartial manner that makes use of 'scrupulous objectivity and maximum technical ingenuity' (2003: 103). Such ideals remain relevant today. When asked about the principles that underpin his approach to implementing media policy, the head of one of the bureaux of the Federal Communications Commission (FCC) who deals daily with highly controversial matters concerning ownership and diversity, responded that policy application is a value-free and non-subjective process:

> Key principles – gee! You make it sound like this is some sort of philosophical inquiry here. As dry as it may sound, what we do is we have a governing statute that we try to implement, we have a series of bureau decisions over the year, sometimes in adjudicatory proceedings and sometimes in rulemakings that have set forth an established regulatory framework, and our job at the bureau level is really just implementing that statutory and regulatory framework. So it's not like we sit around and think big thoughts, about what is in some metaphysical sense good and evil, right and wrong. You know, Congress directs us to do things and we do our best to effectuate that.

'Effectuating' congressional will therefore requires the participation of groups of economists, technologists, legal specialists and government experts who are best able to safeguard the scientific and non-partisan nature of policymaking. Policy, according to this perspective, is the domain of small thoughts, bureaucratic tidiness and administrative effectiveness.

Another reading of Lasswell's work suggests that, far from trying to deny the political imbrications of policy, he was keenly aware that politics constitutes a key context in which policy ideas are developed and rolled out. The task is not to avoid politics per se but the subjective and irrational manner of what passes for much contemporary political discourse. 'Policy science', according to Robert Hoppe (1999: 204), 'was not a technocratic strategy in order to substitute politics with enlightened administration . . . For Lasswell policy science was a vital element in a political strategy to maintain democracy and human dignity in a post-World War II world.' Indeed, Lasswell called for a 'policy frame of reference' that 'makes it necessary to take into account the entire context of significant events (past, present and prospective) in which the scientist is living' (Lasswell 2003: 103). A sensitivity to political problems and aspirations is an essential part of the policy scientist's toolkit.

This book shares Lasswell's belief that policy is part of a strategy to attain specific political goals, and shares even many of his 'value goals' that underpin the definition of what can be considered a problem (if not his solutions to these problems). According to Lasswell, the term 'value' refers to ' "a category of preferred events," such as peace rather than war, high levels of productive employment rather than mass unemployment, democracy rather than despotism, and congenial and productive personalities rather than destructive ones' (2003: 95). Policy practice is a decisive arena in which different political preferences are celebrated, contested or compromised. This is far from the mechanical or administrative picture that is often painted, whereby faceless civil servants draft legislation on the advice of 'experts' and 'scientists', in the interests of a 'public' and at the behest of a 'responsible' government. 'Governing', argues Hal Colebatch (1998: 8), 'does not just happen: it is constructed out of an array of shared ideas, categories, practices and organizational forms. "Policy" is a way of labeling thoughts about the way the world is and the way it might be.' Policymaking can be seen as a battleground in which contrasting political positions fight both for material advantage, for example legislation that is favourable to particular economic or political interests, and for ideological legitimation, a situation in which certain ideas are normalized and others problematized.

This struggle occurs throughout the policy process, from the definition of the policy 'problem' through the selection of a 'solution' to the eventual distribution of that 'solution'. 'How a policy issue area is identified is political', argues Sandra Braman (2004: 154), 'because it determines who participates in decision-making, the rhetorical frames and operational definitions used, and the resources – and goals – considered pertinent.' Every step of the way is marked by fierce competition for, or deployment of, resources, influence and power. This is a conflict that has been theorized in radically different ways by, for example, pluralists who maintain that this struggle is ultimately fair and productive, and more critical voices who argue that there is a profoundly unequal playing field in which talk of fair competition and open bargaining is misplaced and idealized (see chapter 2). Either way, Nicholas Garnham is surely right to assert that media policymaking 'is not and can never be the tidy creation of ideal situations. Compromises and trade-offs are endemic' (Garnham 1998: 210).

This book aims to consider selected media policy developments in the light of these claims that (a) policymaking is a political act and (b) that it is marked by conflict. It focuses on the underlying assumptions and ideas that define policy 'problems', shape policy debates and guide policy objectives. The policy process is both structured – circumscribed by institutional, economic, technological and governmental dynamics – and actor-driven in the pursuit of different norms and goals. The book aims, in particular, to emphasize the importance of political agency in the media policy process. This is not to idealize media policymaking as a battle solely between rival individuals and their different beliefs but to suggest, as Thomas Streeter does in his account of broadcast deregulation in the United States, that 'ideas do matter' (1996: xii). The current system of commercial broadcasting in the USA exists not because it is intrinsically better than other systems or because it is somehow natural, but 'because our politicians, bureaucrats, judges and business managers, with varying degrees of explicitness and in a particular social and historical context, have used and continue to use the power of governments and law to make it exist' (1996: xii). Streeter argues, against those who see politics as marginal to the contemporary policy process, that a highly political concept – corporate liberalism – underpins the policy vision and regulatory behaviour of those who designed, and now sustain, the rules that surround the US broadcast environment.

This book builds on the framework of those theorists like Streeter who have sought to incorporate both agency and structure into their accounts of media policy and who see the policy process as driven by ideology as much as technology or economics. Peter Humphreys attributes the deregulatory transformations in European broadcasting to the 'paradigmatic change' (1996: 299) in the 1980s where pro-market ideas became increasingly hegemonic. Robert Horwitz argues that telecommunications deregulation in the USA in the same decade was due to an 'ideologically diverse regulatory reform coalition' (1989: 6) of social liberals and free-market conservatives, both of these being elements that identified existing regulatory structures as inefficient and undemocratic. Reflecting on the UK,

Goodwin (1998) and Freedman (2003a) identify the historical contradictions of Conservative and Labour politics respectively as central to the direction of British television policies. More recently, Chakravartty and Sarikakis (2006) and Raboy (2002) focus on capitalist globalization as the key influence on contemporary media policy; Galperin (2004) and Hart (2004) prioritize the institutional dynamics and political legacies that have decisively shaped the development of digital broadcasting; while McChesney (2000) and Hesmondhalgh (2005) assert that neo-liberal ideas are a source of inspiration for media policymakers on both sides of the Atlantic.

The intention of this book is to consider a range of contemporary media policy debates in the context of two competing political perspectives: first, through a pluralist account stressing the extent to which media policies are based on wide-ranging, informed and open debates and are aimed at maximizing the democratic, cultural and economic value of the media; and, second, through critiques of the policy process that identify the unequal power relations involved and the lopsided policy objectives that favour business and political elites, hallmarks of a neo-liberal political-economic order that has emerged since the 1980s. Both perspectives focus on the conflicted nature of the policy process, although the former argues that consensus is usually reached after the expression of different positions while the latter insists that such differences cannot be resolved in a just manner as long as access to resources and influence remains so uneven. Given existing levels of social inequality and the rising anger at political and media elites, an assessment is made of the wider implications of pluralist and critical accounts in terms of their ability to help the reader describe, evaluate and intervene in the direction of politics today.

The need for media policy

Media as a key economic sector

Media policy is public policy that responds to the distinctive characteristics of, and unique problems posed by, mass-mediated communications. First, of course, the media are significant economic entities responsible for an increasing amount of domestic and world trade. Figures that account for the specific value of the media are hard to come by and are notoriously unreliable – media, for example, are often counted as part of the 'copyright industries' in the USA and the 'creative industries' in the UK. Nevertheless, it is estimated that the 'core' copyright industries – films, television, home video, DVDs, business and entertainment software, books and music – account for approximately 6.5 per cent of US gross domestic product (GDP), some $819 billion, and employ over five million workers (Siwek 2006: 2, 4). These copyright industries now account for $110 billion in export activity, overshadowing that of motor vehicles ($76 billion), aircraft ($50 billion), food ($48 billion) and pharmaceuticals ($26 billion) (Siwek 2006: 5). The UK's 'creative industries' – as above but with the inclusion of fashion, architecture and design – account for at least £53 billion or 8 per cent of GDP and are one of the fastest-growing sectors, increasing by around 6 per cent since 1997 (Patent Office et al. 2005: 1). Media policies concerning the 'copyright' and 'creative' industries are therefore vital components of both domestic and supranational *industrial* policy.

Media as agents of social reproduction

Policy initiatives are also justified by the argument that media products are not ordinary commodities but systems and networks endowed with special political and cultural significance: that the symbolic transactions facilitated through the media play a key role in the production and reproduction of social relations. Borrowing from Lasswell's transmission model of mass communication, Nicholas Garnham argues the media are decisive agencies of social communication that play a constitutive, not passive, role in the process of social formation. 'Who can say what, in what form, to whom, for what purposes, and with what effect will be in part determined by and in part determine the structure of economic, political and cultural power in a society' (Garnham 2000: 4). The struggles to own and control media outlets, to have a range of perspectives aired, to have access to media technologies and to have the right to answer back – in other words, the struggle to talk to and be heard by others on a mass scale – shape not just individual identities but the broader networks of power in which we circulate. Tessa Jowell, in the same introduction to communications legislation that she described as economically necessary, makes this same point that:

> communications is about much more than economics. The Bill deals with the means by which our society speaks to itself. And, as it were, hears the echo. It is the means by which we talk to the world. It is a shaper of our culture, our identity and our values. (HoC Debates, 3 December 2002: col. 782)

This is an illustration of what Thompson (1995) and Silverstone (2005) refer to as the process of mediation: the rude intervention of the media into our everyday frameworks for making sense of the world. Mediation, argues Silverstone (2005: 189), 'requires us to understand how processes of communication change the social and cultural environments that support them as well as the relationships that participants, both individual and institutional, have to that environment and to each other'. Media are no longer extraneous to spheres of political action, personal identity and cultural belonging but become intimate participants in the way in which we experience these environments and how they are framed. The manoeuvres of politics, the legitimation of war, the conduct of business, the pursuit of fame, the celebration of identity, the search for friends and the naming of enemies are all, to one extent or another, subject to the play of media power. It is hardly surprising then that, in an increasingly mediated world, media systems should be subjected to forms of intervention, surveillance and control that befit their status as crucial agents of social meaning.

This has led to the highlighting of policy objectives that focus, in particular, on the fostering (and protection) of media forms that are seen to play a central role in the exercise of democracy and the involvement of citizens in the formal political process. In a liberal democracy, citizens require free and unfettered access to information and a full range of views if they are to make informed judgements about issues in the public sphere. This is one of the guiding principles of recent media legislation and regulation in the USA and the UK. For example, in a recent review of US broadcast ownership rules:

> the FCC strongly confirmed its core value of limiting broadcast ownership to promote viewpoint diversity. The FCC stated that 'the widest possible dissemination of information from diverse, and antagonistic sources, is essential to the welfare of the public.' The FCC said multiple independent media owners are needed to ensure a robust exchange of news, information and ideas among Americans. (FCC 2003a: 2)

The British government makes similar claims about the significance of the media:

> The functioning of democracy depends on the availability of a range of independent sources of information, views and opinions . . . Given the democratic importance of the media, we are concerned to see that diversity of opinion and expression is actually maintained and increased. Therefore we may continue to need backstop powers to underpin plurality of ownership and a plurality of views in the media. (DTI/DCMS 2000: 36)

The extent to which both American and British governments have actually fulfilled these commitments to diversity and plurality is rather dubious and will be examined in the chapters that follow. Nevertheless, it is the case that policy interventions are justified in the light of their stated desire to maximize the provision of different voices and perspectives in and through the media.

Media and 'market failure'

There is, however, another justification for intervention: that precisely because the media play such a crucial public role, there are particular economic characteristics of media goods that, if uncorrected in a capitalist market, may lead to the under-serving of audiences and further jeopardize the democratic functions the media are assumed to have. Many theorists have written about what they describe as the 'market failure' (Collins and Murroni 1996; Congdon et al. 1995; Graham and Davies 1997; Leys 2001) that arises from the very nature of the media industries. Garnham identifies three specific problems (2000: 55–62):

- Media markets tend towards concentration because of the economies of scale and scope that are used by corporations to offset the unpredictability of public taste and their resulting need for novelty and innovation. This is a situation that tends to favour large organizations that are able to offer a menu of choices and to cross-promote their offerings and therefore to spread risk throughout their portfolios.
- Media products are largely 'public goods' in that the viewing of, for example, a television programme does not compromise someone else's consumption of that programme (unlike eating an apple where one person's consumption of an apple prevents someone else from eating the same apple). This non-rivalrous characteristic of the media commodity means that corporations are forced to devise strategies, such as copyright, advertising and box office mechanisms, that transform public into private goods and introduce new monopolies throughout the media value chain. 'The reason why the media present a constant regulatory problem from the point of view of concentration as market failure is that their economic survival under market conditions depends upon the exploitation of monopolies' (2000: 58). Regulation is needed in order to supervise, control, or break up, these bottlenecks.
- Media systems are most productive when viewed as distribution networks rather than the producers of discrete products. Given that the media 'have been largely defined in terms of, and constructed around, technologies of reproduction and the systems of distribution based upon them' (2000: 59), they have a networked character that works best when

resources are shared rather than fragmented. Once again, this is likely to produce monopolistic, more than competitive, behaviour that is the antithesis of a healthy, open market system. In the era of a 'network society' (Castells 1996), where processes of mediation and information distribution are increasingly important for the economy as a whole, this is a problem that is not confined solely to media markets.

There are two further aspects of market failure that may lead to the need for 'corrective' intervention. First, market forces alone cannot deal with the 'externalities' that arise from media production and consumption – the unintended effects that result from the media's symbolic power that may be either negative or positive, for example the capacity to accelerate or reduce violence in society, to stimulate or distort political debates, and to improve or damage individual self-worth. Reflecting on negative externalities, Garnham describes this as a situation where 'a production process produces the product or service which a set of consumers purchase and, at the same time, a polluting by-product' (2000: 51). Public intervention is therefore required to confront the 'pollution' that arises from the purchase by facilitating the supply of products with positive, rather than negative, externalities. Baker (2002: 90–103) considers some of the policies designed as a response to externalities, for example the creation of antitrust rules, content subsidies, freedom of information legislation and support for public broadcasting.

Second, and related to this, media products are largely 'merit goods', products or services of significant social value but in which individual consumers are likely to under-invest (like, for example, dental treatment or preventative healthcare). Few people disagree that investigative journalism and current affairs programmes are a vital part of the television environment, but it is unlikely that viewers will anticipate their value and freely provide the revenue to sustain them. As Graham and Davies note:

> If all television is elicited by the market, there is a very real danger that consumers will under-invest in the *development* of their *own* tastes, their *own* experience and their *own* capacity to comprehend. This is not because consumers are stupid but because it is only in retrospect that the benefits of such investment become apparent. (1997: 20)

The British government, in particular, appear to agree with this assessment and acknowledge that, left to itself, 'the market may tend to focus investment only on more popular types of content, and therefore not deliver the full diversity of services that viewers and listeners want to receive' (DTI/DCMS 2000: 35). Corrective surgery, in the shape of public service broadcasting and positive content regulation, is therefore needed if the full range of individual and collective benefits that the media may potentially offer is to be guaranteed.

Definitions of media policy

Media policy, it would seem, refers to the attempts to realize the various economic, political and socio-cultural objectives described above, and yet it remains a rather ambiguous and slippery term. Does media policy refer to the actors involved, the instruments developed or the goals pursued? At its most simple, it refers to 'the ways in which public authorities shape, or try to shape, the structures and practices of the media' (Garnham 1998: 210). This definition focuses attention on the agents of change ('public authorities') and the specific mechanisms that are deployed *on* the media. It suggests that media policy is concentrated in the actions of governments, civil servants, regulators and experts – the 'policy communities' referred to in political science literature (Rhodes 1990) – and the development of legally enforceable rules. Denis McQuail defines media policy in a similar vein, as 'projects of government and public administration which . . . are characterized by deploying certain means in the form of regulatory or administrative measures that are legally binding, nationally or internationally' (2000: 21–2).

Media policy, according to this perspective, refers to the drawing up in inter-governmental, governmental or subcontracted institutions of a range of legally sanctioned tools that are designed to modify the structure and behaviour of media markets. Such tools might include:

- public ownership;
- subsidies;
- tax incentives;
- licensing powers;
- ownership restrictions;
- content rules;
- quotas;
- trade barriers;
- trade agreements;
- enforcement of intellectual property rules;
- restrictions on speech rights and information flows;
- codes and protocols;
- non-intervention.

The last method is of some real importance in that the decision not to intervene is, to those who share a neo-liberal conception of the world, a particularly enticing prospect as media markets would be left to govern themselves without outside interference. However, with the exception of the First Amendment to the US Constitution, the classic statement of 'negative policy' (Garnham 1998: 211), non-intervention is relatively rare – even in those states that express a commitment to 'small government' and 'open markets' – as we shall see in the following chapters.

This conception of media policy as the development in government-initiated fora of formal mechanisms for structuring media systems, while useful, is limited in two respects: first, that it provides a restricted account of key actors and venues; second, that it pays too little attention to more informal processes of policy development. Although it is true that the state is the decisive actor in media policy formation – and this book is over-whelmingly concerned with the exercise of state power in this area – it is obviously not the case that media policy is confined to figures in govern-ment and the civil service. Tunstall and Machin's argument that media policy 'seems to be an area in which national politicians combine fantasy, self-delusion, and high moral purpose, with a fondness for seeking crude short-term political advantage' (1999: 4) is perhaps accurate but hardly does justice to the complexity of the media policy field. Indeed, in the world's largest media market, the USA, '[u]nusually large numbers of players, types of players and decision-making venues are involved in the making of media policy' (Braman 2004: 169), including corporate lobbyists, NGOs, social movement activists, law enforcement officials, child protection agen-cies and consumer watchdogs, as well as government officials. While this may not be as exaggerated in a smaller country like the UK (see chapter 4), it is still the case that a growing number of 'stakeholders' in that country are either directly participating in or seeking to influence the policy process (Freedman 2006: 914). Globalization has further enlarged the membership of the media policymaking 'community' to the extent where, according to Sandra Braman (2004: 169), 'it is inappropriate and inadequate to use a venue-based approach (that is, "policy made the by the FCC") to defining media policy'.

It is also true that while the formal, public development of statutory instruments and regulatory tools is the most high-profile aspect of media policymaking, there are other less direct, deliberate and visible mecha-nisms that play an important role in the emergence of media policies and the shaping of media behaviour. Braman describes how 'latent policy', which is 'created as a side effect of decisions aimed at other subjects' (2004:

165), may have unintended consequences for the media – for example, the impact of trade union legislation in the 1970s and 1980s on the British newspaper industry (Seymour-Ure 1991: 206–7) or the effects of the Homeland Security Act on journalistic freedom in the contemporary USA (see chapter 6). Chakravartty and Sarikakis (2006: 5) talk about the impact of the 'politics of everyday life', the routine cultural expression of, as well as the more purposeful political resistance offered by, ordinary people in response to questions of media power. 'Alongside the official, documented and institutionalized realm of policymaking,' they argue (2006: 5), 'we recognize that there is also the ground of politics occupied by publics that engage in more informal ways with the social outcomes of policy shifts whether as audiences, consumers, citizens or merely by exclusion.' The mobilization against the FCC's attempts in 2003 to liberalize broadcast ownership rules is perhaps the clearest recent example of such informal yet determined public action (see McChesney 2004).

Lobbying, as we shall see in chapter 4, is another practice whose influence on the media policy process is hard to quantify, difficult to confirm, but impossible to ignore. Although it is highly regulated (at least in the USA) and subject to rules on transparency and finance, its opacity makes it difficult to pin down. The often unreported conversations between senior politicians and media moguls are a further case of 'informal policymaking' where deals or promises may be made outside the glare of publicity and the formal democratic process. Reflecting on the long-standing relationship between Tony Blair and Rupert Murdoch, Lance Price, a former media adviser to Blair, acknowledges that:

> It's true that Rupert Murdoch doesn't leave a paper trail that could ever prove his influence over policy, but the trail of politicians beating their way to him and his papers tells a different story . . . I have never met Mr Murdoch, but at times when I worked at Downing Street he seemed like the 24th member of the cabinet. His voice was rarely heard . . . but his presence was always felt. (Price 2006: 32)

This suggests a form of 'invisible' but highly effective policy influence that, in this case, has extended across a range of policy issues, from the decision on whether or not Britain should adopt the Euro currency to discussions concerning its rules on cross-media ownership. Private conversations can also spill over into public comment as happened when Rupert Murdoch repeated Tony Blair's alleged criticism of the anti-American tone of BBC coverage of Hurricane Katrina. Given that this conversation was publicized in September 2005, right in the middle of BBC Charter Review and in the run-up to a white paper on the future of the BBC, it would be reasonable to suggest that the media policy process is not entirely immune from the impact of high-level casual encounters and the political preferences stated therein. Indeed, Sandra Braman suggests that the barriers between devising policy (a public event) and formulating strategy (a private matter) are being undermined by the rise of 'purely private sources of decision-making with constitutive impact [and] informal aspects of decision-making processes that are highly influential but have received relatively little analytical attention' (2004: 168).

The central characteristic of media policy, therefore, is not where it is made (a venue-based approach), or about the specific tools developed (an instrumental approach), or the results achieved (an ends-driven approach). Instead, media policy should be defined in a more dynamic way as a process that concerns the interaction between different *actors*, the *institutional structures* within which they work and the *objectives* that they pursue. Media policy refers to the variety of ways in which interested participants seek to develop both formal and informal mechanisms to shape the conduct of media systems, or, as Marc Raboy puts it, to 'the full range of attempts to influence the orientation of these [media] systems by social actors mobilizing whatever resources they can in order to promote their respective interests' (2002: 6). This book focuses, in particular, on assessing the *ideological* resources brought to the media policy process and the contrasting sets of ideas that are either normalized or marginalized in the clashes that take place.

Policy/regulation/governance

It may be useful at this point to distinguish between several terms that are often used interchangeably in media policy literature but which, in the context of this book, refer to separate, although interconnected, phenomena: *policy*, *regulation* and *governance*. If media policy suggests the broader field where a variety of ideas and assumptions about desirable structure and behaviour circulate, then regulation points to the specific institutional mechanisms for realizing these aims. Abramson argues (2001: 301–2) that media regulation 'flows from media policy: where policy sets out the state's role in bringing its preferred mediascape into being, regulation is the instrument through which the state supervises, controls, or curtails the activities of non-state actors in accordance with policy'. Regulation, therefore, consists of the deployment of specific and binding implements used to intervene in media markets and systems: quotas, ownership restrictions, competition rules, and so on. Regulatory bodies may be more or less independent of the state – and many organizations from the FCC to the British media regulator Ofcom and the Press Complaints Commission (PCC) make great play of their 'autonomy' – but they nevertheless operate within an environment, and are responsible for achieving objectives laid down by the state. The practice of industry self-regulation further demonstrates the possible independence of actors in the regulatory process, but those actors are still subject to the codes, laws and regulations drawn up in response to specific media policy concerns and the ideological frameworks on which they are based.

Where regulation implies the application of rules developed through governmental processes, governance is a more contemporary phenomenon that reflects the shifting locale of power towards supra- or sub-national levels as well as the development of non-governmental modes of organization and forms of influence. As distinct from the concept of government, governance 'is seen to imply a network form of control, to refer primarily to a process and to have associated with it diverse agents' (Daly 2003: 115–16). It is therefore broader both spatially and instrumentally than regulation and 'refers not only to formal and binding rules, but also to numerous informal mechanisms, internal and external to the media, by which they are "steered" towards multiple (and often inconsistent) objectives' (McQuail 2005: 234). The increasing importance to the media of supranational bodies like the World Trade Organization (WTO), the World International Property Organization (WIPO) and the Internet Corporation for Assigned Names and Numbers (ICANN) has led to several theorists pronouncing the emergence of a system of 'global media governance' (Ó Siochrú et al. 2002) composed primarily, but not exclusively, of intergovernmental agencies organized around the United Nations.

We may summarize the differences as follows:

- *Media policy* refers to the development of goals and norms leading to the creation of instruments that are designed to shape the structure and behaviour of media systems.
- *Media regulation* focuses on the operation of specific, often legally binding, tools that are deployed on the media to achieve established policy goals.
- *Media governance* refers to the sum total of mechanisms, both formal and informal, national and supranational, centralized and dispersed, that aim to organize media systems according to the resolution of media policy debates.

While we are primarily concerned here with the ideas and values that underpin the process of media policy formation – and less focused on the admittedly crucial technical questions that arise from specific forms of media regulation and governance – some degree of overlap is probably unavoidable as many concepts that underpin policy debates come to be realized and fleshed out through particular acts of regulation and governance.

Media policy or media policies?

There is a further complication in that, to any thoughtful commentator on the issue, there is clearly no such thing as media policy, in the sense of a single or uniform pattern that can describe all the various modes of structuring media performance and media systems. There are, of course, media poli*cies*, hugely different approaches that depend on the specific medium under consideration: daily newspapers or free-to-air broadcasting; the web or pay-television; magazines or recorded music; cinema or computer games. Media policy is, at best, an umbrella term to describe the whole range of discourses and methods used to shape the behaviour of specific media; at worst, it is a loose and highly misleading way of ordering a heterogeneous and multi-layered environment (or series of environments).

One way of dealing with the multiple character of the mass media has been to differentiate media policy systems based on perceptions of their different characteristics and capacities: for example, the extent to which specific media present security dangers or facilitate other forms of 'harm', or around issues such as audience access, scarcity of physical resources and technical ease of regulation. Policies aimed at a medium that is generally diffused (terrestrial television or radio) are likely to be more heavily regulated than those aimed at a medium that is 'called up' by audiences (the web); different perspectives are also likely to be applied to a medium perceived to have limited political importance (the music industry) as compared to one with a clear impact on daily public life (newspapers); a medium that depends on the use of publicly owned spectrum (broadcasting) cannot expect to be treated in quite the same way as one that does not (magazines).

Theorists have therefore made a basic distinction between press and broadcast policies where, in countries like the USA and the UK, newspapers are very lightly regulated and their operations left substantially to market forces, while broadcasting is subject to more extensive policy regimes and required to deliver a range of public policy objectives (Curran and Seaton 2003; Graber 2002: 48–55). However, because of the democratic function that newspapers are perceived to play in facilitating informed debate and checking state power, the press are actually subject to forms of policy action (for example, ownership restrictions, concentration rules and subsidies) along the same 'public interest' lines as broadcasting. Garnham, therefore, presents another way of breaking 'media policy' down into its constituent parts (2000: 48):

- *Mass media policy* focused on press and broadcasting as 'media of public communication and thus as institutions straddling the private economic sphere and the public political sphere' (2000: 48). Policy intervention is justified on the basis that these media are obliged to carry certain social responsibilities and to fulfil certain public obligations.   *passive audience*
- *Telecommunications policy* based on the idea of telecommunications networks that 'developed as carriers of private communication between individual private persons' (2000: 48). Here, 'any regulation of the messages passing over the network was and is regarded as an illegitimate infringement of individual freedom, autonomy and privacy, as indeed an infringement of the right to free speech' (2000: 48). *fair access*

However, the situation has been radically changed in recent years by the phenomenon of convergence and the importance of what McQuail notes as the 'hybrid status' of the internet (2005: 238). Both a telecommunications network and a public communications system, the web, in particular, disrupts any easy distinctions between rival models of media regulation and invites policy interventions from a variety of political, economic, social and cultural perspectives. Internet activity, argues Sandra Braman, involves the 'blending' (2004: 159) of previously distinct communication styles – one-to-many and one-to-one, synchronous and asynchronous, interactive and passive – to the extent that 'point-to-point communication with a single receiver can no longer be excluded from discussions of media law' (2004: 159). Convergence, therefore, muddies the difference between traditional 'mass media' and 'telecoms' perspectives on policy and necessitates, according to Collins and Murroni (1996: 175), a technology-neutral approach – 'fuzzy law' that 'increases regulatory discretion' and relies more than previously on self-regulation and co-regulation. Should traditional forms of content regulation be applied to the burgeoning amount of material facilitated via websites? Should traditional forms of infrastructure regulation be applied to a series of networks that are carrying both private conversations and public communications? These are precisely the sorts of questions that are exercising policymakers as they grapple with issues of 'net neutrality' (in the USA) and the extension of content rules to online media (as in the European Union).

To focus exclusively, however, on the differences *between* media systems is to reify the technological categories on which such distinctions are made and to fix in perpetuity the often historically specific roles assigned to different media. For example, as Curran and Seaton argue, the decision to regulate broadcasting because of spectrum scarcity issues is an 'ideological argument, masquerading as a technical one, since it presupposed that public interest management of spectrum scarcity was best entrusted to the state rather than the marketplace' (2003: 388). Furthermore, the aim of this book is not to address the most economically efficient or socially productive form of regulation for different media (as crucial as that is) but to consider the key arguments posed and objectives sought in the drawing up of policies affecting different media. The focus then becomes less on technological specificity or on whether a *dirigiste* or laissez-faire approach is most appropriate, but about the kinds of values, beliefs and interests that seek to exercise influence in and through media policy formation. As Shalina Venturelli argues: 'the debate over the role of the state in the audiovisual sector does not in reality involve a choice between intervention and non-intervention but rather a choice between forms of intervention and which social interests ought to benefit' (1998: 189). For Robert McChesney, 'the real issue is not regulation versus free markets, but, to the contrary, regulation in the public interest versus regulation to serve purely private interests' (2003: 126). A crucial element of media policy analysis is an assessment of the extent to which certain social groups dominate and certain ones are marginalized from the exercise of power.

The use of the term 'media policy' in this book, therefore, does not imply that there exists a single or predictable account of the structuring of media power; nor does it imply that technological characteristics are of no importance in the development of media policy and the dynamics of media systems. Rather, media policy is understood here as shorthand for the formal as well as informal strategies, underpinned by specific interests, values and goals, that shape the emergence of mechanisms designed to structure the direction of and behaviour in particular media environments.

The scope of the book

Despite the much-needed call in recent years to 'de-westernize media studies' (Curran and Park 2000), readers will have noticed that all examples provided thus far have been confined to two countries only: the United States of America and the United Kingdom. This is not an accident and, indeed, the USA and the UK provide the two case studies on which this entire research is based – a pitifully small sample of the rich and complex media policy debates that are taking place around the world today. In some ways, they are a bad choice: they share a common language, they both have highly developed media environments and similar systems of representative democracy, and they are linked in innumerable historical and contemporaneous ways. In contrast to the 'polarized pluralist' or 'democratic corporatist' models that underpin other media systems, British and American media are both examples of a liberal pluralist model that privileges market forces, self-regulation and strong professionalization (Hallin and Mancini 2004: 67). A focus on an Anglo-American axis is likely to reveal virtually nothing about the wider dynamics of globalization, about emerging centres of media power around the world and the policy regimes that accompany them, about the variety of public policy objectives that are pursued beyond the North Atlantic, or about the movements built and strategies employed by different populations in response to their own systems of media control.

The reason why these two have been selected is not, I hope, an example of the 'self-absorption and parochialism of much Western media theory' (Curran and Park 2000: 3) or an unthinking claim that the lessons from this analysis are easily universalizable. The policy discourses and media structures in both countries are, after all, the products of quite specific historical, political and cultural conjunctures. Yet it would be foolish to deny that the USA and the UK are highly powerful players on the world stage. Not only do their products dominate world media markets – in the area of broadcast television, for example, they account for over 80 per cent of finished programme sales and 65 per cent of formatted programme hours around the globe (TRP 2005: 13, 17) while US companies alone 'own between 40 and 90 per cent of the movies shown in most parts of the world (Miller et al. 2005: 9) – but the structure of their respective media systems and policy orientations have also been influential in shaping the institutional and regulatory forms adopted by other countries, for example with the influence of the FCC model in Latin American countries and the adoption of a version of the BBC model in many European or Commonwealth states. The selection of the USA and the UK as case studies for this book simply reflects their historical, continuing and sometimes decisive impact on media developments beyond their borders and is not meant to suggest that they are the only or the most desirable models available.

It is also the case that the political perspectives that, it is argued here, underpin much contemporary media policymaking emerged from, or were at least influenced by, developments in the USA and the UK. The concept of pluralism was heavily debated by political scientists and sociologists in post-Second World War America and the thesis that the USA provided a model example of pluralist government was one that generated a substantial number of claims and counter-claims (see chapter 2). Similarly, the neo-liberal consensus that is seen by many as the dominant mode of political-economic thinking in the world today originated in the late 1970s in the USA, the UK and China and was popularized, in particular, in the 1980s administrations of Ronald Reagan and Margaret Thatcher (Harvey 2005: 1). The structures and consequences of British and American policy regimes are not, by any means, the only examples of media policy but they are certainly among the most influential. If the call to de-westernize media studies and media systems is to be taken seriously, it requires an accurate assessment of the ideas that are dominant in media policy debates in the USA and the UK – if only that they may be identified and then either modified or rejected.

A further justification for such a narrow sample is that, despite their apparent similarities, the US and UK models of media policy are hugely different. The political systems from which they emerge may share aspects of representative democracy but there are significant contrasts between their respective modes of government, political traditions, party organization and ideological values (crudely expressed as a difference between an attachment to individualism and personal liberty in the USA and a commitment to collectivism and social responsibility in the UK). Their media environments are, of course, also radically dissimilar, with the USA seen as having the prime example of a financially led and commercially oriented system while the UK is seen as having one that embodies ideals of public service and that is based on a mixed economy of public and private ownership. Their approaches to and institutions of media policy also reflect different conceptions of the role of the state. US policy is often perceived as the epitome of a non-interventionist and commercially minded approach, while UK policy embodies the more *dirigiste* outlook and culturally focused set of concerns common to other European countries (Hallin and Mancini 2004: 49). Indeed, there is a strong sense in which British broadcasting policy, for example, was drawn up in direct response to what were seen as the drawbacks of a wholly commercial system such as the one that was emerging in the USA in the 1920s (Hutchison 1999: 21–2).

The book will therefore be comparative in its outlook and seek to evaluate the extent to which these generalizations about the differences between British and American media structures and policy systems hold true. This involves tackling two sets of polarized claims, firstly, that there are clear, almost unbridgeable, differences between the two countries along the lines of Tunstall and Machin's assertion that:

> Whereas Washington does have a general policy for the media and has encouraged an ever more commercial (and exporting thrust), Britain has no such general policy. Like most other European countries, Britain has no overall media policy, no integrated film-and-TV industry, and no real strategy for confronting Hollywood. (1999: 264)

The notion that Britain has no systemic media policy is complemented by the argument that what there is of it is poorly coordinated and inconsistent, particularly in comparison with the USA. Seymour-Ure (1991: 209) talks of the 'fragmentation and unevenness' of the British approach, while Curran and Seaton, in early editions of *Power without Responsibility*, speak of the need for a unified communications ministry to overcome British governments' confused and contradictory attitude towards media policy (1991: 333).

Secondly, and in contrast to this, there is an argument that, while there are clear residual differences between US and UK media policy systems that reflect their particular histories and structures, there are significant and growing points of overlap between the two. This is illustrated by the creation of the 'converged' UK communications regulator Ofcom, partially based on the model of the FCC, as well as the acceptance of many of the pro-market ideas that underpin media policy objectives in both countries and the strategies and mechanisms created to realize these aspirations (Freedman 2006).

The scope of the book is limited in another way: that it is neither possible nor desirable to address all the media policy issues we are facing today. Partly because of the importance of mediation processes and partly because of the increasing complexity and volume of media legislation and regulation, the media policy field has expanded to such an extent that it is rather difficult to identify precisely its boundaries. 'When all surfaces are potential screens and all texts potential commodities', argues Abramson (2001: 312), 'media policy's field of intervention becomes public space itself.' Recent technological innovations have only exacerbated this problem, with the internet alone being the focus of more than 600 bills during the 107th US Congress (Braman 2004: 154). This has also led to tremendous confusion amongst policy players both about how existing policy objectives can be pursued and about whether new objectives ought to be designed that better reflect the dynamism and scale of digital developments. Should traditional concerns about freedom and harm be prioritized or is a new emphasis on technical standards and network rights required? In an era of convergence, are the concerns that dominated the common carrier model of regulation to be automatically applied to other models of media regulation or does it still make sense to separate them out?

The solution employed in this book for dealing with the potentially endless topics and debates that characterize contemporary communications policy is to concentrate on what Robert McChesney (2003: 126) describes as the 'fundamentally public and social nature of media systems', and to select those issues that are most centrally concerned with the facilitation of shared and collective forms of communication through which *public* discourse is produced and controlled. Indeed, it follows from a notion that one of media policy's most important characteristics concerns the mediation of the public itself: that the '*constitutional* functions of media policy, determined by constitutional law, address the conditions under which the public can actively engage in the production and reproduction of the society in which members of the public live' (Braman 2004: 179). This leads to an emphasis on what might perhaps be seen as the more traditional 'mass media' policy issues rather than those that deal with the 'private' issues confronted in 'common carrier' telecommunications policy: issues concerning the ownership of large-scale media organizations, the control of mass mediated content and the fostering of public media systems. While it is true that the internet has problematized the distinction between 'public' and 'private' modes of communication, it is still possible to maintain that there are differences between the policy implications of 'a site for a series of private individual transactions on the model of the market' (the telecommunications model) and, because of its general accessibility, 'a site for public communication within the public sphere with associated rights and responsibilities for those who control and use it' (Garnham 2000: 48). It is this latter site on which the book is predominantly focused.

This means that a whole series of highly significant topics – including the details of the net neutrality debates and questions concerning the digital divide, broadband policy, internet governance and telecommunications ownership – are largely absent. Instead the book addresses:

- The political frames of pluralism and neo-liberalism through which the US and UK media policy systems have been conceptualized and critiqued (chapter 2).
- The shift in meaning of four key principles that underpin British and American media policy development: media freedom, the public interest, diversity and pluralism (chapter 3).

- The dynamics of the media policymaking process and issues of participation, transparency, centralization and rationality (chapter 4).
- The re-structuring of broadcast ownership regulations in the USA and the UK (chapter 5).
- The direction of debates concerning content regulation, including the fining of US broadcasters for obscenity breaches, the commitment in the UK to self-regulation of content and the relationship between security concerns and media policies (chapter 6).
- The future of public service broadcasting in the UK and the controversies concerning the governance of public broadcasting in the USA (chapter 7).
- The arguments for digital switchover in the USA and the UK and the discourses that underpin policy initiatives concerning peer-to-peer networks and intellectual property rights (chapter 8).
- The contribution of the USA and the UK to attempts to build global media policy frameworks and an assessment of the impact of export-led strategies on domestic media systems (chapter 9).

In dealing with all these issues, there is one final point that needs clarification. While we welcome the recent literature that focuses on the challenges posed by under-represented and previously marginalized social groups to dominant concepts of media structure and power (for example, Chakravartty and Sarikakis 2006; Hackett and Carroll 2006; Klinenberg 2007; McChesney 2004), this book is focused on something rather different in that most of the case studies deal with policy debates that are dominated by powerful corporate, political and governmental interests. Media policy *ought* to be a field that is open to resource-poor groups with competing voices and different objectives but, in reality, it is not; it is a process that, for all its conflicts, is ultimately dominated by those with the most extensive financial, ideological and political resources who are best able to mobilize their interests against their rivals. In that sense, it is a study of elite power and not of popular resistance, although, of course, the strategies to be adopted by the latter depend, in part, on understanding the techniques of the former to maintain control. Media policy is not at all a process wholly determined by elites but it is impossible to understand its dynamics – and therefore to change its direction – without an appreciation of the underlying ideas that mobilize its most powerful participants. As Aeron Davis argues:

> Unequal power relations are thus maintained less by mediated elite persuasion of the masses and more by numerous micro-level decision-making processes within elite networks. The communication which takes place

between powerful elites – either through the mass media or in more private communication spheres – in fact excludes the mass of consumer-citizens. (2003: 684)

This book will examine the extent to which contemporary media policy – despite the formal transparency and accountability of many of its procedures – is one such sphere in which this inter-elite communication (and public exclusion) takes place.

This approach is therefore a determined way to assess fully the discourses that dominate media policy today and, in so doing, to help illuminate and resist what many see as the thoroughgoing neo-liberalization of the media systems to which we regularly turn for a variety of our social, political and personal needs. The spirit of the book is unashamedly critical: to subject 'common-sense' media policy objectives and instruments to detailed interrogation in the spirit of Nicholas Garnham's assertion that 'we always need to ask the question why this policy in this form now and in whose interest is it designed? Neither policies nor their presentation should ever be taken at their face value' (1998: 210). That is, of course, true both for the subject of this book and for the arguments contained within it.

2

Pluralism, Neo-liberalism and Media Policy

The contention of this book is that media policies are not merely techno-logically determined or economically inevitable, but are the products of systematic interventions into media systems based on a complex range of political values and objectives. These are not necessarily narrowly partisan operations that only reflect the interests of an identifiable party clique, a potentially conspiratorial notion that separates the performance of specific Labour/Conservative, Republican/Democrat administrations from wider social forces. Instead, policies can be seen as political actions designed to promote more general ways of organizing public life – to defend national security, to protect the public, to increase efficiency or to maximize the flow of market forces – and to produce mechanisms to realize these aims. Policies emerge from a combination therefore of (often short-term) party political visions and more structural factors that include the influence of other social groups and institutions, including business, the civil service, media professionals and even the public.

This chapter focuses on two political perspectives that underpin contrast-ing accounts of media policy processes, the narratives of liberal pluralism and neo-liberalism, and considers 'ideal type' scenarios of both pluralist and neo-liberal media policies. There is, of course, an important distinction between the ways in which the two terms are used: pluralism is often deployed by participants to describe and justify existing media policy arrangements, while neo-liberalism is more likely to be used in a way that critiques, rather than defends, the current terms and conditions of media policy. It is also the case that they are by no means the only two political frames for contextualizing media policy. Peter Humphreys (1996), for example, summarizes the differences between majoritarian and consensus forms of broadcast governance; Baker (2002) considers elitist, liberal plural-ist, republican and complex theories of democracy in relation to media performance and policy; Hallin and Mancini (2004) contrast the workings of liberal versus welfare state democracies, individual versus organized pluralism, bureaucratic versus clientelist administrations and moderate versus polarized pluralism in relation to the regulation of different types of media systems (2004: 50–61). Although these all contain useful points of reference, they lack the analytical power both of liberal pluralism's continuing ability to provide the explanatory framework for modern liberal democratic politics and of neo-liberalism's capacity to provide a coherent explanation for the obsession with free markets sweeping the world today. They may be relatively broad (and often internally contradictory) brushes to do justice to the specific dynamics of British and American policy, but they nevertheless connect to core ideas, values and beliefs concerning media policy in both countries and will serve as the main conceptual frameworks that are relevant to the policy case studies in the following chapters.

Pluralist perspectives on politics and policy

Many of the assumptions about the political character of contemporary western societies and the balance of power in policy formation emanate from the rich debates in US political science that emerged in the second half of the twentieth century. Responding to criticism that American society was dominated by political and financial elites that skewed the operations of democracy, liberal pluralists argued that US politics was a competitive arena in which different interests vied for power and influence but in which there was no single dominant voice. US-style liberal democracy was cemented by transactions that took place in a 'political marketplace where what a group achieves depends on its resources and its decibel rating' (Ham and Hill 1993: 29), a measure determined less by fixed notions of class or financial power than by the more subjective variables of status and insider knowledge.

Pluralists did not deny, however, that there were inequalities in the political process and that some participants were better resourced and connected than others. Indeed, the most famous statement of pluralism, Robert Dahl's *Who Governs?* (Dahl 1961), opens with the following question: 'In a political system where nearly every adult may vote but where knowledge, wealth, social position, access to officials, and other resources are unequally distributed, who actually governs?' (1961: 1). Dahl's answer was that – at least in his case study of the political system of New Haven, Connecticut – politics was dominated by coalitions, by rival groups of actors and interests, none of whom could be said to exercise complete control. According to Dahl, 'there was no clear center of dominant influence in the [political] order. No single group of unified leaders possessed enough influence to impose a solution' (1961: 198), certainly not the economic or social 'notables' who had only a limited and shifting impact on New Haven politics. Pluralist politics, argued Dahl, was notable for its 'dispersion of political resources' and the 'disappearance of elite rule' (1961: 85, 86) that resulted in polyarchy, a benign, if not fully democratic (at least in its classical Athenian sense) mode of politics.

Pluralist arguments were especially influential in analyses of US public policy dynamics where discussion was focused on the potential threat to democracy posed by the rising number of special interest groups in the political marketplace. As well as Dahl, theorists including Cater (1965), Freeman (1965) and Truman (1951) argued that no one group dominated the policy process which was instead marked by vigorous competition between different participants drawn from Congress, federal agencies and specialized interests. Freeman (1965: 5) called for an emphasis on 'subsystem actors', a crucial element of 'the plural patterns of power and decision-making within the national government as they mirror the functional specialization and diversity of American society' (1965: 6). Cater (1965: 17) described these highly segmented new policy spheres as 'subgovernments', compact networks of people with shared interests and the potential to challenge executive power. Freeman spoke of the triangular arrangement of congressional committees, executive bureaus and interest groups which add to the 'complex and pluralistic committee matrix within which so many decisions are reached in a decentralized fashion' (Freeman, 1965: 25). Public policy influence is therefore simultaneously dispersed and contained within these subsystems.

Pluralists argued that any danger of undue private interest group influence would be countered by the openness of and multiple access points into the policymaking process which would actually add to the stability of the system. Far from one group being able to hegemonize control, these arrangements were designed to produce consensual and particularistic policymaking bodies and coherent policy outcomes. Influence stemmed not only from economic power but also from the prestige, profile and vision of the participants. The policy process, they argued, was therefore a mirror of US society, itself described as a fairly open 'mosaic of overlapping groups of various specialized sorts' (Truman, 1951: 43). This picture of an open yet stable policy system relies on a conception of power as decentralized and multifaceted: both formal and statutory (as in executive power) and, as Cater puts it (1965: 4), 'mobile and transitory' in the bargaining-led atmosphere of subgovernment.

It is significant for the argument of this book that many leading pluralist thinkers of the time emphasized the importance of the mass media in facilitating pluralist arrangements. Cater (1965), Dahl (1961), Freeman (1965) and Truman (1951) all argued that a 'free' communications system was necessary to provide the information through which citizens would be able to evaluate the claims of competing groups and thus ensure the creation of public opinion that 'must play a continuous role as arbiter among the contestants' (Cater 1965: 15). Dahl devotes a whole chapter in *Who Governs?* to the issue of information control and newspaper influence. Describing the media as key participants in the framing of politics, he paints the picture of a pluralist media environment where the impact of the press is restricted both by the multiplicity of information sources as well as by the 'low salience of politics in the life of the individual' (1961: 264) which makes the citizen a difficult target for straightforward political propaganda. This combination of instrumentalism and limited media influence embodies what James Curran describes as the 'liberal functionalist' approach to the mass media – that their role is 'to assist the collective self-realization, co-ordination, democratic management, social integration and adaptation of society' (2002: 136).

Critics from *within* the pluralist tradition later came to recognize some of the limitations of the policymaking system and acknowledged the potentially de-stabilizing impact of privately held power on US public policy. In a system described by Theodore Lowi (1979: 51) as 'interest-group liberalism', the notion of subgovernments and subsystems was now seen as too rigid and narrow to articulate the pervasiveness of private interests as they were thoroughly mobilized throughout a policymaking process described by Charles Lindblom as coming under 'a special control by business' (1980: 74). Reflecting on the increasing influence of lobbyists and experts in Washington, DC, Hugh Heclo spoke of the 'fairly open networks of people that increasingly impinge on government' (Heclo, 1978: 88) and whose impact depended not necessarily on money but on knowledge of the specific policy debate. These highly specialized 'issue networks' were not replacing the more formal and consensual subgovernment model but were complicating policy scenarios and increasing unpredictability with their more ad hoc, dynamic and non-consensual style. Despite these changes, however, pluralism remained for many theorists a powerful frame with which to conceptualize US government and politics.

These models of and approaches to public policy were taken up and developed by British researchers, who settled on the concepts of 'policy communities' and 'policy networks' in their conception of a pluralist arrangement of power. Grant Jordan (1990: 325) argues that while there has been 'no straight-line application of the US ideas to a British context', there are clear genealogical similarities between US accounts of subgovernments and UK 'policy community' models as stable forms of decision-making based on shared values amongst long-term participants. The policy community model has proved to be a very tempting normative concept, allowing theorists to assess whether a specific policy field is based on a highly integrated, long-term, consensual and select arrangement of people (in which case it qualifies as a policy community), whether it is a more loosely organized, short-term, open and discontinuous grouping (in which case it may be considered as an issue network), or any number of intermediate structures (see Rhodes [1990] for a typology of policy networks).

The model of a highly cohesive, segmented policy community also reflects the idea of a peculiarly British policy style described by Jordan and Richardson as bureaucratic accommodation, where the 'mode is bargaining rather than imposition' (1982: 81), involving civil servants and a range of interest groups. The US public policy process, on the other hand, is an 'intrinsically political and highly complex policymaking system' where the key task is to form a 'coalition across a number of different institutions and levels of government' (Peters 1986: 20). So, while the British system appears to privilege the idea of disinterested civil servants reaching out to different groups in order to produce a consensus, the US approach is more politically motivated with participants constantly manoeuvring for advantage. Both systems, however, adhere to a perspective of what David Marsh calls 'reformed pluralism' (2002: 16) where power is less diffuse than previously but where politics is nevertheless marked by the interaction of, and increasingly intense competition between, different groups.

The language of subgovernments, issue networks and policy communities has allowed researchers to focus on specific instances of policymaking in order to identify participants, the relationships between them, the objectives set and the policies produced (see, for example, Marsh and Rhodes [1992] with reference to British examples). It is much less successful, as even many of its adherents admit, in assessing why some issues come to be classified as policy 'problems' and in illustrating the balance of power in the policymaking process. As Jordan comments about the UK, although it is just as applicable to US models, a 'policy community is a type of policy setting but it is not a statement about who has power' (Jordan, 1990: 333). To get to grips with power, we need to focus on another set of rather more critical approaches that largely reject the pluralist conception of power that still dominates the majority of thinking about contemporary public policy.

Critiques of pluralism

Radical sociologists and contemporaries of Truman, Dahl et al. in the USA were quick to dismiss the notion that, as Todd Gitlin summarizes the pluralist position, 'there are elites, but there is no elite' (quoted in Miliband 1973: 154). C. Wright Mills (1956) identified a ruling 'power elite' drawn from big business, the military and government that undermined the possibility of any truly competitive bargaining arrangements in the public policy process. Eleven years later, William Domhoff (1967) continued this line of attack, arguing that the answer to the question of 'who owns America?' was a very powerful corporate community that dominated the policymaking process for its own ends. Domhoff argued that the policy process 'begins in corporate boardrooms where problems are informally identified as "issues" to be solved by new policies. It ends in government, where policies are enacted and implemented' (Domhoff, 1983: 84).

Many issues, however, are *not* identified as problems to be tackled, meaning that pluralist confidence in the scope of public policy action and the competitive allocation of power is misplaced. According to Bachrach and Baratz (1962), pluralists miss out on the 'second face of power' – the identification of *non*-issues and the consequences of policy *in*action. 'Of course power is exercised when A participates in the making of decisions that affect B', they write, acknowledging Robert Dahl's famous conceptualization of power.

> But power is also exercised when A devotes his energies to creating or reinforcing social and political values and institutional practices that limit the scope of the political process to public consideration of only those issues which are comparatively innocuous to A. (Bachrach and Barataz, 1962: 948)

This form of 'nondecision-making' highlights the material and symbolic resources that powerful players have at their disposal in aiming both to dominate the visible policy process and to 'limit the scope of actual decision-making to "safe" issues' (1962: 952). This capacity to dominate the definition of policy problems is not shared equally by all participants in the policy process and challenges the notion that public policy is a transparent or egalitarian process. If Bachrach and Baratz are correct, policy formation, far from being a technical or administrative procedure, is a highly ideological process that privileges the frameworks and priorities of the powerful and marginalizes those who challenge these priorities.

In Britain, the Marxist writer Ralph Miliband provided a sustained attack on pluralism in his influential *The State in Capitalist Society* (1973). Firstly, he rejected as totally false the pluralists' claim that 'the major organized "interests" . . . compete on more or less equal terms, and that none of them is therefore able to achieve a decisive and permanent advantage in the process of competition' (1973: 131). Such is the power of business that the chief threat to a democratic policy process does not come from interest groups or lobbying but from the 'pervasive and permanent pressure upon governments and the state generated by the private control of concentrated industrial, commercial and financial resources' (1973: 132). Private capital, with its stranglehold on economic life (and resulting sway on government), makes its influence felt before its representatives walk through the door to lobby policymakers. Miliband also rejected the idea that British civil servants or US officials might be able to shake off this influence. People in these positions 'are not likely to be free of certain definite ideological inclinations, however little they may themselves be conscious of them; and these inclinations cannot but affect the whole character and orientation of the advice they proffer' (1973: 108). Civil service impartiality and expertise is therefore undermined by the structural constraints on a policy process tainted by the domination of private over public power.

The debate between pluralists and their critics continues. While David Marsh accuses pluralists of neglecting 'the pattern of structured inequality that is reflected in political institutions and processes' (2002: 19), William Galston, formerly President Clinton's deputy assistant for domestic policy, defends pluralism as a 'limited and robust' form of government that 'does all that is necessary to secure the theoretical and institutional bases of respect' (2005: 4–5). For some, pluralism is the most effective form of politics in its recognition of difference and its combination of competitive behaviour and consensual outcomes; for others, pluralism refers to the means by which inequalities are embedded into a political system that claims to celebrate the existence of different social groups and then finds a mechanism for prioritizing the interests of some over others. How is this debate expressed normatively inside media policy?

Characteristics of pluralist media policy

According to James Curran, the 'liberal approach is the dominant way of thinking about the media in the United States and increasingly around the world' (2002: 127). If we take Curran's use of the term 'liberal' in terms of its European meaning that privileges the dynamism of market forces and the principle of individual freedom from the state (as opposed to the American definition that emphasizes 'progressive' or critical ideas), then we can agree that pluralism is a powerful discourse underpinning not just popular conceptions of the role of the media but the development of media policies as well. Pluralist media policy should, in theory, assist the functioning of democratic life through, for example:

- ensuring the circulation of a wide range of voices and opinions, no matter how 'marginal' or 'unpopular' they may seem to be;
- facilitating a competitive environment in which multiple outlets, voices and representations are made available to citizens 'without discrimination on the basis of race, color, religion, national origin, or sex' as the 1934 US Communications Act put it;
- stimulating the creation of public opinion that acts as a communication channel between private individuals and the state;
- fostering a climate in which citizens are informed about issues perceived to be important to their daily lives;
- protecting the freedom of individuals from the state as well as the state's ability to protect its citizens from harm;
- stabilizing society by maximizing the expressive and cultural rights of all social groups.

These normative principles have largely guided the development of media policy in the USA and the UK and shaped the eventual emergence of the range of regulatory tools, legislative instruments and administrative procedures designed to achieve the objectives stated above. Here, we focus briefly on three areas – the media policymaking process, ownership rules and content regulation (all of which will be examined in more detail in later chapters) – to illustrate how pluralist discourse has, for many years, been incorporated into policy practice.

The media policymaking process

It is axiomatic for pluralists that decisions about the media are made in the most transparent and accessible ways with an emphasis on expert advice, open discussion and public participation. Opportunities are given to all interested parties to contribute to the policymaking process in such a way that no single 'stakeholder' is able to gain hegemony. The pluralist argument runs as follows: governments are democratically elected and therefore free to press for legislation that is written with the assistance of experts, fully debated and scrutinized in Congress or Parliament, open to rebuttal or praise by the media, and subject to extensive industry and public consultation. Bill Bush, the special adviser to Tessa Jowell, the

Secretary of State for Culture at the time of the 2003 Communications Act, provides a useful illustration of the pluralist workings of Parliament:

> The truth is that the [Communications] Bill was not the work of one hand or even a small number of hands. It was the work of very great many people. The regulators contributed enormously. Tessa [Jowell] spoke extensively to broadcasters right across the spectrum, communications companies, radio companies, press, local and national, UK companies, European Union based companies, and non-EU, spoke to a huge public consultation, but also spoke to the representatives of the public, many of them self-appointed, but nevertheless you talk to people and take them into the account. Just because no one individual in that enormous cobweb of conversations, discussions, seminars, and formal and informal meetings, just because there is no one person who absolutely gets their way all the time on everything, does not mean that there was a tight conspiracy to do down any one particular viewpoint. (Bush 2005)

Another marker of a pluralistic system is the importance attached to the independence of policymaking and regulatory institutions. In the case of the FCC, while it is true that Congress appoints its five commissioners, the organization operates relatively freely in implementing Congressional will and devising (or choosing not to devise) new rules concerning media structure and behaviour. The fact that Congress has only passed two major pieces of legislation covering the communications industries as a whole, the 1934 Communications Act and 1996 Telecommunications Act, is a further sign that the FCC is relied on to oversee the day-to-day running of these major industries. To what extent, however, is the FCC's autonomy undermined by the power of special interests? According to one official in the Media Bureau:

> The people that come in here [the lobbyists], it doesn't do them any good to buy me lunch for instance. First of all, there are some severe limits. I mean you can buy me a McDonalds hamburger or something but beyond that you're over the limit. But that's not going to change anything and the people that come in here that are effective are the ones that come in with real facts or solid legal arguments about why their side should prevail.

In Britain, one of the most senior figures inside the Press Complaints Commission (PCC), the organization that deals with complaints about misleading or inaccurate press coverage, refutes the notion that the PCC is susceptible to interest group pressure. When asked how much outside interference there is in its decision-making, he replied:

> None at all, none at all. When I say that, what I am saying is that the PCC stands or falls by its demonstrable independence from all forms of external

pressure. So, for example, the newspaper and magazine industry pays for this building, my salary and the salaries of the staff here. But we have to be and be seen to be independent from our paymasters and from politicians and from all the pressures that come from the House of Commons.

The normative characteristics of pluralist media policymaking are therefore its accountability, impartiality and autonomy that are designed to insulate it from the domination of special interests and to incorporate the views of multiple stakeholders. As Jonathan Adelstein, a Democratic commissioner on the FCC, put it when objecting to the launch of a media ownership proceeding in July 2006 (dissent that, for some, illustrates the inherent pluralism of the process), the task ahead 'requires transparency, leadership, bipartisanship, consensus building, thoughtful deliberation, and genuine participation by the American people' (FCC 2006a: 34), a succinct summary of pluralist principles.

Ownership and other structural rules

As we saw in chapter 1, the media industries have a tendency towards monopolistic behaviour. 'For the liberal pluralist', argues Ed Baker (2002: 176), 'monopoly is intrinsically objectionable. Monopoly overtly threatens pluralism.' For this reason, measures are necessary to promote competition within media systems and to introduce artificial market barriers beyond which no single media corporation is allowed to go. These mechanisms include antitrust or competition laws and media-specific ownership rules designed to ensure that a wide range of voices and outlets take their place in the media marketplace and to prevent the emergence of overly dominant corporations or individuals. This can take the form of restrictions on cross-media or foreign ownership, limits on the number of stations or share of audience controlled by one company in local and national markets, and special controls on high-profile or significant media mergers. Back in 1995, the British Conservative government provided an admirably clear justification for the need for such ownership restrictions:

> A free and diverse media are an indispensable part of the democratic process. They provide the multiplicity of voices and opinions that informs the public, influences opinion, and engenders political debate. They promote the culture of dissent which any healthy democracy must have. In so doing, they contribute to the cultural fabric of the nation and help define our sense of identity and purpose. If one voice becomes too powerful, this process is placed in jeopardy and democracy is damaged. Special media ownership rules, which exist in all major media markets, are needed

> therefore to provide the safeguards necessary to maintain diversity and plurality. (DNH 1995a: 3)

This approach is not confined to European media systems only. In the broadcast ownership review of 2002 that sought to loosen ownership rules, the FCC stated that:

> We adhere to our longstanding determination that the policy of limiting common ownership of multiple media outlets is the most reliable means of promoting viewpoint diversity. Nothing in the record causes us to reconsider this conclusion . . . We therefore continue to believe that broadcast ownership limits are necessary to preserve and promote viewpoint diversity. A larger number of independent owners will tend to generate a wider array of viewpoints in the media than would a comparatively smaller number of owners. (2003a: 11)

A pluralist approach, therefore, looks to market mechanisms to foster the greatest number of viewpoints, reserving the right to intervene in the media marketplace only when necessary. Indeed, pluralist-minded policymakers point to criticisms of existing rules from both the right and the left – that rules are either anti-competitive or too mild to facilitate real diversity – as evidence of a consensual approach that does not bow down to special interests and powerful lobbyists.

Other forms of structural regulation have been introduced in order to undermine monopolies or to discriminate positively in favour of local, less commercially popular or more challenging media output. Baker's assertion that liberal pluralists 'should favor any policy that supports more robust media conduits for pluralist groups not adequately nurtured by the market' (2002: 184) partly explains the emergence of:

- The Financial Interest and Syndication Rules, introduced in 1970, that weakened the power of the US networks by taking away their rights to profit from syndication and preventing them from owning the production companies that provided their programming. The aim was to boost the power of independent producers and 'to cultivate more diverse and innovative television content' (McAllister n.d.).
- The Prime Time Access Rule, also introduced in 1970, that mandated that one hour of prime-time programming should be reserved for locally produced, and not network provided, material.
- Lower postal rates to assist non-commercial media and subsidies, particularly common in Scandinavian countries, where state support is provided to civil society organizations to allow them to produce and distribute their media. Such financial assistance 'is a way of facilitating

the working of democracy, and supporting collective organizations as a public interest counterweight to private corporate interests' (Curran 2002: 242), once again in the interests of developing and safeguarding pluralistic media structures.

- Public service broadcasting systems that are designed to produce high-quality material of different genres, aimed at a wide range of audiences, and not dependent on or reducible to high ratings in the broadcasting market.

Content regulation

Pluralist media policy speaks of the need to maximize the number of media outlets and voices and also to protect the public from harm. This involves a balance between ensuring freedom of expression – most famously through the First Amendment's constitutional protection of free speech – and the obligation to 'safeguard the interests of citizens' as the title of a chapter in the British government's communications White Paper put it (DTI/DCMS 2000: 58–69). While the default position of the pluralist imagination is of limited intervention into the flow of information provided by print media, it is recognized that, given the influence of the broadcast media, certain types of media content need to be regulated in order to maintain quality and to protect viewers and listeners from offence, misleading advertising, invasions of privacy and unbalanced coverage.

This approach has given rise in the UK and the USA to a number of instruments and institutions over the years including:

- The Fairness Doctrine that required US broadcasters to cover topics of political importance, no matter how controversial they may have been, and to give equal time to political candidates to express their differences (Horwitz 1989: 249). *FOX news - Rep./Conservative*
- Rules prohibiting 'obscene, indecent or profane language by means of radio communication' (18 United States Code 1464) have been followed by an order from British regulators that material 'that might seriously impair the physical, mental or moral development of people under eighteen must not be broadcast' (Ofcom 2005: 8). This has led to the establishment of a 'watershed', a time (9 p.m.) before which material that is unsuitable for children should not be shown.
- Restrictions on sponsorship in the UK, including limits on product placement, a ban on the sponsorship of news and current affairs programmes and the insistence on editorial independence from the influence of sponsors.

- Restrictions on advertising in terms of products that may be advertised (most famously cigarettes) and upper limits on the proportion of the schedule given over to advertising.
- The requirement that news 'must be reported with due accuracy and presented with due impartiality' (Ofcom 2005: 24).
- Rules on unwarranted infringements of privacy and the recognition by broadcasters of the 'legitimate expectation of privacy' (2005: 42) that leads to a prohibition, unless specifically justified, on surreptitious filming, doorstepping and filming without consent. *reality TV*
- Quotas designed to protect cultural diversity and social cohesion in the face of increased cultural imports (mostly from the USA) and potential loss of national identity. The declaration in the European Union directive on *Television without Frontiers* that European broadcasters should reserve a majority of transmission time for works of European origin (EC 1989) is a much-quoted and highly controversial attempt to stimulate media pluralism (see Collins 1993). Quotas, however, are used to bolster and protect independent producers and local content in many parts of the world (see Machet and Robillard 1998; Messerlin 2000: 297–9).

In summary, pluralist approaches to content policy require a balancing of principles concerning freedom of expression and the fostering of a responsible media climate in which citizens are protected from harm and their rights to representation and privacy are respected. While US policymakers, guided by the spirit of the First Amendment, are generally more reluctant to intervene in media content debates than their British counterparts, it is nevertheless the case that both countries have developed media policy systems that focus on structural as well as behavioural issues. The extent to which these systems have actually delivered pluralist outcomes – evaluated in terms of the development of competitive environments in which multiple outlets facilitate the airing of diverse views in the interest of sustaining group identity and political consensus – is, however, a far more problematic question and will be assessed in the chapters that follow.

Neo-liberal perspectives on politics and policy

Neo-liberalism's discursive attachment to free markets, individual rights, personal choice, small government and limited regulation is now a firmly established part of contemporary life, celebrated and publicized by powerful voices in politics, business, media and academia across the world, but also extensively critiqued by activists, theorists and commentators. Robert McChesney (1999) argues that neo-liberalism is the 'defining political economic paradigm of our time' while Dan Schiller insists that the 'neoliberal freedom to fashion [communication] networks into instruments of enterprise' is at the heart of contemporary 'digital capitalism' (2000: 1). Jim McGuigan is struck by 'the command of neo-liberalism over popular consciousness and everyday life' (2005: 232) and argues that it wields such ideological power that it has become 'common sense' (2005: 233). The neo-liberal desire to 'bring all human action into the domain of the market', as David Harvey (2005: 3) puts it, shapes both the objectives of government action and the structures and policies that emerge (in part) from this action.

At one level, neo-liberalism and pluralism share many of the same underlying features of classical *liberalism*: commitments to the democracy of the marketplace, freedom from the state and the fruits of competition. Yet, where pluralism is based on the recognition of group diversity and the attempt to maximize the productivity of group bargaining to achieve social cohesion, neo-liberalism holds up individual responsibility, personal gain and private property as fundamental principles. In perhaps the most famous declaration of neo-liberalism, Margaret Thatcher, then prime minister, declared that too many people 'are casting their problems on society and who is society? There is no such thing! There are individual men and women and there are families and no government can do anything except through people and people look to themselves first' (Keay 1987: 9). Hostility towards the state and an emphasis on the sanctity of the individual in a free market have led to many of the trends and instruments that are intimately associated with neo-liberalism today, including deregulation, privatization, liberalization, tax cuts, austerity measures, imposition of free trade disciplines, attacks on barriers to capital accumulation, and cultural homogenization.

There is a danger, however, that, in providing long lists of its negative tendencies, neo-liberalism is itself flattened and homogenized, that it comes to be an umbrella term for all that is wrong with a more commercially minded society. The risk is that, by talking about neo-liberalism as a steamroller laying waste to public culture and paving the way for market forces, more complex and precise accounts of the agents, arguments and mechanisms involved in neo-liberal practices may be sacrificed in order to emphasize, in this context, the undesirability of the project itself. Treating neo-liberalism as simple shorthand for marketization not only runs the risk of dehistoricizing the process (as if the obsession with markets and capital flows was only invented recently), but also marginalizes the tensions and competing interests that lie at the heart of neo-liberal projects.

We can identify several overlapping critical perspectives on neo-liberalism that coalesce around the regeneration of laissez-faire economics in the increasingly interdependent circumstances of the late twentieth and early twenty-first centuries. At the heart of each perspective is a recognition of the damaging impact of the neo-liberal commitment to market transactions above all other forms of exchange, although there are contrasting points of departure and of emphasis.

A new economic paradigm

Perhaps the most common approach is that neo-liberalism has become the new 'economic orthodoxy' (Callinicos 2003: 2) and a 'governing economic paradigm' (Hay 2004: 505). It emerged as a response to the crisis of 'embedded liberalism', the post-Second World War western economic order based on state direction of macro-economic matters and the provision of welfare structures to provide a 'cushion' (or a ladder) for citizens in need of support. Keynesianism, as it came to be known, was under increasing pressure in the 1970s as a combination of falling rates of growth and rising inflation – together with the 'threat' of new centres of production in Asia and insecure oil supplies – helped to undo what was left of the corporatist consensus that had largely dominated for thirty years. The collapse of the Soviet Union and its satellite states further suggested to those eager to listen that there was little alternative to the replacement of social partnership with a more entrepreneurial and vigorous form of capitalism.

This involved a challenge to the existing patterns and rules of both national finances and international trade. The new financial regime necessitated 'a shift away from Keynesian macroeconomic demand management to a more structural approach to fiscal and monetary policy' (Cerny 2004: 12) with the lowering of personal and corporate taxes, the pursuit of labour-market flexibility, the promise of balanced budgets and a move to release central banks from state control. Neo-liberalism also sought to extend the disciplines of 'free trade' across national boundaries by challenging the logic of protectionist tariffs and constructing new supranational trade agreements and financial institutions that would oversee and embed the supremacy of free-market transactions. A higher profile for institutions such as the International Monetary Fund and the World Bank, together with the transformation of the post-War GATT into the World Trade Organisation and the construction of supranational agreements like TRIPS

(Trade-related Intellectual Property Rights) and the GATS (General Agreement on Trade in Services), are all features of a new trading environment which, more than ever, favours the owners of capital and their agents and embeds private capital into the supply of public services. As Colin Hay puts it (2004: 508), economic neo-liberalism displays a confidence 'in the allocative efficiency of market and quasi-market mechanisms in the provision of public goods'.

A new political project

Neo-liberal economic practices did not emerge spontaneously or naturally, but took hold as a result of the intellectual and political activities of a range of figures from the 1970s onwards. According to Andrew Gamble (2001: 128), the 'spearhead' of the attack on Keynesianism was 'the doctrine of monetarism' associated with economists like Milton Friedman, Alan Walters and Friedrich Hayek and think tanks like the Institute of Economic Affairs and the Heritage Foundation in which these ideas found their expression. What was more surprising, Gamble argues, 'was the speed with which the ideas of neo-liberalism jumped the barrier into practical politics' (2001: 128). Most famously championed by the administrations of Thatcher in the UK and Reagan in the USA during the 1980s, but also implemented in Australia and New Zealand at the same time, neo-liberalism rapidly became the inspiration for a new political project.

David Harvey (2005) argues that this is, fundamentally, a project of capital re-distribution (upwards) rather more than a system of marketization for its own sake. He focuses on the 'creative tension' (2005: 19) between the utopian aspects of *neo-liberalism* – as a society in which market forces work seamlessly and productively to provide for all – and the material practices of *neo-liberalization*, a process that seeks, following the turmoil of the 1970s, 'to re-establish the conditions for capital accumulation and to restore the power of economic elites' (2005: 19). What we have seen since the early 1980s is a profoundly contradictory phenomenon where free-market enthusiasts who sing the praises of open markets subsequently impose tariffs to protect domestic industries, usually for electoral gain. Public denunciations of interfering in the market are sometimes followed by government bail-outs of failing firms in order to protect national prestige and calm business interests. Tensions are, therefore, particularly evident in Harvey's theorizing of the neo-liberal state which has a minimal role in the 'pure' expression of neo-liberalism but a rather more significant one when it comes to concrete actions of neo-liberalization. Given that the present consensus is based on the rejection of 'embedded liberalism' which saw massive public intervention into industrial, social and cultural life, continued state intervention into the economy would seem to be a major paradox.

Harvey (2005: 2) argues, however, that the role of the neo-liberal state is 'to create and preserve an institutional framework' appropriate to the project of capital restoration, far more than it is to address long-standing problems of falling rates of profit and capital investment. This means, for example, supporting private property rights in existing markets and extending these rights to new markets where these rights do not currently exist. Through, for example, laws on corporate taxation, secondary picketing, export subsidies and intellectual property rights, recent British and US governments have contributed to a trading environment that favours business interests and is designed to generate private rather than public dividends. The neo-liberal state, therefore, has a *different* role from the one it had under embedded liberalism but is no less central in shaping social forces, even if the state itself is often formally absent from the structures and institutions that it creates (see Majone 1996 and Moran 2003 for a contrasting argument that the enormous growth in rules and regulations affecting both public and private sectors is evidence not of neo-liberalism but of a 'regulatory state'; and Rhodes 1994 on the 'hollowing out' of the state).

Harvey stresses the significance of the contradictions of the neo-liberal state that lay it open both to external dissent and internal tension. For example, he argues (2005: 79–81) that its authoritarian behaviour in enforcing market disciplines runs counter to its celebration of personal freedom, just as rampant individualism and corruption in the financial system results in volatility and risk-taking that lead to calls for further regulation. Furthermore, the state's celebration of competition runs counter to the oligopolies and monopolies created through the process of neo-liberalization, while its reduction of the notion of 'freedom' to 'freedom of enterprise' creates potential negative externalities and undesirable social outcomes that, again, require state intervention. Neo-liberalization, he concludes, is a far more fractured and insecure process than the hegemony of neo-liberal ideas would suggest – an insecurity that paves the way for the possibility of resistance to its practices. Indeed, neo-liberalism's lack of success in stimulating sustained economic growth and overcoming economic instability – as opposed to its achievements in creating a growing economic elite – draw attention to its underlying weaknesses.

A powerful ideological system

For any new social, political or economic order to be sustained, it has to sink roots far beyond its immediate protagonists and cheerleaders and to produce a set of ideas that are eventually accepted as 'natural' and logical. As we have already seen, minority ideas concerning monetarism and anti-statism preceded neo-liberalism's viability as a political project and were initially 'regarded as purely "ideological" in a pejorative sense, meaning that they . . . had no purchase on the realities of modern capitalism' (Gamble 2001: 128). Their eventual success depended not only on external economic factors (such as rising unemployment and inflation), but also on the internalization and normalization of underlying concepts of, for example, competition, entrepreneurship, individual responsibility and rational calculation. 'An open project around the restoration of economic power to a small elite would probably not gain much popular support. But a programmatic attempt to advance the cause of individual freedoms could appeal to a mass base and so disguise the drive to restore class power' (Harvey 2005: 40).

There has been no lack of institutional support for such a project emanating from a range of sources including political parties, the academy, the media, think tanks and, of course, boardrooms themselves. Neo-liberalism has therefore acquired a discursive power that articulates its resonance throughout these key organizations in its pursuit of wider (although clearly not uncritical) acceptance. Nick Couldry uses the term neo-liberalism 'to identify under one label a range of discourses, operating as a form of "common sense", that absolutely legitimates the market and delegitimates the social' (Couldry 2006: 2). Neo-liberal ideology assists here in the naturalizing of key transformations in capitalist labour practices concerning the extension of working hours and increased employer control, disguised in language of individualization and flexibility. Many other critics refer to the discursive and narrative power of neo-liberalism, for example that it has provided the 'ideological software' (Peck and Tickell 2002: 33) for systematic economic re-structuring, that it has helped to 'internalize neoliberalism in the way people frame political and economic issues' (Cerny et al. 2005: 20) and that, in the context of the UK, the crisis in the late 1970s 'came to be *narrated* in neoliberal terms' (Hay 2004: 507 – emphasis added) by populist politicians like Reagan and Thatcher.

Pierre Bourdieu has written extensively about the discursive impact of this 'magic word' (1998: 34). For Bourdieu, neo-liberalism is a 'strong discourse' (1998: 95) backed by powerful symbolic and economic forces that have helped to transform what he sees as a utopian ideal into a serious political programme. It is a utopia because it is a 'pure mathematical fiction, based, from the outset, on a gigantic abstraction' (1998: 94), based, that is, on a distorted and narrow view of individual rationality that dehistoricizes and desocializes the structures from which it emerges. Neo-liberalism has even produced a new vocabulary – of freedom, openness, flexibility, dynamism, novelty, diversity and democracy that are facilitated by market practices – that 'rests on a series of opposition and equivalences which support and reinforce one another to depict the contemporary transformations advanced societies are undergoing . . . as in turn benign, necessary, ineluctable or desirable' (Bourdieu and Wacquant 2001: 4). Neo-liberalism, to its proponents, is truly an ideal world.

Neo-liberalism should be seen therefore as a dynamic and volatile process. We can point to specific instruments of neo-liberal restructuring – for example, liberalization, privatization, deregulation, openness to foreign direct investment, fiscal discipline, lower taxes and outsourcing (Tabb 2003) – but the overarching aim of neo-liberalization is to transform the balance of forces inside different economies and states in order to facilitate capital accumulation (if not sustained growth). These political-economic objectives depend on a thick ideological layer that attempts to root neo-liberal ideas of competition and individualization throughout the population. Neo-liberalization is, above all, a project and not an endgame: an 'historically specific, ongoing and internally contradictory process of market-driven socio-spatial transformation, rather than . . . a fully actual-ized policy regime, ideological form, or regulatory framework' (Brenner and Theodore 2002: 6).

Varieties of neo-liberalism? Neo-conservatism and Third Way politics

Andrew Gamble warns against the 'tendency to reify neo-liberalism and to treat it as a phenomenon which manifests itself everywhere and in everything . . . Far better to deconstruct neo-liberalism into the different doctrines and ideas which compose it, and relate them to particular prac-tices and political projects' (Gamble 2001: 134). This call to avoid over-generalization has been taken up by numerous writers so that we can now read about multiple forms of neo-liberalism: the 'social neoliberalism' of Lula in Brazil (Cerny et al. 2005: 21), 'circumscribed' neo-liberalization in Sweden and 'sustained' neo-liberalization in the UK (Harvey 2005: 156), 'deep' and 'soft', 'roll-back' and 'roll out' neo-liberalisms (Peck and Tickell

2002: 37) and, finally, 'spectacular' and 'vernacular' forms of neo-liberalism (Hay 2004: 514). This sensitivity to local adaptations of a broader theory is best expressed by the claim that we are now witnessing 'the emergence of *varieties of neoliberalism*' (Cerny et al. 2005: 21 – emphasis in original). Rather than working to a general model, states are experimenting with and internalizing different aspects of the neo-liberal agenda and we are therefore in the presence of 'diversity within convergence' (2005: 21). This point becomes important when we consider the extent to which the two governments within whose periods of office the case studies in this book mainly lie, George W. Bush's Republican and Tony Blair's New Labour administrations, may be described as neo-liberal in character. While theirs is clearly not the only influence on media policies during that time, their 'steering' of the policy process is, nevertheless, enormously significant.

It is perhaps not too contentious to suggest that George W. Bush's Republican administration is a prime example of neo-liberal government. The US commentator, Thomas Frank, argues that Bush is the latest in a long line of conservatives who, in the last thirty years, have 'smashed the welfare state, reduced the tax burden on corporations and the wealthy, and generally facilitated the country's return to a nineteenth-century pattern of wealth distribution' (Frank 2006: 6). Yet George W. Bush is far more than a simple purveyor of neo-liberal economic policies, but the embodiment of a politics of *neo-conservatism* that is rooted in a variety of economic, political *and* social issues. William Kristol, editor of the neo-conservative *Weekly Standard*, identifies four dimensions of neo-conservative thinking (Kristol 2003):

- An aggressive foreign policy in which it is argued that the USA has a responsibility to intervene, pre-emptively if necessary, to make the world safe for its version of democracy. This was a theory developed by Dick Cheney (then Defense Secretary, later Vice-President) in his *Defense Strategy for the 1990s* (Cheney 1993) that, in an increasingly uncertain world, it was the duty of the USA to 'preclude hostile nondemocratic powers from dominating regions critical to our interests and otherwise work to build an international environment conducive to our values' (1993: 1). Critics argue that this has led to the pursuit of a 'neo-imperial foreign policy' (M. Cox 2004: 31), the use of military power to secure and extend US interests across the globe. Post 9/11, this has involved its waging of a 'war on terror' that has seen American troops deployed, most famously, in Iraq and Afghanistan and the imposition of aspects of

US liberal democracy (notably market structures) on what the US government chooses to describe as undemocratic states. Only under the neo-conservative administration of George W. Bush has Cheney's plan, sometimes referred to as the 'Project for a New American Century', been effectively realized with the export, often at the barrel of a gun, of American values across the world.

- A commitment to cutting taxes in order to stimulate the economic growth that is seen as providing modern democracies with their 'legitimacy and durability' (Kristol 2003).
- A more relaxed attitude towards the role of the state than previous conservatives and a recognition that it is not 'strong' or 'weak' but 'intrusive' government that is the problem.
- A concern with social issues, for example, pornography, abortion, quality of education, relations between Church and state and, in particular, a belief that American culture is 'sinking to new levels of vulgarity' (Kristol 2003). This is the argument taken up by Frank (2006) in his explanation of popular support for Bush's neo-conservative politics: that it is the result of a misconceived and profoundly contradictory cultural backlash against the 'liberal' media, political correctness and elite politicians. 'While earlier forms of conservatism emphasized fiscal sobriety, the backlash mobilizes voters with explosive social issues – summoning public outrage over everything from busing to un-Christian art – which it then marries to pro-business policies' (Frank 2006: 5).

Neo-conservatism, therefore, combines the neo-liberal emphasis on free markets and individual liberty with a concern about social issues in a way that some theorists have found paradoxical. Wendy Brown argues that while the two perspectives share some common ground, there are also serious tensions between them. 'Neo-conservatism's strong moral positions – on abortion, homosexuality, the family, etc. – have nothing to do with neo-liberalism and actually fly in the face of the economic rationality neo-liberalism promulgates at the social level' (Brown 2003: note 5). David Harvey argues that, for all their points of agreement, there is a key difference between the two perspectives. The concern of neo-conservatism 'for an overweening morality as the necessary social glue to keep the body politic secure in the face of external and internal dangers' (Harvey 2005: 82) helps to explain a coercive streak in the current US government as it seeks to maintain political stability and social order. Yet neo-conservatism has its own contradictions, particularly in its attitude towards commercialism and culture. As Thomas Frank notes (2006: 248), 'American conservatism depends for its continued dominance and even for its very existence on people never making certain mental connections about the world . . . For example, the connection between mass culture, most of which conservatives hate, and laissez-faire capitalism, which they adore without reservation.' The concerns of neo-conservatives are not reducible to those of neo-liberalism, but they are just as wedded to market transactions and a deregulatory logic when it comes to economic matters.

The question of whether Tony Blair's record in office can be described as neo-liberal is more contested. New Labour came to power in 1997 committed to providing a 'Third Way' between traditional welfare-based social democratic and conservative free-market policies. In an early statement of New Labour values, he asserted that:

> My vision for the 21st century is of a popular politics reconciling themes which in the past have wrongly been regarded as antagonistic – patriotism *and* internationalism; rights *and* responsibilities; the promotion of enterprise *and* the attack on poverty and discrimination. (Blair 1998: 1)

This involved the rejection of previous Labour commitments to nationalization and redistribution (as illustrated by the abolition in 1995 of Clause IV of the party's Constitution that committed it to 'common ownership of the means of production') and the embrace of market forces and new technologies as vehicles for establishing a dynamic and competitive economy (Anderson and Mann 1997; Panitch and Leys 1997). But the Third Way, according to its chief theorist Anthony Giddens, was also deeply concerned with issues of social justice and a more cosmopolitan outlook on the world. It required the creation of a mixed economy – a 'social market' – that referred to 'a balance between regulation and deregulation; and between the economic and non-economic in the life of the society' (Giddens 1998: 19). It also involved an explicit rejection that it could, in any way, be described as neo-liberal: 'Third Way politics' argued Giddens (2000: 32), 'is not a continuation of neoliberalism but an alternative political philosophy to it.'

New Labour's combination of market-driven politics with its stated commitment to the renewal of public services and community cohesion has led to some confusion about its relationship to neo-liberalism. Martin Smith (2004: 224) asserts that 'New Labour is hydra-headed. The project is difficult to define because it is full of contradictions and it presents a "head" to suit the occasion.' Douglas Jaenicke (2000) and Rordan Wilkinson (2000) also argue against characterizing New Labour as a simple expression of neo-liberalism. Colin Hay distinguishes between what he calls the 'normative' neo-liberalism of the Conservatives and the 'necessitarian' character of New Labour's forced embrace of neo-liberal-ism (2004: 525) in the context of its acceptance of and adaptation to the imperatives of globalization. Trapped by the need to compete with global markets, New Labour's character 'derives less from its neoliberalism than the manner in which it comes to accommodate itself to neoliberalism' (2004: 524). Neo-liberalism, according to this perspective, lies on New Labour's shoulders like a light cloak which can be thrown aside at any moment, rather than developing into an iron cage with its associated marketized rationality. Even some of New Labour's fiercest critics dismiss the idea that it is fundamentally neo-liberal in character. David Hesmondhalgh argues that New Labour 'represents a new hybrid' (2005: 99) of neo-liberal and more traditional social democratic ideas and that this combination is clearly expressed in an approach to media and cultural policies that mixes elements of hard-headed marketization with a 'com-mitment to expansive notions of public service and the public interest' (2005: 102). Colin Leys claims that, given New Labour's intimate involve-ment with the commodification of key areas of British public life, it has 'become a vehicle for a variant of economic neoliberalism with social-democratic overtones' (2001: 79).

New Labour's record of extending privatization, pressing for trade lib-eralization and overseeing increased levels of inequality suggests, however, a more singularly neo-liberal political approach. In their analysis of Blair's economic record, Arestis and Sawyer identify the emergence of a 'new monetarism' and argue that the 'Third Way' 'is no more than "neoliberal-ism with a human face"' (2001: 275) while, for Alex Callinicos, New Labour, along with other 'Third Way' governments in Europe, 'have embraced and in certain respects radicalized the neo-liberal policies of their predeces-sors' (2001: 107). Bob Jessop rubbishes claims that New Labour represents a mixture of market capitalism and social democracy and argues instead that it involves a 'continuation of neo-liberalism by moralizing Blairite "christian socialist" means that owe more to American neo-conservatism and American neo-liberalism than they do to an institutionalized, Euro-pean christian democratic tradition' (Jessop 2004).

George W. Bush's neo-conservatism and Tony Blair's 'Third Way' poli-tics occupy distinctive positions in relation to neo-liberalism. While both share an understanding of market relations as intrinsically productive and desirable and both agree that their political perspectives are not reducible to economic matters alone, they are the products of different political and cultural traditions and accountable to different political forces. Bush is sympathetic to (and pulled by) a more conservative social agenda, to the ideas of the Christian right and a cultural backlash against 'liberal' (progressive) values. Tony Blair relies on a different social base, one that is tied historically through the Labour Party to working-class interests and a collectivist and welfarist set of values. The particular nuances they bring to government are not the same but, nevertheless, perhaps secondary in the sense that they have both inherited neo-liberal agendas from their predecessors and have done little to deviate from or challenge key neo-liberal assumptions and goals in terms of the cementing of market forces at the heart of their respective societies.

Characteristics of neo-liberal media policy

Neo-liberalism has emerged recently as a dominant frame not just as '*the* explanatory term for contemporary forms of economic restructuring' (Larner, 2003: 509) but also for progressive critiques of current media and communications policies. Scholars including Flew (2002), Harvey (2006), Hesmondhalgh (2002, 2005), McChesney (2000), McGuigan (2005) and Mosco (2004) all identify neo-liberal pressures as a key feature of today's media environment that shape everything from the role of the state to the character of the content produced. The politics of neo-liberalism, according to Chakravartty and Sarikakis (2006: 18), 'has succeeded in *defining* the ways in which we debate the role of the state in communications policy' (emphasis added), while Cees Hamelink (2002: 252–3) talks of a neo-liberal 'agenda' where audiences are conceptualized as consumers, knowledge is commodified, commercial space expanded, trade prioritized, ownership concentrated and common resources siphoned off into private enclosures. For all the different points of emphasis in these critiques, there is an assumption that there are some defining instruments of neo-liberal media policy and a shared agreement that, as Robert McChesney puts it, neo-liberal policies 'maximize the role of markets and profit-making and minimize the role of nonmarket institutions' (2000: 6). Neo-liberalism, therefore, has come to be intimately associated with the trends of deregulation, liberalization, privatization and marketization that have worked their way through the British and American media since the early 1980s.

Deregulation

One of the most visible features of neo-liberal media policy concerns deregulation, the desire to reduce the role of, or remove entirely, the state from the regulation of media industries that ought instead to be controlled through the creative and dynamic play of market forces. Neo-liberal governments from the 1980s on promised to roll back the structural and behavioural restrictions that had been put in place throughout the twentieth century to stimulate and sustain plurality. 'The rhetoric of deregulation,' according to David Hesmondhalgh (2002: 108), 'was particularly powerful in the cultural industries, because the notion of freedom from government intervention fed on anxieties about government interference in personal and political expression.' Indeed, advocates of deregulation in government were able to draw on both left-wing critiques of 'regulatory capture' as well as free-market opponents of 'big government' (Horwitz 1989). The political commitment to deregulate was further intensified by the emergence of a number of interlocking factors: a period of sustained technological innovation that saw the development of cable, satellite and computer technologies that undermined the need for and possibility of spectrum-based arguments for regulation; the rise of globalization arguments that challenged the existence of national forms of regulation; and the desire, especially in countries like the USA and the UK following the economic instability of the 1970s, to develop new information-based economies in which communications and media industries would be central.

Deregulatory measures were pursued vigorously, in particular by FCC commissioners operating with unbridled enthusiasm for the free market. Charles Ferris, FCC chairman from 1977 to 1981, licensed thousands of new broadcast stations and justified entry liberalization for new media and telecommunications ventures in the following terms: 'Remove the [Federal Communications] Commission from the marketplace. Force it to justify the need for regulation. Get it out of the way of industry driven by new technology. If a company has the money to invest in a telecommunications service, let it, and leave it to the public to determine whether the service will survive' (quoted in Horwitz 1989: 259–60). His successor, Mark Fowler (1981–7), oversaw the break-up of the monopoly telephone company AT&T and the creation of a liberalized telecommunications market with the emergence of regional 'Baby Bells' in 1984. He also famously described television as 'just another appliance. It's a toaster with pictures' (quoted in Horwitz 1989: 245) and proceeded to undo many of the rules governing ownership and content – for example, rules requiring broadcasters to transmit minimum amounts of news and children's programming – that had been developed over the years (see Fowler and Brenner 1982 for a rationalization of this approach). The highpoints of 'pluralist' policy, the Fairness Doctrine and the Fin-Syn rules, were themselves finally abolished in 1987 and 1995 respectively because of what were claimed to be damaging effects on free speech and free trade. Deregulatory rhetoric could also be heard in Britain in the 1980s where think-tanks such as the Institute for Economic Affairs and the Adam Smith Institute pressed for the break-up of the BBC and the liberalization of ownership controls, although with admittedly less immediate impact than in the USA.

The 1990s witnessed further deregulation on both sides of the Atlantic. The 1996 US Telecommunications Act, the product of systematic lobbying by corporate interests (Aufderheide 1999: 42), allowed, for example, cable and telephone companies to enter each other's markets and to merge, deregulated most cable rates, abolished audience limits for radio, extended broadcast license periods, relaxed ownership rules and handed digital bandwidth to existing broadcasters for free (1999: 55–6). In Britain, the 1996 Broadcasting Act followed a similar (but far more modest) agenda, permitting increased cross-ownership between media companies and 'steering the redesign of policy inexorably . . . towards a widespread liberalization of media ownership' (Doyle 2002: 102). Broadcast deregulation also took hold in the rest of western Europe (Humphreys 1996; Papathanassopoulos 2002: 9–32) and, after the collapse of the Communist bloc after 1989, across the media in eastern Europe (Sparks 1998).

However, many critics saw in this process not the withdrawal of the state from media regulation but the pursuit of specific ideological ends: to reshape media markets in order to provide increased opportunities for accumulation and profitability. In other words, this was a state-driven initiative to change the terms of trade that drew on arguments about 'technological imperatives' and 'consumer sovereignty' but was primarily a '*political* process, whereby politicians and regulators changed their minds about the benefits of regulation and defeated the entrenched industry interests that wanted maintenance of the regulatory status quo' (Horwitz 1989: 264–5). A more adequate description for the dismantling of existing regulations and fostering of new modes of behaviour was, therefore, *re-regulation* (Murdock 1990: 12), rather than a genuine disengagement of the state from policymaking. For its supporters, 'strategic reregulation' (Vogel 1996: 18) could be a creative process of economic restructuring whereby 'state actors took the initiative in proposing reforms and in molding politically acceptable bargains' (1996: 5); for its opponents, re-regulation was a political tool used to steer economic life not necessarily towards greater competition but certainly towards greater marketization.

Marketization

Neo-liberal media policy relies not simply on the use of market mechanisms in media environments, but on the recognition that market forces provide the most powerful logic for the organization of the environment as a whole. David Hesmondhalgh describes marketization as the idea that 'the production and exchange of cultural goods and services for profit is the best way to achieve efficiency and fairness in the production and consumption of texts' (2002: 109) and sees it as the overarching principle governing recent changes in the media policy landscape. Here we touch on three areas of activity in which the pursuit of profit has been intensified: the marketization of non-market institutions, privatization and commercialization.

Colin Leys (2001: 84) argues that the transformation of a 'non-market field' into a market consists of four features:

- the reconfiguration of goods and services so they can be priced and sold;
- the creation of demand for these goods and services;
- the conversion of the workforce into one subject to market disciplines;
- the support of the state in reducing the risks associated with these activities.

Leys argues that this process of neo-liberal marketization has occurred in the UK particularly in the areas of health, education and public service broadcasting (PSB) where, in the case of the latter, goals of social responsibility, education and collective, public use have been transformed into ones concerning ratings, entertainment and individual consumption (2001: 161–2). Continuing financial support for PSB has been compromised in the last twenty-five years by the growing commodification of British television as a whole – with its ever-increasing tendencies towards spin, sensationalism and segmentation – and the requirements, in particular, for institutions like the BBC to introduce efficiency measures, cut costs, develop more public–private partnerships and compete more effectively on a world stage. In order to maintain the release of licence fee revenue, the BBC has all too often taken these instructions on board, for example, in its introduction of an 'internal market' and the emergence of a 'culture of accountancy' under the leadership of Director General John Birt in the 1990s (see Born 2004), as well as the casualization of staff and sell-offs of units that followed. The BBC remains a not-for-profit organization but its survival is predicated on the extent to which it competes with its commercial competitors and learns how to operate in a market environment. The increasing involvement of the pro-competition regulator Ofcom in both defining and structuring the future of public service broadcasting in the UK is another powerful example of marketization (see chapter 7).

This aspect of marketization has been less prominent in the USA for the simple reason that there are fewer non-market operations to be transformed in the first place. This is also the case with our second example, privatization, where, in an environment in which publicly owned media play a negligible role, there are few public assets to sell off to the private sector. This is not the case with communications infrastructures where the US state has been more proactive in switching forms of ownership. It privatized the NSFNET, the backbone of the internet, in 1995 and carried out wireless spectrum auctions 'as part of the most aggressive agenda ever put forward by any American administration in favor of perfect enclosure of the public domain' (Benkler 2006: 152). There is, of course, another definition of privatization: the purchase of existing companies by private equity funds that, according to *Advertising Age* is like a 'tsunami' sweeping the US media. In late 2006, major brands like Clear Channel, Cablevision, the *Los Angeles Times* and the *Boston Globe* were all targeted by private equity in a situation in which 'going private is the emerging business model for traditional media firms' (Atkinson 2006).

In Europe, and indeed most of the rest of the world, where public and state ownership of the media was more common, privatization of state assets was a significant part of the restructuring of communications systems in the 1980s and 1990s. Not only national Postal, Telegraph and Telephone authorities (PTTs) were sold off but also government-run newspapers, state broadcasters and even some public service broadcasters like the French channel TF1, privatized in 1987 (see OSI 2005 for an inventory of changes to European media). In the UK, however, despite all the proposals in the 1980s by free-market enthusiasts to break up the BBC (Goodwin 1998: 69–76) and, more recently, to dispose of Channel Four, privatization has been used as more of a threat than a reality inside the media industries.

One way in which the lure of privatization has expressed itself inside US and UK media policy concerns the extent to which decision-making and regulatory powers have been subcontracted out. The neo-liberal argument for 'slimmed-down' government and less interventionist regulation finds its reflection in current trends towards light-touch regulation, self-regulation and co-regulation – forms of media governance that involve the active participation of the private sector (although not necessarily the reduced involvement of government). Self-regulation, to its supporters, is seen as preferable to direct government intervention and as a flexible and efficient form of control that urges industry players to act responsibly and collectively. Price and Verhulst, reflecting on the advantages of self-regulation when applied to the dynamism of the internet, argue that it consists of a 'series of representations, negotiations, contractual arrangements and collaborative efforts with government' (2000: 60). A network of self-regulatory bodies is seen as complementary to what they describe as the 'global, essentially private and decentralized network' (2000: 75) that is the internet.

Critics point out that self-regulation, in the context of market-friendly communications environments, often excludes the public from these 'negotiations' and 'contractual arrangements' Instead, it is a further way of privileging private interests and a particularly useful way of warding off any government interference in the attempts by corporations to shape the structure of media markets. Even those generally sympathetic to the adaptability and flexibility of self-regulation note that 'it may allow strong market players to set up rules that favour their interests to the detriment of competitors and users' (OSI 2005: 91). This can be seen clearly in the performance of organizations like the British Advertising Standards Authority (ASA) and the Press Complaints Commission (PCC), which are dominated by industry voices and unaccountable in their decision-making to the public.

The third illustration of marketization refers to attempts in all media environments to secure the highest ratings and extract the greatest profits by commercializing media content. Robert McChesney has written extensively on what he dubs the 'hypercommercialism' (2000: 34) that he sees as endemic, particularly in the US media system. This refers to the practices of branding, cross-promotion and product placement, the reliance on celebrities, the expansion of advertising and the fragility of the barrier between 'corporate' and 'creative' sides of media organizations that has helped 'increasingly to subordinate editorial fare to commercial values and logic' (2000: 42). The other side of 'hypercommercialism' is the expansion of media into other areas of social life: the ownership of sports ventures by media organizations, the consumer boom in media-related goods aimed at children, the extension of popular children's films into large-scale musical theatre and the growing involvement of media firms in amusement parks, entertainment centres and shopping malls. The mediation, on increasingly commercial terms, of daily life 'may be producing a qualitative change in its role and impact in our society' (2000: 48) that is of great concern to democratic and collectivist values.

Conclusion

This chapter has considered two contrasting political perspectives that have influenced the emergence, implementation and criticism of media policies in the USA and the UK. Both liberal pluralism and neo-liberalism are committed to the deployment of market forces in the media environment but they have very different normative accounts of media policies. Pluralism is the language often adopted by policymakers who speak of the importance of the expression of multiple voices, opinions and outlets in the interests of social stability and consensus. Neo-liberalism is a discourse that describes attempts by political and economic actors to roll back barriers to profitability and to inscribe market dynamics in *all* areas of media activity. The chapter has described some of the 'ideal type' features of both pluralist and neo-liberal approaches to media policy and has argued that an understanding of the shared and distinctive characteristics of liberal pluralism and neo-liberalism is essential if we are to make sense of the contemporary policy developments and regulatory initiatives that are discussed in later chapters.

3

The Reinterpretation of Media Policy Principles

Even the most hardened cynic would probably agree that not all media policy initiatives are carried out purely on the basis of short-term political or economic gain. Indeed, even when policymaking does take place for narrowly instrumental reasons, it is still likely to be justified with reference to concerns that are broader than 'profits' or 'electoral success' alone. Media policies have, over the years, been conceptualized according to entrenched political values and commitments. Philip Napoli describes these as the 'foundation principles [that] have long served as the analytical guideposts for policymakers facing the challenges posed by new communication technologies' (2001: 3). These principles underpin the development of media policies and, at the same time, serve as 'the enduring normative goals that policymakers have pursued' (2001: 3). In other words, they are simultaneously the driving force and the desired result of media policy actions.

This chapter considers four of the most resilient principles that underlie media policymaking: freedom, the public interest, pluralism and diversity. There are, of course, a whole range of other values that have influenced and been promoted through media policies. Napoli (2001) suggests that competition, universal service and localism have been key to US communication policies; McQuail argues that values of justice / equality and order / solidarity 'seem to be basic principles which lie at the heart of most expectations concerning public communication' (1992: 67); for Gibbons, themes of independence and accountability are central to the relationship of media and democracy (1998: 35–54). The list could go on: public service, citizenship, social welfare and mutuality, to name just a few, are other important values served by the media. The point is that it is not possible to do justice to all these themes in one chapter and, in any case, many of them emerge as constituent elements of the principles on which we focus. This chapter evaluates how these core principles have been conceptualized in relation to media, their realization in specific policy and regulatory instruments, and the re-evaluation of these principles – from a largely neo-liberal perspective – in the latter years of the twentieth century.

Freedom

Freedom is perhaps the most fundamental principle guiding media policy initiatives over the last several hundred years. A 'free media' is seen both as one of the main features of a free society *and* as a key mechanism through which democracy is sustained and extended. The ability freely to circulate a range of ideas, no matter how marginal, unwelcome or uncomfortable, to audiences who are equally free to consume and contest these ideas, is a basic feature of democratic theory. As a communication principle, freedom has often been defined 'in terms of an unrestricted right to publish without prior permission or licence and without reprisal, aside from the normal provisions of the law, which apply to all citizens' (McQuail 1992: 68–9). This depends on a belief that individuals have the sovereign right to express themselves without reservation and that, therefore, similar rights are granted to institutions that facilitate this communication. Moves to revoke or restrict these rights are seen as authoritarian, evidence of a weak commitment to freedom and democracy.

In this view of media freedom, the state is conceptualized as the main danger and state power viewed as potentially the main barrier to the unrestricted circulation of ideas. Freedom, here, involves the ability of the media to be free *from* state interference and control as well as the capacity to be free *to* challenge arguments proposed by representatives of the state and to monitor their activities. The emergence of 'free media' is the story of the titanic struggle against government licensing and control, and the establishment of a system committed not to the exercise of power but to the service of individual readers, listeners and viewers (and, in more recent years, users, bloggers and downloaders). This is what James Curran (2002: 4–8) describes as the 'liberal narrative' of media history, a powerful account of the positive impact of firstly the press and latterly cinema and broadcasting on democratic life. It is a comforting story 'of progress in which the media became free, switched their allegiance from government to the people, and served democracy' (2002: 7).

The legacy of John Stuart Mill

This narrative of media history, and the concept of freedom on which it is based, is strongly influenced by the writings of the British philosopher John Stuart Mill and, in particular, his essay *On Liberty* (Mill 1989 [1859]). Here Mill makes an impassioned argument for the sovereign right to individual self-expression as a principled feature of any democratic society. 'No society in which these [individual] liberties are not, on the whole, respected, is free, whatever may be its form of government; and none is completely free in which they do not exist absolute and unqualified (1989: 16). There is, however, one significant qualification: that one person's freedom cannot be justified if it involves denying another's. 'The only freedom which deserves the name is that of pursuing our own good in our own way, so long as we do not attempt to deprive others of theirs, or impede their efforts to obtain it' (1989: 16). This argument remains relevant to this day: Tony Blair's historic speech to the US Congress in July 2003, shortly after the invasion of Iraq, does not mention Mill by name but his spirit is certainly present.

> We are fighting for the inalienable right of humankind – black or white, Christian or not, left, right or a million different – to be free, free to raise a family in love and hope, free to earn a living and be rewarded by your efforts, free not to bend your knee to any man in fear, free to be you so long as being you does not impair the freedom of others. (Blair 2003)

Mill's commitment to individual freedom is based not just on principle but also on the practical benefits that may be accrued in allowing arguments to flourish and truths to be uncovered. Minority positions must be respected and disseminated if public opinion is to assume a vibrant and meaningful existence. 'If all mankind minus one, were of one opinion, and only one person were of the contrary opinion, mankind would be no more justified in silencing that one person, than he, if had the power, would be justified in silencing mankind' (Mill 1989: 20).

Mill's seemingly absolutist stance on freedom of expression has been deployed in relation to media freedom, in particular the freedom of the press, because of his equivalence – or at least his lack of differentiation between – 'freedom of opinion, and freedom of the *expression* of opinion' (1989: 53 – emphasis added). In part, this is because Mill himself refers to the 'liberty of the press' (1989: 19) in relation to general liberty of thought and discussion; more substantially, it is because, according to Onora O'Neill (2004: 5), Mill argues that freedom of expression 'has to be embedded in communication if it to support truth-seeking and the emergence of true beliefs'. From this perspective, the same rights and guarantees awarded to individual freedom of expression should be handed to those institutions that most fully articulate and embody these expressions. This idea, that the press should be treated 'as a voice, albeit a more powerful one, on a par with individual voices' (Lichtenberg 1990: 105), remains as the basis on which many contemporary debates concerning free speech and media freedom are played out.

The impact of the First Amendment

The liberal approach to press freedom is premised on the right of the individual to pursue his or her own beliefs in a contest with others and is nurtured in a narrative that assigns a primary role to the responsibility of the press to act as a 'watchdog' (Curran 2002: 217). Public policy in this area is therefore aimed at ensuring the maximum freedom of individuals to engage in debate and the minimum ability of government to curb such debate. The most celebrated policy instrument that expresses this commitment is the First Amendment of the US Constitution that 'Congress shall make no law . . . abridging the freedom of speech, or of the press', described by Napoli as the 'boundary-setting foundation principle of communications policy' (2001: 29). It still provides the marker against which free-speech principles are measured, as demonstrated by George W. Bush's reluctance, in front of an audience of broadcasters, to criticize First Amendment principles: 'Look, I'm a First Amendment guy. Anyone running for President is a First Amendment person. You gotta honor that. How can you not be a First Amendment guy?' (Bush 2005).

Liberal pluralist accounts of media history can point to Supreme Court rulings on free speech that were guided by expansive and sympathetic readings of the First Amendment. For example, in a decision that made it more difficult for powerful public figures to bring libel actions against their critics in the press, Justice Brennan argued that 'debate on public issues should be uninhibited, robust, and wide-open, and that it may well include vehement, caustic, and sometimes unpleasantly sharp attacks on government and public officials' (*New York Times* 1964: 270). An even fiercer defence of the rights of the press to publish, free from censorship, material against the wishes of the government was provided by the Supreme Court in its ruling on the *New York Times'* decision to publish a leaked internal report on US involvement in the Vietnam War. In words that have a particularly contemporary resonance, Justice Black argued that:

> In the First Amendment the Founding Fathers gave the free press the protection it must have to fulfil its essential role in our democracy. The press was to serve the governed, not the governors. The Government's power to censor the press was abolished so that the press would remain forever free to censure the Government. The press was protected so that it could bare the secrets of government and inform the people. Only a free and unrestrained press can effectively expose deception in government. And paramount among the responsibilities of a free press is the duty to prevent any part of the government from deceiving the people and sending them

off to distant lands to die of foreign fevers and foreign shot and shell. (*New York Times* 1971: 717)

The high point of pluralist interpretation of constitutional free speech rights for the media can probably be dated to 1969 with the application of the First Amendment to broadcasting and support for the FCC's Fairness Doctrine (see chapter 2) in the famous 'Red Lion' case. Here, the Court went beyond a 'negative' understanding of media freedom as freedom *from* the state and instead argued that regulation was appropriate to secure the speech rights of those normally excluded from the media through a right-to-reply mechanism. The Court argued that 'it is the right of the viewing and listening public, and not the right of the broadcasters, which is para-mount' and subsequently that the First Amendment 'does not protect private censorship by broadcasters who are licensed by the Government to use a scarce resource which is denied to others' (*Red Lion* 1969: 368). The First Amendment could be invoked, therefore, to defend both the rights of journalists against the state as well as the interests of the public against media corporations.

A further illustration of the pluralist commitment to vigorous debate and freedom of expression may be seen in the widely used metaphor that a free media is one that facilitates a 'marketplace of ideas'. This is a concept that combines liberal belief in the dynamism of economic transactions in the free market with the importance of the circulation of ideas in a democracy and has, according to John Durham Peters, 'become a fixture in legal and public debates about freedom of expression and the social responsibility of the media' (2004: 65–6). It is eloquently articulated in a dissenting opinion by Justice Oliver Wendell Holmes (in a case that ruled against criticism of the USA during the First World War) that 'the ultimate good desired is better reached by free trade in ideas – that the best test of truth is the power of the thought to get itself accepted in the competition of the market' (*Abrams* 1919: 630). The phrase is then echoed in the 'Red Lion' case where the Court argued that it is 'the purpose of the First Amendment to preserve an uninhibited market-place of ideas in which truth will ulti-mately prevail, rather than to countenance monopolization of that market, whether it be by the Government itself or a private licensee' (*Red Lion* 1969: 390). The metaphor has been used extensively both by the Supreme Court (Peters 2004: 77) and the FCC (Napoli 2001: 109–21) in relation to decisions concerning speech rights, oligopoly, pornography and editorial balance. It has also been used in the UK, for example, to justify the need for media ownership rules where market forces alone 'cannot necessarily provide the market-place of ideas that enables democracy to prosper' (DTI 2004: 10).

Limitations of media freedom instruments

Despite the attractive quality of many of these arguments – after all, who would not *like* to believe that we have a thriving marketplace of ideas? – pluralist interpretations of media freedom based on Mill, the First Amendment and the 'marketplace of ideas' have nevertheless been extensively criticized.

First, these interpretations exaggerate the extent to which instruments like the First Amendment were ever reliable guarantors of press freedom. For example, according to media historian Paul Starr, the First Amendment was scarred by the political tension of the time in which it was drafted. 'By itself, the mere wording of the First Amendment did not guarantee freedom of speech, broad or narrow in construction . . . The real meaning of the amendment was determined through political conflict, and this conflict was not long in coming' (2004: 77). Sure enough, shortly after the Amendment was adopted, the Federalists had managed to silence much of the opposition Republican press by threatening newspaper editors under the Sedition Act.

'Absolutist' claims to free speech were further challenged by a ruling during the First World War in which the Supreme Court refused to defend the right to circulate leaflets that denounced conscription and the war. According to Justice Holmes:

> the character of every act depends upon the circumstances in which it is done. The most stringent protection of free speech would not protect a man in falsely shouting fire in a theatre and causing a panic . . . The question in every case is whether the words used are used in such circumstances and are of such a nature as to create a clear and present danger that they will bring about the substantive evils that Congress has a right to prevent. (Quoted in *Abrams* 1919: 52)

This notion of 'clear and present danger' remains the yardstick against which claims to free speech must be judged. In the same speech in which George W. Bush declared his commitment to the First Amendment, he also noted that freedom comes with restrictions:

> A free society is where people feel free without retribution to speak . . . On the other hand, there's some information which could damage our ability to collect information, and that's where the real rub has been so far from my perspective . . . And it's a delicate balance. (Bush 2005)

The 'clear and present danger' doctrine justifies a range of government constraints on an individual's right to know and to speak, including the

Homeland Security Act in the USA and the Official Secrets Act in the UK (see chapter 6).

The First Amendment is ambiguous on another point: whether it refers 'only to an individual right to publish or to the distinctive rights of the press as a political institution' (Starr 2004: 76). Napoli (2001: 44–52) traces this confusion to rival 'individualist' and 'collectivist' interpretations of the amendment, while Stein (2004) notes the existence of conflicting 'defensive' and 'empowering' approaches to speech rights. The latter draws on participatory democratic theory and suggests that state action can be used to facilitate the rights of the public to speak; the former draws on a neo-liberal philosophy that 'presumes that freedom exists in privately controlled spaces that have been secured against government coercion' (2004: 105). This is best illustrated by the Supreme Court's decision in 1974 to rule against a right to reply in the press on the basis that this would be a form of 'governmental coercion' which would bring about 'a confrontation with the express provisions of the First Amendment' (*Miami Herald* 1974: 255).

Second, many of the assumptions on which pluralist arguments for media freedom are based are outdated. As James Curran puts it (2002: 217), 'the classic liberal theory for a free press on which we still rely was refined and elaborated in the nineteenth century as part of a political campaign for press deregulation'. This involved a very different media environment to the one we have today, one in which small-scale political publications competed for scarce readers and the main threat to the ability of the press to report independently and accurately was the power of the state. In such a situation, it was not surprising that the 'early liberal thinkers took it for granted that free enterprise was the foundation of freedom of expression' (Thompson 1995: 239). Today, however, the western media is characterized by transnational corporations, oligopolistic markets, literate audiences and fierce competition for revenue. In such a situation, appeals to the sanctity of individual rights to self-expression and the equation of these rights with those of the media is extremely problematic. 'According unrestricted freedom of expression not only to individuals but also to powerful institutions, the media among them, is not *necessary for* but *damaging to* democracy' (O'Neill 2004: 8).

Third, it is the case that liberal narratives of media freedom are easily superimposed on to events that require a quite different interpretation. For example, the abolition of press taxes in Britain in the mid-nineteenth century is often heralded as a key victory for freedom and democracy that gave birth to the modern press. Its real objective, however, was to marginalize the impact of the radical press and to create the conditions for a commercial newspaper market: 'the parliamentary campaign for a free press was never inspired by a modern libertarian commitment to diversity of expression . . . [but] the subordination of the press to the social order' (Curran and Seaton, 2003: 22). More recent interpretations of phenomena such as the First Amendment and the 'marketplace of ideas' metaphor are misleading in that they are often the result of a highly contemporary and inflexible attachment to the desirability of market forces that was lacking in the original formulations. Jean Seaton (1998: 124) argues that neo-liberal interpretations of Mill and the First Amendment, that treat ideas as ordinary commodities to circulate in the free market, have become increasingly important in media policy discussions. Yet this is not what Mill implied in his defence of free speech and advocacy of open debate where he was more concerned to secure the right political conditions for argument than a formal legal framework. Seaton's impression of Mill's position:

> is not of a so-called 'neo-liberal' free-market view of the battle of ideas, in which the right of expression is sacrosanct, and the best idea is 'bought' and therefore triumphs. Instead of a Darwinian jungle, he sees the argument-market as a kind of cauldron, in which ideas of varying strength and merit are adapted and fuse. (1998: 127)

On a similar note, Cass Sunstein attacks interpretations of the First Amendment that reduce its scope to an economically based activity that protects the speech acts of sovereign individuals from government interference. Instead, he argues that 'democratic deliberation' lies at its heart and that the author of the amendment, James Madison, 'saw "free communication among the people" not as an exercise in consumer sovereignty, in which speech was treated as a kind of commodity, but instead as a central part of self-government, the "only effectual guardian of every other right"' (Sunstein 2001: 10) An absolutist interpretation of the amendment, that government should never intervene in the communications market, plays a 'large role in public debate' but remains, nevertheless, a 'myth' (2001: 9).

John Durham Peters (2004) provides a particularly elegant account of the way in which a strange assortment of figures – from the poet John Milton to the economist Adam Smith, John Stuart Mill and Supreme Court Judge Oliver Wendell Holmes – are all credited with inventing the 'marketplace of ideas' metaphor, even though Peters can find no evidence of any of them ever having used the phrase. In what he calls an example of 'imaginative retrojection' (2004: 72), contemporary faith in market forces is backdated so that historic commitments to freedom of expression come to be articulated through concepts concerning economic exchange rather than political struggle. This involves a misunderstanding of these writers' *qualified* support for the ability of the market to deliver social justice. 'The main sin of attributing the notion to Milton, Smith, Mill, or Holmes', argues Peters (2004: 80), 'is missing their warnings about the kind of people and society we would become if marketplace values of getting and spending alone prevailed.'

This attachment to market-led readings of the origins of free-speech commitments has, not surprisingly, shaped the actual application of these instruments in such a way as to privilege private economic interests rather than public democratic ones. The media economist Bruce Owen antici-pated the attitude of the FCC in the 1980s towards creating a 'marketplace of ideas' when he argued that, contra the ideas of those who believed in a 'truth-seeking' perspective, 'I want to take the "marketplace" notion quite literally. There is a market in which information and entertainment, intel-lectual "goods" are bought and sold' (quoted in Napoli 2001: 105). Perhaps the clearest example of this reinterpretation of free-speech principles in the USA was the extension of First Amendment protection to commercial speech at the end of the 1970s (Creech 2000: 143). Until that point, 'the consensus within the US Supreme Court, and the legal culture in general, was that the First Amendment did not protect commercial speech at all' (Sunstein 2001: 9). However, faced with 'aggressive media, advertising and corporate lobbies ever eager to eliminate government regulation of their activities' (McChesney 2000: 268), the Supreme Court caved in and pro-vided an admirably forthright definition of corporate speech as 'expression related solely to the economic interests of the speaker and its audience' (*Central Hudson Gas* 1980: 561).

The result of this has led to multiple warnings about the extent to which, using Stein's language (2004), neo-liberal 'defensive' interpretations are now dominant over participatory democratic 'empowering' views of the First Amendment. Thomas Streeter (1996: 191) argues that conservatives have hegemonized 'free speech' discourse while Robert McChesney claims we now have a 'new theology of the First Amendment' (2000: 257) in which corporate claims to free speech are systematically valued over all others. Robert Entman (2003 [1993]) conducted a content analysis of the use of the First Amendment by the FCC in rulings between 1981 and 1992 concerning the Fairness Doctrine, radio deregulation and children's television rules. He discovered that the vast majority of the Commission's references to free expression referred to either the protection of editorial autonomy by corporate owners against all forms of government interference or to the need for debate in a 'marketplace of ideas'. He concludes that the primary meaning of the First Amendment increasingly refers to 'maximizing media owners' rights to expression unimpeded by government. This now-dominant view subsumes other interpretations of First Amendment goals in its determination to shield owners from formal governmental intrusion' (1993: 470) and, according to Entman, the amendment in its current form and determination 'has had a chilling effect on discourse regarding communications policy' (1993: 470).

This does not mean that the First Amendment, and other instruments pertaining to speech rights and freedom of expression, have been unilaterally captured by corporate voices. However, it is the case that their ambiguities and inconsistencies have been exploited in disturbing ways with the emergence of 'absolutist' approaches to free speech that reflect neo-liberal certainties about the efficacy of the market. Media freedom, despite the claims of well-intentioned liberal theorists, is not an absolute principle but an instrumental right that should be claimed only insofar as it promotes socially desirable values – for example, equality, tolerance, knowledge, justice, empowerment and citizenship – and, crucially, does not prevent others from realizing these values. Onora O'Neill is right to be concerned about a situation in which individual speech rights have been all too easily granted to powerful media institutions: 'we are now perilously close to a world in which media conglomerates act as if they too had unrestricted rights of free expression, and therefore a licence to subject positions for which they don't care to caricature and derision, misrepresentation or silence' (2002). If this question of unequal power is ignored, then we are perhaps still no further away from the idea that 'freedom of the press is guaranteed only to those who own one' (Liebling 1964: 30–1).

The public interest

The concept of the public interest has played a major role in the development and application of media policies, regularly serving to justify particular policy initiatives and providing a yardstick against which these initiatives can be measured. Napoli argues that it 'functions as the broad umbrella concept from which all of the other foundation principles in communications policy stem' (2001: 63), while McQuail insists that media policies should be seen as 'projects of government and public administration which have particular goals and a certain legitimation in terms of the wider "public interest" ' (2000: 21–2). The phrase was first and most famously applied to US communications media in the 1934 Communications Act that authorized the newly formed Federal Communications Commission to regulate the airwaves 'in the public interest, convenience, or necessity'. Indeed, it would be fair to say that the First Amendment's protection of speech rights is in the public interest and that, as the UK Press Complaints Commission argues in its Code of Practice, there is 'a public interest in the freedom of expression itself' (PCC 2006). The impact of the phrase on US policy is demonstrated by the fact that it appeared 11 times in the 1934 Act, 40 times in the 1996 Telecommunications Act (Napoli 2001: 63) and 207 times in the FCC's review of broadcast ownership rules in 2003. Given that the phrase was also invoked 24 times in New Labour's Communications White Paper of 2000 and 23 times in its consultation on media ownership in 2001, the public interest remains to this day a central principle of media policy on both sides of the Atlantic.

Its definition, however, is a more contentious matter. Does it refer, on the one hand, to the realization of the desires of the public as a collection of individuals or does it imply a normative commitment to a principle that expresses their best interest? One survey into perception of the public interest noted real confusion about the term, that it is seen both as 'whatever the public is interested in knowing' and 'whatever is in the interests (to the benefit) of the public to know' (Morrison and Svennevig 2002: 66). Our discussion will focus on how these two contrasting conceptual approaches have contributed to different policy instruments and objectives, one that reflects pluralist sentiments about social consensus and the 'common good', the other more concerned with the interplay of private individual interests that is at the heart of neo-liberalism.

McQuail argues that the public interest concept derives from debates in economic regulation and refers to a contractual arrangement whereby, in return for securing trading rights, producers had to accept certain obligations to the community as a whole, for example universal service, minimum standards and fair pricing (1992: 21). This applied, in particular, to industries and services that were seen as essential and related to the 'general welfare' beyond that of private individuals – in particular the public utilities of gas, electricity, water, sewage and basic telecommunications. This kind of 'public interest' approach is therefore generally connected to the protection of consumer rights through the regulation of private economic activity by public authorities. While this approach is by no means hostile to private property, it nevertheless suggests that there is a certain tension between private and public interests and that the former cannot be relied upon voluntarily to respect the latter. Intervention is required to curb the excesses of corporate behaviour and to steer it towards serving the public as well as its shareholders. 'In the view of Progressive public interest theory, regulation was imposed by government to correct inefficient or inequitable market practices . . . the regulatory agency would function as a watchdog for the general welfare through the oversight of rates and profit levels' (Horwitz 1989: 25). The state is conceptualized here as a mediator between the power of corporations and the interests of the public.

Public interest regulation that presupposes the existence of a 'common good' above and beyond the interests of particular political or economic elites is especially relevant to the media. According to Horwitz, the status of press or broadcasting as a public good predisposes them to regulation in the name of social objectives: 'Certain industries, and certain types of industries, appear historically always imbued with something larger, something more general than private interest. This "something" is what we intuitively understand as the public interest' (1989: 11). McQuail argues on the same lines that policy instruments – for example, content rules, ownership restrictions, frequency allocations and press subsidies – 'are often justified on grounds of a wider "common good", transcending individual choice and preferences, with more reference to experts or to tradition than to the balance of popular opinion' (1992: 24). According to Croteau and Hoynes (2001: 150), 'media are fundamentally intertwined with matters of the common good rather than just private profit,' and they point to four possible objectives for media systems run in the public interest: diversity, innovation, substance and independence.

This was the approach adopted by US regulators when drawing up the first rules that allowed private broadcasters access to the public airwaves on the understanding that they had to respect certain public interest obligations. To begin with, there was little clarity as to what these obligations should be apart from some very broad indications. Napoli argues that one of the earliest attempts to 'operationalize' the public interest concept was the Federal Radio Commission's statement in 1928 of key principles for broadcasters that included freedom from signal interference, provision of different programme types, a commitment to localism and evidence of the character and integrity of broadcast licencees (2001: 83). With the expansion of the broadcast system, however, it became necessary to codify unwritten rules and assumptions into a set of requirements that would help regulators evaluate the extent to which broadcasters were meeting their public interest obligations and to ensure a smoother licence renewal process. In 1960 the FCC adopted a programming policy statement which listed the 'major elements usually necessary for the public interest' and included requirements for opportunities for 'editorializing', the use of local talent, weather and market reports, services for minority groups and children's, educational, public affairs, political, agricultural, news, sports and entertainment programming. In return for the right to have exclusive access to public airwaves, broadcasters were forced to meet these obligations. One commentator has described this trade-off as a 'social contract' between broadcasters and the public (quoted in New America Foundation 2004: 1).

Under attack from broadcasters for being vague and inconsistent, the Supreme Court defended the public interest as the 'touchstone for the exercise of the [Federal Communication] Commission's authority' (*FCC* 1940: 138) and indicated that the public interest was a crucial way of evaluating whether broadcasters were serving their publics effectively or not. However, the Court also acknowledged that it was an instrument whose precise meaning could not be pinned down easily:

> While this [public interest] criterion is as concrete as the complicated factors for judgment in such a field of delegated authority permit, it serves as a supple instrument for the exercise of discretion by the expert body [the FCC] which Congress has charged to carry out its legislative policy. (1940: 138)

This description of the 'supple' nature of the public interest is confirmation of a more 'procedural' (Napoli 2001: 74) definition – that it is whatever those charged with enforcing its remit decide it is – but also a clear admission of the ambiguities and inconsistencies that dog interpretations of the public interest to this day.

For example, the public interest is still referred to regularly in the UK as a yardstick by which to justify the publication or broadcast of particularly sensitive or controversial material. If the dissemination of this material is likely to contribute to the 'common good' through the making available of new information or the correction of false allegations, then breaches of privacy or consent may be sanctioned. The problem is that interpretations of what the public has a 'right to know' vary greatly depending on political perspectives and professional responsibilities. While the Press Complaints Commission, the self-regulatory body paid for by the newspaper industry, lists a mere three examples of public interest contexts in its Code of Practice (PCC 2006) – detecting and exposing crime; protecting public health and preventing the public from being misled – the journalists' union has a much more extensive list that includes exposing corporate greed, exposing hypocritical behaviour by those holding high office and revealing conflicts of interest of those in positions of power and influence (NUJ 2004). A similar discrepancy can be seen in relation to broadcasting. The BBC's editorial guidelines recognize that there is 'no single definition of public interest', but provide a list that includes the exposure of anti-social behaviour, the uncovering of corruption and injustice, and the disclosing of information likely to allow people 'to make a significantly more informed decision about matters of public importance' (BBC 2005: 44–5). Rather significantly, the commercial regulator, Ofcom, makes no mention of any of the above in its much shorter discussion of what constitutes the public interest (2005: 42). Evoking the public interest in this fashion may be a useful way of reminding us, in Horwitz's words, of the existence of 'something more general than private interest', but its operational utility is undermined by the fact that it is open to conflicting definitions.

A more robust 'common good' interpretation of the public interest sees it not as an accessory to market relations but as a countervailing force to them, as a pole of attraction with a very different dynamic to that of private accumulation. We can see this in some of the institutions of the public sector in the UK: the National Health Service, comprehensive education and the BBC. Here, it is not the concept of public interest but of public *service* that provides the rationale for democratic citizenship. Colin Leys argues that these public services 'are the defining features of a civilized society, which capitalist market production, if it persists at all, should exist to pay for, and to which it should be subordinate' (2001: 220). This refers to a 'non-market domain' (2001: 224) in which essential services are provided, the market is kept at bay, and boundaries between the public and the private are well policed in order to prevent the infiltration of the former by the latter.

Nowhere has this concept been more influential than in the sphere of British broadcasting which has been operating, in part, as a public service for over seventy-five years. Rather than being held to a narrowly consumer-oriented public interest standard, government and regulators have sought to develop a more systematic basis on which the public, seen as a collective, can be served. According to Curran and Seaton (1991: 348), the 'central credo' of public service is that:

> Broadcasting should be publicly owned or regulated so that it serves the public good rather than private gain. Only in this way, it is argued, can broadcasting be prevented from becoming subservient to the

commercial forces that make for low quality, cultural uniformity, and right-wing bias.

This idea has been applied most significantly to the BBC, one of the key non-market British institutions, as well as to other commercial broadcasters who have been forced to use their profits – in a more vigorous interpretation of the American public interest standard – to produce programmes and cater to audiences in ways specified by public authorities. It is a conception of broadcasting that is 'rooted in a view of society that stresses social association and mutual obligation, and tacitly rejects the neo-liberal view of society as an aggregation of contracting and exchanging individuals' (1991: 356).

Privatizing the public interest

Yet it is precisely this latter view that has come to challenge the 'common good' interpretations of public interest and public service in recent years. The emergence of neo-liberalism in the early 1980s together with its associated trends towards deregulation and marketization involved a reconsideration of the definition of the public interest. Far from there being an identifiable 'common good' that lay beyond the sum of individual transactions facilitated by the market, the public interest was best expressed in relation to public preferences and individual consumer choices. This had the benefit, at least, of avoiding some of the ambiguities that accompanied the interpretation of the public interest that had characterized most broadcast regulation up till that point. The public interest could now be proved and quantified – using opinion polls, ratings, surveys and circulation figures – and legitimized according to this data. The downside was that more subtle and broad conceptions of the public as a diverse group of citizens were sacrificed for a far more instrumental view. Members of the public were now seen either as customers of media corporations or, as an antitrust expert from the Department of Justice put it, 'as the shareholders of the companies involved [in a merger]' (Majure 2001: 31).

Horwitz (1989) describes how the concept of the public interest was transformed by the deregulation that occurred in the US telecommunications and broadcast industries in the 1970s and 1980s, and notes that this transformation involved 'a shift away from concern with stability and a kind of social equity to a concern with market controls and economic efficiency' (1989: 21). The new marketplace approach to the public interest was best expressed by FCC chairman Mark Fowler and his legal adviser from 1981–6, Daniel Brenner:

Communications policy should be directed towards maximizing the services the public desires. Instead of defining public demand and specifying categories of programming to serve this demand, the Commission should rely on the broadcasters' ability to determine the wants of their audiences through the normal mechanisms of the marketplace. The public's interest, then, defines the public interest. (Fowler and Brenner 1982: 3–4)

This new populist conception of the public interest justified the rolling back of many traditional public interest obligations and was marked by the 'near exclusive emphasis on economic values, reflecting the core liberal emphasis on the individual' that, Feintuck argues, 'results in a failure to serve the "public interest" that exists in the fundamental democratic expectation of equality of citizenship' (2004: 24). This is illustrated by the following events in 1981 alone:

- The abandonment by the National Association of Broadcasters of its Code of Conduct after its advertising portions were found illegal on antitrust grounds;
- The elimination by the FCC of radio rules concerning programming logs, commercial time limitations and non-entertainment requirements;
- The simplification of license renewal application forms containing only five questions;
- The refusal by the FCC to establish concrete requirements for children's programming.

(New America Foundation 2004: 4)

This was followed by the more sustained deregulation of the broadcast industries in 1984 and, of course, by the decision in 1987 to abolish the Fairness Doctrine on the basis that the doctrine was inconsistent with both the public interest and the First Amendment principles it was intended to promote.

It is not that the concept of the public interest is disappearing but that its meaning as a counterweight to private pressures is being evacuated. While many of the obligations that formed the basis of the original 'social contract' between broadcasters and the US public have been scrapped, market-friendly regulators are now crowing about the ambiguity of the public interest concept. For example, Michael Powell, FCC chairman from 2001–5 and a commissioner from 1998, admitted that, having searched through the archives for a viable definition, he was still no nearer to understanding what the public interest referred to.

The night after I was sworn in, I waited for a visit from the angel of the public interest. I waited all night, but she did not come. And, in fact, five months into this job, I still have had no divine awakening and no one has issued me my public interest crystal ball. But I am here, an enlightened wiseman without a clue. The best that I can discern is that the public interest standard is a bit like modern art, people see in it what they want to see. That may be a fine quality for art, but it is a bit of a problem when that quality exists in a legal standard. (Powell 1998a)

The opacity of the public interest that Powell refers to did not, of course, prevent him from launching a series of deregulatory initiatives in the name of the public interest during the years of his chairmanship. A senior figure in the FCC, charged with overseeing the review of broadcast ownership rules, also admits that the notion of the public interest is a 'largely empty vessel, and it can be filled up with whatever one might want to fill it up with'. This reflects a problem not just to do with the elasticity of many of the principles that inform media policymakers, but also of the latter's determination to use their interpretation of these ambiguous ideas to justify the need for specific policy instruments and, in recent years, deregulatory initiatives. It is further proof of the politicized nature of the media policy field.

Marketized interpretations of the public interest have also entered the debate in Britain. For example, the 'public interest test', introduced by the New Labour government in 2003 to adjudicate on media mergers, depends on a definition of public interest based on plurality of ownership, diversity of sources, economic benefits and market effects (DCMS/DTI 2001: 47), a concept of the public interest that is responsive rather than counterposed to commercial forces (see chapter 5 for more details). While the 'common good' understanding of the concept is still present (witness, for example, the introduction in 1998 of a Public Interest Disclosure Act to protect whistleblowers from reprisals, a move that partially softens the blow of the scrapping in 1989 of a public interest defence in the Official Secrets Act), an alternative definition of the public interest based on consumer sovereignty and market competition is increasingly influential. Perhaps the best example of this was a high-profile speech in 1999 by the then chief executive of ITV, Richard Eyre (Eyre 1999). He argued that in a multi-channel, viewer-dominated digital world, the old paternalistic system of public service broadcasting would die out to be replaced by the more dynamic and less regulated system of 'public interest broadcasting'. This is an explicitly commercial view in which the BBC is reduced to filling the gaps left by the other broadcasters and in which 'regulation as a sort of conscience by rulebook won't exist. What will replace it? You and me . . . and the viewers' (Eyre 1999). It is a further vision of the 'privatization' of the public interest

– or, in Habermasian terms, of the 'refeudalization' of the public sphere (Habermas 1989) – an individualization that threatens to eliminate 'a common public realm of discourse' (Baker 2002: 290).

Perhaps it is the case that the concept of the public interest was always a blunt tool to use against the incursions of the market, especially in the USA. While neo-liberals have appropriated the terminology to argue for a populist, ratings-led conception of media responsibility that has shielded media corporations from outside interference, pluralists have turned to the 'angel of the public interest' as a source of minimal protection for the public in a commercial environment. The problem, however, is that it is a concept lacking an account of social life that is independent of or counterposed to those commercial forces – indeed it is, as Horwitz asserts, 'inescapably bound to the commerce origin' (1989: 15). Most importantly, he argues that 'because public interest theory is tied to a pluralist theory of power, it slights the structural importance of the economy and of economic power' (1989: 26), and therefore fails to construct adequate barriers against private capital or against state involvement on behalf of private interests. Its ambiguity is a sign of weakness and not of strength. Unless it is attached to a positive expression of non-commercial ideas and related to the construction of a viable non-market domain, the concept of the public interest is likely to remain a flimsy defence against the encroachments of private capital.

Pluralism and diversity

The desire to foster a wide variety of voices, opinions and outlets in the media is a long-standing policy commitment, but the terms under which this objective is conducted are by no means always clear. According to an influential commentator on British media policy, '[n]otions of pluralism, diversity and the marketplace for ideas are at best vague and malleable, at worst adjusted to the purpose of whoever invokes them' (Tambini 2001: 26). Writing about the search for diversity in the US media, Napoli (2001: 126) argues that 'policymakers and policy analysts have yet to reach a consensus in terms of what constitutes an adequate definition or measure of this rather ambiguous concept'. For this reason alone, it is worth attempting to clarify and disentangle the two terms and to evaluate the conflicting interpretations that have been given to them by US and UK policymakers.

Diversity and pluralism are frequently used either consecutively or interchangeably in many discussions of media performance and policy.

Thomas Gibbons simply equates the two, distinguishing between internal pluralism as 'a diversity of programming content within the [single broadcast] service' and external pluralism as 'a diversity of media sources' (1998: 31). Another definition argues that:

> Pluralism is generally associated with diversity in the media; the presence of a number of different and independent voices, and of different political opinions and representations of culture within the media. Citizens expect and need a diversity and plurality of media content and media sources. (Doyle 2002: 11–12)

This highlights the key issues – of the democratic requirement for contrasting sources, ideas, forms, and images present in the media environment – but does little to clarify the distinction between the two terms. The confusion is not helped by the fact that US media policy debates generally focus on securing diversity, whereas European ones are increasingly coalescing around the objective of pluralism (which, as we shall see, is itself closer to what US policymakers describe as competition).

Denis McQuail (1992) offers a useful way of understanding the relation between the two terms. Pluralism, he argues, refers to a political conception of independence from the state combined with vigorous competition for the allocation of resources. What McQuail describes as 'pluralistic political arrangements' are required for the mass media to be seen 'as essential weapons in resisting trends to centralized control and uniformity' (1992: 141–2). A structurally pluralistic media system is a prerequisite for media diversity, itself understood as the 'variability of mass media (sources, channels, messages and audiences) in terms of relevant differences in society (political, geographical, social-cultural, etc.)' (1992: 147). A plural media should facilitate reflection of the contrasting voices and interests in society, provide access to the channels that do this, and offer a full menu of products and services to audiences. So, while pluralism refers to the wider political context in which media operate, diversity is related to the media's ability to acknowledge and express existing social differences through maximizing the choices offered to audiences, who are in turn able to take advantage of this provision.

Approaches to media diversity

In the United States, media diversity policy focuses on two interconnected phenomena. The first relates, broadly speaking, to the participation by and representation of ethnic minorities in the creative process and is part of a larger debate concerning cultural diversity (described as 'cultural pluralism by Doyle 2002: 12). The second is based on the classic liberal paradigm of media freedom and an interpretation of the First Amendment that, in a famous phrase of Supreme Court Judge Justice Black, 'rests on the assumption that the widest possible dissemination of information from diverse and antagonistic sources is essential to the welfare of the public' (*Associated Press* 1945: 20). Media diversity is therefore seen as a key objective of a vigorous 'marketplace of ideas' through which the First Amendment is expressed and cemented and actively promoted by specific policy instruments. All major US broadcast regulatory innovations, such as the Prime Time Access Rule, the Fin-Syn rules, the Fairness Doctrine and broadcast ownership restrictions, have been carried out under the aegis of the 'marketplace of ideas' metaphor for the express purpose of the promotion of media diversity.

In contrast to this expansive definition, Napoli (2001: 125–52) outlines the main ways in which broadcast diversity has actually been operationalized by regulators, the courts and corporations themselves. He identifies three main dimensions – source, content and exposure diversity – and breaks this down into further subcomponents concerning ownership, workforce, format, demographic (or representational) and viewpoint forms of diversity. The guiding assumption has traditionally been that greater source diversity is likely to lead to enhanced content diversity. According to the FCC (1999: 9): 'One of the most important purposes of our multiple ownership rules is to encourage diversity in the ownership of broadcast stations so as to foster a diversity of viewpoints in the material presented over the airwaves.' This is the premise of modern market liberals who argue that a plethora of media outlets will ensure that no single outlet – or voice – dominates: 'So long as there are reasonably competing media sources as there are today, these can cancel each other out. Why is it that everyone does not eat Wheaties or use Exxon gasoline?' (Compaine and Gomery 2000: 568). The problem is that there is no systematic proof that multiple media ownership by itself guarantees the provision of different or conflicting voices; external pluralism does not magically lead to the airing of 'diverse and antagonistic' ideas. 'Despite the common assertion of a causal relationship between source diversity and content diversity,' argues Napoli (2001: 134), 'policy and legal decisions have often been made without empirical evidence supporting the existence of such a relationship.' According to Napoli, 'the expectation that increased diversity of sources leads to increased diversity of content is far from a certainty' (2001: 137).

However, since the abolition of many of the aforementioned regulatory instruments in the deregulatory climate of the 1970s and 1980s, any

residual commitment on the part of regulators to ensure a robust interpretation of diversity has ebbed away. What seems to be largely underpinning the FCC's conception of diversity in recent years are beliefs in variety
and competitiveness, of a smorgasbord of companies, formats, opinions,
styles, niches, and narratives from which audiences are free to pick and
choose. Diversity here refers not so much to what distinguishes one
choice from another but to the size of the menu as a whole. It is a highly
consumerist construction that privileges the act of individual selection far
more than the social obligation to provide choices that are fundamentally
in opposition to each other – or, in the words of Justice Black quoted
earlier, viewpoints that are 'antagonistic'. Robert Horwitz argues that this
points to a fundamental difference between *variety* and *diversity*:

> Variety refers to more choices within a relatively narrow set of market-
> determined formats. Diversity is a more philosophically based concept
> than simply a market-based notion of consumer choice. Diversity is
> ensconced within the values which underlie the freedom of speech, values
> which demand divergent points of view both because they nurture an
> informed, self-governing citizenry and because they promote cultural
> pluralism. (1989: 280)

Some regulation continues to be necessary, but it is increasingly structural
rather than behavioural, maintaining some restrictions on ownership of
multiple media outlets rather than positively fostering or enforcing a
commitment to publicize less popular or non-consensual viewpoints, an
approach that is itself problematic because of recent neo-liberal interpretations of the First Amendment. Furthermore, the protection of viewpoint
diversity, one of the core objectives in recent reviews of broadcast ownership rules, is now to be achieved by matching consumer appetites to the
instincts of the market. The effect of this policy approach – of linking
increased choice to increased diversity – has been to blur any meaningful
distinction in regulatory activity between competition and diversity.

Approaches to media pluralism

In Europe, media pluralism (rather than diversity) has become the more
prevalent policy objective, but there has also been more attention aimed
at highlighting the differences between the two. Pluralism gained currency
in media policy debates in Britain in the late 1970s (Freedman 2003a;
Gibbons, 2000), a response to the emergence of more mixed, multicultural
populations as well as to increasing levels of dissatisfaction with existing
media structures. For example, the 1977 Annan Committee on the future

of broadcasting articulated real concerns about the ideological narrowness of the broadcasting 'duopoly' of the BBC and commercial sector, and argued that contemporary culture 'is now multi racial and pluralist . . . [t]he structure of broadcasting must reflect this variety' (Annan 1977: 30). This laid the basis for a 'pluralist' approach that sought to open up broadcasting to new and previously marginalized voices, but also led to a more decentred view of broadcasting as catering to different parts of the community through the introduction of choice and competition – very much related to the definition of diversity earlier in relation to the USA. This new notion of a marketized 'liberal pluralism' led to the abandonment of policy objectives concerning social consensus and the emergence of a 'free marketplace in which balance could be achieved through the competition of multiplicity of independent voices' (Curran and Seaton 1991: 296).

This anticipated the deregulatory and liberalizing initiatives of the 1980s and 1990s, where it was argued that market mechanisms together with the introduction of the new technologies of cable and satellite would expand the choices available to all audiences. Media policy was designed to facilitate the entrance of new players and outlets to media markets in an attempt to boost competitiveness and profitability. Media pluralism, in this context, began to be intimately associated with processes of commercialization and marketization. According to Thomas Gibbons:

> media pluralism was not promoted for the purpose of supporting a more democratic role for the media, as might be supposed from its content. Instead, the idea was adopted as a transitional concept that conveniently assisted a shift from public service dominance to a market approach. The broad strategy was to identify the pluralistic aspects of public service and then to claim that they could be provided as effectively through competition. (2000: 307)

This new emphasis on pluralism led to a clarification of the differences between pluralism and diversity and the distinctive policy responses required by each. This was an approach in the mid-1990s closely identified with the future New Labour government of Tony Blair. The Institute for Public Policy Research (IPPR) think tank, closely associated with New Labour, published the results of its investigations into the changing media in the book *New Media, New Policies* (Collins and Murroni 1996). In the chapter on concentration of ownership, the authors distinguish between 'plurality of sources and diversity of content' (1996: 58) and claim that competition legislation, in conjunction with other regulatory instruments, is necessary to deliver plural ownership structures and a 'democratic marketplace for ideas' (1996: 63). However, although the authors argue that there is no straightforward or predictable connection between pluralism (of outlets and of ownership) and diversity (of content), their emphasis is very much on developing quantitative measures (around market share, for example) designed to produce pluralistic ownership structures, in the hope that diverse content and voices will flow from this. The incoming New Labour government adopted this approach and further specified the difference between pluralism and diversity in the Communications White Paper (DTI/DCMS 2000), and especially in its consultation on media ownership rules (DCMS/DTI 2001). The latter argued succinctly that:

> Diversity refers to the variety of different programmes, publications and services that are available, whereas plurality is about the choice people can make between different providers of those services. Both are key to the quality of service and the range of news and opinion we as citizens receive from the media. They are, however, delivered by different means. (2001: 6)

The traditional mechanism for ensuring media diversity is through positive content regulation, for example, public service broadcasting, independent production, local content quotas, subsidies, and statutory programming requirements (precisely the behavioural regulation that is largely absent in the United States). Pluralism, on the other hand, is delivered through competition legislation backed up by media-specific ownership restrictions that are designed to curb bottlenecks and excesses of power, to maintain entry to media markets, and to encourage competition within these markets. There is little difference between this and the fostering of competitive media markets to secure 'viewpoint diversity' in the United States.

Pluralism and diversity today

Although this is a helpful step forward in distinguishing between plurality (of sources) and diversity (of content), the underlying principles separating them are becoming less distinctive. Both objectives are now defined along familiar contours of variety and choice, and both are to be realized through a combination of market forces and limited regulatory intervention. For example, according to the section on 'maintaining diversity and plurality' in the 2000 White Paper, convergence has inspired companies to increase content production across a range of platforms – market forces, it argues, are already 'delivering a large element of the diverse services which our society requires' (DTI/DCMS 2000: 35). We are therefore left with a situation in which the discourse of pluralism and diversity is extraordinarily common in British media policymaking, being eloquently defined and clearly distinguished, but increasingly conceptualized in terms of efficiency, consumer satisfaction and customer choice. Philip Napoli notes a similar 'shift in orientation' in the USA from looking at diversity as a public good towards one that is a 'tangible and empirically assessable construct' (1999: 8), an illustration of the contemporary neo-liberal interpretation of the 'marketplace of ideas' metaphor. Policy objectives concerning media diversity and media pluralism may be expressed differently in the USA and the UK but they are both converging around the rhetoric of competition and choice.

Contemporary media policies are now littered with positive references to diversity and pluralism. These twin objectives are key justifications for the rewriting of rules affecting the media industries in the twenty-first century. There are, for example, 35 mentions of pluralism and 42 of diversity in the British government's White Paper (DTI/DCMS 2000) that underpinned the 2003 Communications Act; there are 67 mentions of pluralism and 24 of diversity in its consultation on media ownership rules (DCMS/DTI 2001); and there are an impressive 599 references to diversity in the FCC's review on broadcast ownership rules (FCC 2003a) that recommended raising the national television ownership cap from 35 per cent to 45 per cent of the total audience (see chapter 5).

These references to diversity and pluralism feature in policy documents that are highly deregulatory and liberalizing in character, relaxing media ownership restrictions and increasing the relevance of competition legislation to the media industries. Indeed, some of the strongest supporters of market liberalization insist that they are motivated by the desire to increase diversity. Former FCC chairman Michael Powell introduced the 2003 broadcast ownership review by claiming that the revised rules would 'promote and protect diversity, competition and localism in the 21st century broadcast media marketplace' (FCC 2003b: 1). Even Rupert Murdoch, the chairman of News Corporation, has attached himself to the diversity bandwagon, arguing that:

> we are a relatively small part of an ever-widening rainbow of outlets for the dissemination of diverse views. The media sector is experiencing an historic growth spurt. Pluralism and diversity are growing *organically* under our very noses while we agonize about their shrinkage. (Murdoch 1998 – emphasis in original)

This is potentially somewhat confusing. Policies designed to maximize pluralism and diversity were initially introduced specifically because of the perceived inability of market forces fully to allow a wide range of outlets to articulate a wide range of opinions to a wide range of audiences. Now it appears that market forces are seen as not only *not* inimical to diversity and pluralism but as the main guarantors of such aspirations. This involves a process of conceptualizing media diversity and media pluralism as twin outcomes of strategies designed to maximize consumer choice and market competition.

Media policymakers in the USA and the UK are, therefore, in danger of neutering expansive concepts of diversity through neo-liberal reforms. Diversity ought not to be simply about celebrating choice and recognizing demographic differences but about acting on them, acknowledging the social, political, and economic divisions that mark contemporary life, and using the media to articulate them in the hope that solutions may be identified and pursued. This requires something more than merely expanding the number of media outlets or paying lip service to cultural differences; what is needed is the integration of fundamental arguments and disagreements about key issues into the fabric of the media to realize the First Amendment commitment to publicize 'diverse and antagonistic sources'. Diversity need not be limited to the provision of rival views expressed under (and often artificially imposing) a consensus, but should flourish by challenging consensus views about the key debates of the day. This will also require a challenge to the idea that the market is best placed to achieve this ambition. As James Curran argues (2000: 138), diversity and pluralism cannot just be equated with competition.

> It needs to mean more than this: namely media diversity supported by an *open* process of contests in which different social groups have the opportunity to express divergent views and values. This broader definition implies a commitment to extending freedom of expression, broadening the basis of self-determination, and promoting equitable outcomes informed by awareness of opposed opinions and interests.

Contemporary policymakers are more than likely to ignore this expansive view and instead to equate aspirations towards pluralism and diversity with initiatives solely designed to maximize consumer choice and market penetration.

Conclusion

It is not the case that contemporary media policymaking is devoid of foundation principles but that these are based on an increasingly narrow and instrumental commitment to market forces as the central dynamic of contemporary communications. It may the case that, as the UK government minister responsible for culture and the media put it, 'we know that markets don't always act fairly. That they don't always follow the public interest. And that there is more to life than the bottom line' (Jowell 2003). The fact remains, however, that meeting the 'bottom line' is increasingly the main objective of policymakers as well as media executives. Many of the other principles that underpin media policymaking are flexible enough, as Napoli argues, to function 'primarily as rhetorical tools for advocating particular policy actions, as opposed to analytical tools for the rigorous assessment of these actions' (2001: 3). In the context of the grip of neo-liberal ideas at the heart of the US and UK governments, what are held up as firmly held beliefs – a desire for increased diversity, that media should serve the public interest, that freedom of expression is a basic human right – are often no more than convenient justifications to secure public consent for policy actions that increase corporate control of the media.

4

Dynamics of the Media Policymaking Process

This chapter expands on the argument initially proposed in chapter 2 that a central feature of a pluralist approach to media policy is a decision-making system that is accessible, accountable and rational. A democratic policy environment would suggest the existence of a plethora of competing voices and perspectives that interact with each other in an open, non-discriminatory and vigorous way in order to reach agreement on policies that maximize the welfare of the majority as opposed to the interests of a few. This is best expressed by Krasnow and Longley's positive characterization of the communications policy process (1978: 101): 'In a pluralist complex . . . policy-making power tends to be somewhat divided and dissipated . . . In such a system, policy making results from the agreement – or at least the acquiescence – of all the participants, not from domination by one.' According to this perspective, contemporary media policymaking is a relatively 'open' field involving a variety of 'stakeholders' engaged in a 'conversation' about the future of the media industries.

Others paint a far more critical picture, arguing that there is an unmistakably neo-liberal character to contemporary policymaking that subsumes the distinctive characteristics of media goods and flows in a market-driven approach. Reflecting on the US experience, Robert McChesney argues that there has been a progressive deterioration of transparency and public participation and a 'decisive increase in the business domination of media policy making' (McChesney, 2004: 48). Colin Leys attributes the 'new dominance of business in the so-called "policy communities" or "networks" in every field of public policy', including British broadcasting, to 'the importance all politicians attached to adapting policy to the interests of corporations' (2001: 56). Media policymaking is, therefore, exclusive, unequal, distorted and fundamentally undemocratic.

There are also those who adhere to neither of these positions and who believe that while policymaking is affected by the unequal distribution of resources there is, nevertheless, no predictable outcome to media policy debates. Hesmondhalgh, for example, recognizes that the policy process is shaped by social and economic inequalities, but also notes that 'policy is not utterly at the mercy of the wealthy and powerful. Political institutions and processes have some autonomy' (2005: 97). Far from media policy being a simple tale of corporate capture, we need instead to assess carefully 'the balance of social forces (patterned by structured inequality), the different resources available to agents, the relative autonomy of political institutions and process from such factors, and the strategic alliances made by policy-making parties with other social institutions' (2005: 107–8).

A focus on the policymaking process is needed because, at a time of considerable change in the global media environment, new actors, technologies and paradigms are emerging that are creating new or accelerating established conflicts in media policymaking, for example in terms of national vs supranational levels of policymaking, public vs corporate interests, centralized vs dispersed policy networks, secretive vs transparent forms of decision-making, and qualitative vs quantitative forms of policy data. This chapter aims to illuminate the dynamics of and balance of power in the media policymaking process in both the USA and the UK, in order to examine these conflicts in more detail and to assess the legitimacy of the perspectives on policymaking presented above. It concentrates, in particular, on the extent to which contemporary decision-making can be said to be competitive, transparent and scientific.

A competitive process?

With the increasingly global organization of media businesses, the impact of digital technology and new platforms on media distribution, the economic importance of content industries, and the hegemony of market-led approaches to the provision of goods and services, it is hardly surprising that media policymaking has expanded in scale and scope. The number of 'stakeholders' has mushroomed in recent years, and voices that were traditionally peripheral to media policy debates have come to play a central role, crossing both departmental and geographical borders. The traditional 'subsystem' of dedicated civil servants, legislators and select industry players has had to come to terms with the interventions of personnel from other domestic government departments, supranational institutions and processes (like the EU or the WTO-administered General Agreement on Trade in Services [GATS] agreement) and finally a whole range of religious, moral, consumer, activist and voluntary groups.

Media policy has rarely been confined to a single location in government. In the USA, both House and Senate subcommittees have overseen the work of the FCC and the Department of Justice has long been involved in anti-trust cases. Policy in Britain has traditionally been even more fragmented (Seymour-Ure 1987) with responsibilities still divided between, for example, the Department for Media, Culture and Sport (DCMS), Department of Trade and Industry (DTI), the Foreign Office and the Treasury. However, 'ownership' of media policy has become increasingly blurred – all major communications policy initiatives since the New Labour government took power in 1997 have been co-authored by the DCMS and DTI, resulting in a vigorous debate about whose imprint is the more dominant. Even in the USA, policy is increasingly 'splintered' as agencies like the National Telecommunications and Information Administration and the Federal Trade Commission, along with the State Department and Department of Homeland Security, all play an important role in shaping the US media environment.

Also, policymaking is not confined to the national level. Domestic media systems are subject to a complex barrage of rules from bilateral trade deals, regional directives and multilateral trade disciplines. For example, the behaviour of national public service broadcasting channels in Europe is monitored by the European Commission's Competition Directorate who check whether tight 'state aid' rules are being breached (see Tryhorn, 2005); many domestic copyright regimes have been transformed by treaties launched by the World Intellectual Property Organization (WIPO); and current negotiations under the auspices of the GATS are attempting to impose strict trade disciplines on domestic audio-visual industries (see chapter 9). Many of these developments are far from complete and policymaking power remains largely nationally based, yet we are certainly seeing the emergence of new international pressure points on the media policymaking process.

The explosion of stakeholders

The participation of an expanded number of interest groups is perhaps the greatest challenge to traditional modes of media policy formation. The influence of corporate lobbyists and trade associations is well-established, particularly in the USA, but increasingly so in Britain as well. 'Pressure groups' too have existed for a long time, but without the power and influence they now appear to wield. For example, in the USA, the Parents Television Council is credited with being a key influence on recent legislation to increase fines for 'broadcast indecency' on American networks (see chapter 6). Consumers Union and Consumer Federation of America are highly significant mass-membership organizations that have prioritized issues such as media ownership and broadband access to great effect. The impact of media activist groups is more surprising. In the UK, the intervention during the passage of the 2003 Communications Act of campaigning group Public Voice helped to secure a 'public interest test' in the case of major media mergers (see chapter 5), while the court case in the USA that formally derailed the FCC's broadcast ownership review in June 2004 was launched by the Promotheus Radio Project, a small collective of radio activists working in conjunction with a legal team from the Media Access Project.

Many policymakers agree that the policymaking universe is becoming increasingly crowded. Reflecting on his experience of legislation for web content, the head of public policy for one of the largest web portals comments that:

> More and more stakeholders are seeing themselves as such and are seeking to represent their interests more and more strongly and in more innovative ways with the decision-makers. So there's no doubt that, say in the example of child safety online, the number of stakeholders seems to grow almost monthly . . . There are now maybe fifteen representatives of industry, a dozen children's charities, a dozen law and order agencies and different Home Office departments involved. So these things certainly do mushroom.

A lobbyist for one of the biggest radio companies in the USA notes that, because of consolidation, there are fewer licence holders but 'a lot of other non-licence holders in the policy business right now'. This changes the whole dynamics of the policymaking process in that, according to him, it is now a

> public relations battle as opposed to a legal battle and many of the major companies in the industry are now establishing government liaison officers and have retained press consultants and even damage control press people who they can call in to deal with media issues at a moment's notice. And that is pretty foreign to what we did a couple of years ago.

Organized interests are complemented by the growing numbers of individuals seeking to make their voices heard. A reporter at the trade magazine *Broadcasting and Cable* in Washington, DC, argues that 'there is much more public involvement now in the issues that I cover. I think in part it's because people have realized how important media policy is and what an impact media consolidation has had.' One public policy advocate talks of the 'unprecedented public involvement in media policy debates. Nothing has happened like this since the advent of radio in the late 1920s and early

1930s.' This perspective is shared even by one senior vice-president at a powerful media trade association:

> I believe that the 3rd Circuit decision [overturning the FCC's 2002 broad-cast ownership review] was influenced by an interesting sense of a grass-roots feeling . . . This was the first time I had ever seen a Court that was interested in 'wait a minute. There was this hearing that was held out in South Dakota somewhere' and that was part of the discussion.

Reflecting on these changes, a senior British civil servant involved in broadcasting issues confirms that, although there is little need for the process itself to change, 'it may be more complicated in practice in that there are so many more interests to take account of'. According to another experienced industry figure who remains close to the Labour government: 'one of the virtues of being my age is that you do see it [the policy process] over a long period, and like a simple childhood period when I was younger and the people involved in terms of numbers were small. Now it is much more complicated and vastly more folk are involved in it. But is that good or bad?'

It is also the case that media policymaking is a highly contested process that is marked by divisions at a number of levels. Policy on issues like obscenity, privacy and the future of the BBC has rarely developed exclusively on party lines, with intra-party disagreements often as frequent as inter-party ones. However, as the decision-making process has become more complex, the divisions themselves have multiplied and there is no predictable or comfortable way of delineating how splits occur. One basic difference is between 'insiders' (regulators, civil servants, politicians and major media business interests) and 'outsiders' (other lobbyists, think tanks, academics, public interest advocates) struggling to have their voices heard. There are also significant differences of interest and perspective:

- between government departments (where the DTI and DCMS may have different responsibilities and client groups or where Congress and the FCC are subject to very different pressures);
- within regulators (one Ofcom official suggested that there is a 'war' inside the regulator between 'free marketeers' and the 'ex-Oftel [former telecommunications regulator] guys' who have a stronger commitment to public service);
- between rival commercial interests (particularly between rights holders and intermediaries in emerging online policy battles or even different corporate perspectives on ownership rules).

The mere existence of these divisions, the participation of the public and the growing influence of interest groups is evidence, for some, of the pluralist character of contemporary media policymaking. According to one enthusiastic supporter of the current media ownership regime in the USA, the 'messiness' of the media policy process is a price worth paying:

> In democracies, there is no universal 'public interest.' Rather there are numerous and changing 'interested publics' which fight battles issue by issue, in legislative corridors, regulatory commission hearings and ultimately at the ballot box. That it is sloppy and imperfect is beside the point. To loosely paraphrase Winston Churchill, it works better than any alternative that's been tried or proposed. (Compaine 2001: 5)

This paints a picture of a policy domain littered with participants, pulled in different directions by competing interests, but nevertheless fundamentally democratic. To what extent is this perception true and how does it impact on the idea of a powerful policy 'centre'?

First, there is no necessary relationship between the number of participants in a decision-making process and the eventual decision that is taken. Being a 'stakeholder', identifying yourself as someone who has an interest in the outcome of a decision, is in no way a statement about your power. The explosion of 'stakeholders' is more likely related to the expansion of the media industries than it is to their ability to change the balance of power in a decision-making situation. As a member of a Washington, DC, think tank puts it, 'the fact that there is so much more legislating taking place is the key to understanding why there are so many more lobbyists and lobbying'.

Second, when it comes to specific media policy issues, there is little evidence that we are dealing with a more devolved policy structure. 'Ultimately,' argues a senior policy adviser to the British government, 'policymaking reflects the structure of the industry rather than the other way around.' In the case of distribution-led media industries, this suggests a high degree of centralization and control. This is illustrated by the adviser who complains that 'as a sector, it [media policymaking] is amazingly insular and small. Another part of my job involves working in other stakeholder areas and there are very few industries and sectors [like media] where everybody knows each other and everyone worked together at one stage.'

This seems particularly to be the case in the UK where the deregulatory 2003 Communications Act was driven by a handful of figures inside Downing Street (most notably Ed Richards inside the Number Ten Policy Directorate) in close consultation with relevant ministers and special advisers. It is borne out by the inclusion of rules in the legislation that allow foreign ownership of television channels and, in particular, permit Rupert

Murdoch to expand into terrestrial television – decisions that emanated, after heavy lobbying, from 'behind the heavy front door of No 10' (Bell 2005b: 5). One very experienced contributor to British media policy debates recalls:

> My sense of it was that there was an agenda being run by a very small tightly-knit clique of people, who were to some extent prepared to listen, but only within the very narrow bounds of their own idea of what should be done. So they had pretty clear parameters, they were prepared to listen to outsiders within those parameters, but actually I think it was more of a lobbying and PR effort.

The head of public policy for a large online company praises the way in which government and regulators 'involve industry from an early stage in new legislation', but also admits that 'government departments clearly have their own client groups that they rely on to function properly'. While the Home Office is 'pretty anti-industry', the DCMS

> seems to be pretty much in thrall to rights holders . . . rather than inter-mediaries in the online space. So these are all client groups that they natu-rally gravitate to because those client groups are saying what they [the various government departments] want them to say. It bolsters their position.

There is a slightly larger group of politicians at the core of media poli-cymaking in the USA. According to a public policy advocate on media issues:

> The most important players in communications policy are the members, and especially the chairmen, of the Energy and Commerce Committee on the House side and the Commerce Committee on the Senate side. All of whom are heavily lobbied by industry players . . . They are the ones that makes the laws and the FCC tries to enforce them. The FCC can only operate within the parameters set by Congress. Most members of Congress haven't got any idea about communications policy. They get beyond the surface level discussion of the issues and they are completely lost. So you're really talking about 30 to 40 members of Congress on House and Senate side in total who understand the issues well enough to legislate on them.

An aide to a senior senator involved in the 2002–3 broadcast ownership proceedings admits that, while there were increased opportunities for public interest groups to intervene in what was becoming a national debate, the policymaking venue failed to expand accordingly. 'I did not see sena-tors that were not on the Congressional committee taking strong stands and being the face of this issue. It stayed mostly within the committee of jurisdiction and the senators who had studied the issue previously.'

There is, therefore, an important distinction to be made between the size of the pools which surround the decision-making process – inhabited by an increasingly volatile mixture of civil servants, private and public lobbyists, regulators, individual citizens, politicians and academics – and the core members of this process who may choose to swim in the pools but who retain their own interests. This is summed up by the head of public policy of a major UK broadcaster who argues that:

> Media policy is paradoxical. Because the media affect everybody, politicians and policymakers care more about media policy than they do about steel policy or car policy. So in one sense everybody consumes it, but in another sense, the number of people making decisions is fairly small . . . *The decision-making is tight but the influence is broad.*

When debates and disagreements do take place in the process of policy formation, both the terms of these conflicts and their eventual resolution in specific policy instruments are drawn up, not by members of a dispersed policy 'network' but by a small decision-making elite.

The media's influence on policymaking

The notion that contemporary media policymaking epitomizes the pluralist model of a vigorous and competitive bargaining arena is further challenged by the increasingly active role of the media themselves as highly influential policy participants. The American media, according to Spitzer (1993: 9), 'plays a pivotal role in influencing policy because it is the conduit, the pipeline, the funnel regulating the flow of communications between the policymakers . . . and others in the political system who might seek any different policy'. Others attribute a similarly decisive role to the media: Graber (2002: 174–5) describes journalists as key political actors who are either 'surrogates' and 'mouthpieces' for public officials or interpreters who frame coverage 'in such a way as to exert pressure for policy action', while Davis (2002: 179) characterizes the media as a public relations vehicle through which powerful actors are able to communicate with each other in order to manufacture 'elite rather than mass forms of consent'.

The problem is that the media form a largely unaccountable force and that this policymaking influence is wielded without a democratic mandate and reserved for some of the wealthiest and most powerful corporate figures, who have their own economic and ideological interests. Critics (for example McChesney 2004: 63) have identified a conflict between media organizations keen to see the passing of particular laws or deregulatory initiatives and their reporting of these policy developments. Boehlert

(2003), for example, notes that there was a virtual news 'blackout' in the run-up to the FCC vote on 2 June 2003 on loosening ownership rules, in particular by news organizations such as Fox and CBS, subsidiaries of companies 'with the most to gain from a lenient FCC ruling'. There is also the other 'face' of media power: government's attitude towards, for example, sanctioning more stringent cross-media ownership restrictions or introducing statutory privacy legislation can be seen as linked to its desire not to antagonize powerful newspaper proprietors or media commentators and risk unfavourable coverage. This is a particularly strong argument in relation to the UK, where the close relationship between Tony Blair and Rupert Murdoch, owner of the best-selling *Sun*, *Times*, *News of the World* and *Sunday Times* newspapers, has long been seen as shaping the direction of Labour Party policy (Freedman 2003a: 158). The argument that policy initiatives are taken partly on the basis of their likely popularity in the media is, not surprisingly, fervently denied by a senior Labour adviser:

> I know what the perception is and it is not accurate, because it implies or assumes that the interests of media companies are the primary motivation or the final straw, or the weightiest issue you would consider when making a policy decision. And that is not the case at all. You have a multiplicity of issues to look at and how the media might react to certain things is one of those issues, but it is by no means the weightiest.

A lobbyist for one of the largest media companies who has good access to Tony Blair is rather more pragmatic about media influence.

> Do politicians respond to the media? Well of course they do. But that's OK. Especially in a country where you have a parliamentary dictatorship like you do here, where you have no checks and balances like we have in America, the press is a very important player. When you have an ineffectual opposition, which is true for the bulk of the Labour terms, the press plays an important role. I can't imagine any politician ignoring it at all. That's why they put out press releases, and that's why they have parties in which they suddenly invite editors and stuff, because they want to influence them. That's OK. I don't see anything wrong with that.

Another government supporter and experienced broadcaster takes an equally down-to-earth view of press influence on policymaking:

> For God's sake, that's inevitable isn't it? We have been living through 15 years of increasing media power. They have always been powerful, but the rules under which they operated 15 years ago meant that politicians and newspapers knew where they were. That has changed quite dramatically . . . and we are struggling to come to terms with it.

The growth of newspaper power is illustrated by one government adviser who blames the press for constraining public debate on key policy issues. Reflecting on the controversy over allowing foreign ownership of British terrestrial television in the 2003 Communications Act, he recalls that the government had to keep the proposals confidential for a long time and hope that they would not be leaked.

> The nature of the perverse and shallow media coverage in this country is that all consideration of this became to do with Rupert Murdoch because there are journalists out there who are obsessed with very narrow concerns . . . the important thing to establish was that we wouldn't let fictions that exist in the minds of journalists define the legislative content . . . It would be wonderful to have a media discourse in this country where you could float these ideas and have a full and open consultation, but it is very difficult.

The acknowledgement that 'full and open consultation' remains a 'difficult' proposition does not, in any way, refute claims that a major influence on government decisions to pursue or bury specific policy proposals is the likely reaction of powerful media moguls, hardly a glowing endorsement of a fully competitive and decentralized bargaining system.

A transparent process?

If there is a general perception that the number of stakeholders has increased, there is an even stronger belief amongst many participants that the media policymaking process (and, to a certain extent, media regulation) has become more open, accountable and subject to scrutiny. A high-profile example of this was the pre-legislative joint committee, set up in 2002 and chaired by Lord Puttnam, to examine the draft communications bill in the UK. After convening ten hearings and thirteen private meetings, considering some 200 pieces of written evidence and listening to over 100 individuals from more than fifty organizations, the committee produced a report (Joint Committee 2002) that had a significant and positive impact on the eventual passage of the legislation. Yet, according to one experienced regulator who monitored the debates, there were still

> large parts of the Communications Act that went through without any significant debating in the committees or on the floor of either of the Houses. So one of the things that you might construe is that media policymaking has become more a factor of government, civil service and its interaction with stakeholders, and less subject to parliamentary scrutiny in the old-fashioned sense of the word.

Pre-legislative scrutiny in both the USA and the UK seems likely to improve the *efficiency* of the legislative process (in comparison to the 1990 Broadcasting Act in the UK where over 1,000 amendments were tabled), but there is less certainty that such procedures will either expand the range of contributions made to the process or guarantee that new and minority voices will be listened to with the same gravity as the submissions made by commercial bodies.

Many of the claims of increased openness are based on technological innovations, especially the emergence of the internet as an informational tool. Congressional hearings are streamed online with easy access to speakers' transcripts, notices of forthcoming hearings and details of relevant legislation. Access to both current FCC investigations and past FCC decisions has been transformed by the internet. Every piece of correspondence and every meeting that relates to a particular proceeding is recorded online and any member of the public can contribute to FCC rule-making through its electronic filing system. As one corporate lobbyist puts it, 'we are in the digital era where anyone, through either the FCC's website or a public interest website, can chime in to any process'. According to an official in the FCC's Media Bureau:

> There's a lot more accessibility of FCC decisions . . . When I started practising, if I wanted to get an application filed at the FCC when I was not at the FCC, and see what a broadcaster was doing in terms of increasing power or whatever they might be applying for, I had to physically send someone down here, make a copy, bring it back to the office and review it. Now I can make a couple of clicks online and I can review what they are proposing to do and any member of the public can.

'Everything', according to another senior FCC official involved in ownership policy, 'is out in the open. We are the most transparent agency that I know of.'

In the UK, the most recent DCMS-led BBC Charter review process has been trumpeted as a model of transparency. Again, technology was central: thirteen seminars organized by an 'expert panel' set up by the government to reflect on the future of the BBC were webcast and a dedicated website was provided, containing transcripts, research findings, a summary of responses to the public consultation and other background information. But here openness was seen not simply in technological terms, but as a means of ensuring the widest possible participation and debate. One of the civil servants responsible argues that it was quite different from previous reviews, given the level of public consultation, survey research and analysis carried out to 'make for a better informed outcome' (see chapter 7 for discussion of the outcome).

Yet even this level of public consultation does little to undermine government control of the policymaking process or of the decisions eventually taken. Transparency *follows* the decision about how to 'construct' the debate, i.e. a decision on what issues are, or are not, permissible. A further shortcoming of this approach to transparency is that while some parts of the media policy process may now be better publicized, the actual details of how decisions are reached remain far more obscure. One trade reporter in Washington, DC admits that while the 'FCC is more open than other regulator agencies in providing public access or information to the public about what media companies have asked the FCC to do . . . they are less accessible in talking about their internal deliberations'. This is perhaps even more of a problem in the UK which lacks an Administrative Procedures Act which forces at least some degree of accountability on the US decision-making process. Indeed one of the main exemptions of the recently introduced Freedom of Information legislation in the UK concerns material which relates to the formulation of government policy. Participants may be invited into the room, but there are no requirements to reveal how seriously their views are taken or the means by which decisions are finally made. A highly experienced corporate lobbyist who works on both sides of the Atlantic argues that a degree of 'intellectual transparency' is needed.

> [There is a problem with] the procedure of white papers and green papers. Mr A said, Mr B said that, Mr C said this, Mr D said that and then they say we have decided this. How did you get there from a, b, c, d? No indication. I think there should be a requirement for analytical pathways so that the decision-makers must say how they got there from the evidence put in front of them . . . If you read some of the green and white papers, it's a nod to this guy and to this guy as if to prove that somebody showed up and then they say, 'and we decided'. How the hell did you get there?

Without detailed information about whose arguments are most persuasive and how competing arguments are settled, and there is no evidence that the British government is willing to provide such information, claims that the media policymaking process is a model of transparency and openness are exaggerated.

In any case, a commitment to transparency does not, in itself, make policymaking more accessible and indeed is more likely designed to legitimize the process in the eyes of the public. One critic of recent UK media legislation argues that the plethora of advisory groups, feedback loops and consultations (embodied by the UK regulator Ofcom's launch of dozens of consultations in its short life)

> are meaningful to the extent that if there was an overwhelming response from the public in one direction or another, which was in direct contradiction from the way that the government wants them to go, it would be very difficult for them to hold that line. So I think in that sense, they are an exercise in validating democracy, rather than real transparency or openness.

Another head of public affairs comments that, while the internet has made it much easier for the public to contribute to these consultations, this does not necessarily translate into a shift in the balance of power in the decision-making environment. The process 'is much more demystified to some extent and there is much more easy public access. But the idea that it gives those [public interest] groups much greater weight against the [core policymaking] institutions I don't think is necessarily true.' Indeed the association of transparency with good communication may itself be flawed:

> Shovelling enormous numbers of documents onto web sites is seldom a good way of communicating with wider audiences. Transparency leaves many audiences unable to see the wood for the trees, unable to understand what is disclosed, unable to assess what they understand or to judge its accuracy, and ill-equipped to take an active and constructive part in democratic debate' (O'Neill 2004: 15).

Despite claims that the process is more open and accessible than it was previously, the public therefore remains a largely peripheral force when it comes to influencing the media policymaking agenda. While its general opinions are collected in surveys and consultations and are then used to justify particular outcomes – for example, the preservation of public service broadcasting or the strengthening of obscenity regulations – there are few opportunities for individual members of the public to come into direct contact with and actively shape the core policymaking process. First, they are excluded from the main forums in which policymakers and 'stakeholders' come together – either because these are private occasions or because the costs are prohibitive. Second, there is no guarantee, even when they do respond in numbers, that policymakers will listen to them. The most vivid example of this was the refusal of the FCC to take seriously the 2.3 million separate submissions, 99.9 per cent of which, according to FCC commissioner Michael Copps (2004), *opposed* the loosening of ownership rules in 2003, on the basis that these comments were ill-informed and biased. In the consultation on UK media ownership in 2001, the government ignored the vast majority of the submissions that overwhelmingly opposed the opening up of terrestrial television to foreign companies on the basis, as one participant put it, 'that this is what the government wanted to do and felt was the right thing to do'.

Lobbyists and policymaking

The biggest threat to transparent policymaking, however, derives from the continuing and intimate relationship between key corporate interests and government policymakers, a relationship whose bonds are rarely exposed to the public. This is partly a structural connection of the sort identified by Mitchell (1997) in his analysis of the 'conspicuous corporation'. Business does not simply share common class interests with a political elite; corporations also 'devote more attention and time to policy issues of concern to them, hire more lobbyists, commit more money in support of their political activities and goals, and have more mobility than other organized interests' (1997: 220). It is not the case that lobbyists necessarily operate in secret nor indeed that they always get their way, but that corporate interests increasingly circumscribe and swamp the policymaking sphere.

This is, of course, far more of an issue in the USA where lobbyists have long operated as a very visible part of the policymaking process. As one seasoned observer of Washington politics comments:

> [The lobbyists'] leverage is much more open, you know you see them in halls of Congress and they don't have to grease a deal in a back room because they're going to do it with a sledgehammer right there in front of every trade reporter and every Congressional hearing . . . It's not like you have to secretly cut Rupert Murdoch a deal when you can cut him a deal and the entire industry at the front end.

An aide to the chair of one of the most powerful Congressional committees reveals that they have 'a lot of contact' with lobbyists. 'We rely on them for statistics, data, policy opinions. You know, lobbyists have a bad name sometimes but they shouldn't because it's a lot easier for me to do my job when I'm being given information from various sources.'

However, many lobbyists deny that they have such power and instead describe themselves as 'educators', saving legislators time and money through the provision, when requested, of important data. Their role as 'persuaders' is significant but harmless: 'what you're attempting to do is to take the body of fact as it exists and present it in a favourable fashion' as one senior vice-president puts it. Another insists that 'every one of us is a public interest group' and that 'the ability to petition your government is for me absolutely paramount'. Lobbying, according to this perspective, is simply where 'groups bond together to petition the decision makers to see it their way. Nothing more, nothing less.' Arguments about regulatory and policy capture are dismissed – indeed, the outcry over the proposed loosening of media ownership rules and various examples of broadcast indecency shows that the notion that 'legislators are simply marching to the industry's beat is far from true'.

This idea that lobbyists for the media industries are just harmless educators is somewhat disingenuous. The highly deregulatory 1996 Communications Act, for example, was the result of systematic pressure applied by leading corporate interests and, indeed, parts of the legislation were actually drafted by lobbyists (Aufderheide 1999: 42–3). Recent figures revealing that the communications industry alone spent more than $1.1 billion lobbying federal government from 1998 to 2004, and that some 398 personnel passed through the 'revolving door' between government and industry during that time (Centre for Public Integrity 2004), demonstrates both the continuing involvement of the largest communications companies in extensive lobbying and the everyday interactions between government and media businesses. Former FCC chair Michael Powell was just the latest in a long line of FCC luminaries who moved from the public sector into, in his case, a lucrative position with Providence Equity Partners, one of the largest private equity firms in the media and communications world. Lobbying remains at the epicentre of the US government. 'Here in Washington', writes a local journalist, 'there's hardly a day of the week that Congress' senior lawmakers and staffers don't consult with large groups of corporate lobbyists at regularly scheduled meetings' (Birnbaum 2004). Perhaps the best proof that lobbying is a valuable and effective strategy is the scale of media companies' investment in their 'government relations' operations – Time Warner alone has about thirty-five people involved in lobbying and pays its 'executive vice-president for global public policy' more than $3.2 million a year (Sarasohn 2004).

The power of the commercial lobbyists may not completely remove the ability of government to act independently but it certainly makes it difficult to ignore their concerns. Policymakers are more likely, in this situation, to act as brokers, arbitrating between rival commercial interests rather than confronting corporate power as a whole. As Tunstall and Machin put it (1999: 51), policymakers in Washington 'umpire the lobbying contest and approve the final agreed consensual lobbying outcome'. This is illustrated by advice given by a former FCC chair to William Kennard when he took over as chair in 1997:

Bill, you have to realize that when you are chairman of the FCC, you're basically a referee of big money fights and they are fights between the rich on the one hand, and the very wealthy on the other. The key to being a successful chairman is to keep the power in equilibrium. So you give something to one powerful lobby one week, you better it out by giving their opponents something the next week. (Quoted in McChesney 2004: 48)

The implications of lobbying are not confined to the USA. From the campaign for commercial television in the early 1950s to the British Media Industry Group in the mid-1990s that pushed for liberalization of owner-ship laws (Goodwin 1998: 143), corporate lobbyists have also been active in Britain for some time. Their influence, however, was constrained by the existence of a mixed media economy and a residual commitment to public service broadcasting. Now, given the pro-market perspective of the New Labour government, they find themselves operating in a far more welcom-ing environment and the 2003 Communications Act was a particularly fertile period for lobbyists. For example, recent papers released from gov-ernment archives reveal that representatives of Rupert Murdoch's Sky Television met with ministers six times during the short passage of the communications bill in 2003. They show that 'Mr Murdoch secured private reassurances from ministers during heavy lobbying that he would be able to buy Channel Five if he wanted to' (Leigh and Evans 2005). Such an outcome is perhaps not surprising given Murdoch's economic clout and political influence, as well as his long-established relationship with Tony Blair. One lobbyist who dismisses regulatory 'capture' as too 'simplistic' a theory, nevertheless agrees that 'the idea that regulators as well as politicians don't take into account factors revolving around power is ridiculous'.

Consider the case of the government's decision, under pressure from evidence of increasing obesity and poor nutritional habits, to restrict televi-sion advertising of 'junk food' aimed at children. Instructed by the culture minister to investigate the issue, Ofcom published proposals in March 2006 that involved scrapping the use of celebrities and promotional offers in food advertisements for the under-tens as well as four options for further restrictions on advertising, none of which included the one clause that public health campaigners had demanded: a ban on junk food advertising before 9 p.m., a measure that Ofcom insisted would be 'disproportionate'. 'The food industry's extensive lobbying appears to have paid off,' argued one campaigner for the charity Sustain. 'Ofcom has put the interests of the food and advertising industries before the interests of kids' health' (quoted in Gibson 2006: 4). During the consultation that followed, it was revealed that the regulator 'consulted industry groups 29 times when it drew up its proposals, compared to just four meetings with health and consumer groups . . . This style of regulation means they are umbilically linked with industry' (Watts 2006). In November 2006, Ofcom published the results of its consultation, introducing a total ban on advertising foods high in salt, fat and sugar during children's programmes and a small number of adult programmes, a result that would still allow junk food advertising in soap operas and entertainment shows watched by millions of children. Health campaigners were not impressed: an official at the British Media Association argued that Ofcom 'does not have the courage to recommend a more comprehensive ban', while the chief executive of the British Heart Foundation asserted that 'Ofcom has acted in the interests of the advertising and junk food industry, not our nation's children' (quoted in BBC 2006).

A more resourceful example of lobbying concerns the UK independent television production sector whose trade association, Pact, claims success for introducing sixty-six points into the 2003 communications bill, whose first draft made no reference at all to independents. An imaginative and persistent lobbying campaign, aimed at securing the expansion of independent production, focused on wining and dining parliamentarians ('I almost lived in the Cinnamon Club around the corner from Westminster for about nine months,' recalls one participant), and met with a positive response from a government that was receptive to arguments about granting a higher profile and more financial autonomy to the independent sector. Responding to the government's desire to secure a more competitive media system, the campaign deliberately focused on themes of creativity and innovation.

> It was a deliberate strategy. We could see where the government wanted to go on this and, in fact, I think it was a recognition of what our sector does. But what we did was make sure we crafted the language better. So the whole thing about creative competition, freeing up markets, freeing up global competitive [flows], these were all things that we wanted to do but we recognized that this played into a government agenda as well.

This suggests that a successful lobbying campaign depends on resources and political influence, but also on a sense that the issue connects with the broad ideological stance of key policymakers. Lobbying is therefore not necessarily about *overt* corruption but also about common values. As one commentator on British policy puts it:

> We are not talking about huge amounts of money being poured into almost bribing senior officials into taking the right line. I think it is more

a question of pushing at an open door, building up the arguments that are sympathetic to their natural instincts.

Measures that are based on arguments about increasing competition, building up exports, expanding the marketplace, and maximizing value and efficiency are likely to be warmly greeted by current governments. But this emphasis on 'pushing at an open door' also explains why some less powerful 'stakeholders' are able to make their voices heard. For example, disabled groups have made full use of sophisticated lobbying techniques and have embraced new technologies in order to apply maximum pressure on policymakers. According to one regulator in the UK, the disability lobby was

> moderately vocal in 1990, but by the time you got to 1996 and certainly for the [2003] Communications Act, they were a very vociferous and influential lobby, particularly within the Lords, and brought about real change. I suppose that part of that was that they got the force of the Disability Discrimination Act [DDA] to wave at the policymakers and say 'there is no hiding place now because under the DDA we have rights'.

This example, however, does little to support the claim that media policymaking is a model of transparency and accountability. The extent to which policymakers are able to act autonomously of industry interests is severely constrained by the scale and influence of 'powerful [corporate] lobbies that effectively control the debate and impose boundaries on the "legitimate" range of discussion' (McChesney 2000: 64). The limited public involvement and parliamentary and congressional scrutiny that does take place is marginalized by a relationship between industry and government that is marked by its intimacy, lack of transparency and shared objectives concerning the desirability of introducing more and more market-friendly measures into contemporary communications environments.

A scientific process?

Decisions made about the structure of complex symbolic media forms like press and broadcasting are made, in the eyes of many policy participants, with a Gradgrind-like commitment to facts. As few are able to agree on the meaning of foundation principles like diversity, pluralism, the 'public interest' and localism, US policymakers in particular are turning to what they see as more reliable quantitative methods. According to one corporate lobbyist, the FCC is 'economics-driven now . . . anyone who wants to try and make an impact files economics studies now'. 'We really are driven by the experts: the economists' agrees a senior FCC staffer. This reflects an instrumentalism at the heart of US media policymaking, that decision-making about the media, like any other area of public policy, should be guided by scientific, rather than abstract, principles and by objective, not politicized, sources of information.

While British policymakers are still prepared to turn to deliberative polling and focus groups to provide background information, they too are far from immune from the attractions of hard *data*. One lobbyist involved with raising the profile of the independent production sector during the passage of the 2003 Communications Act argues that his success was partly due to the fact that 'we presented the case on economic grounds where we had really good economic analysis. Most politicians are more than happy to have a debate if you show them evidence that stacks up.' Ofcom, the converged communications regulator, boasts of an 'evidence-based approach' – using techniques like consumer research, market data, market intelligence and technology research – that is as relevant to amorphous concepts like 'public value' and 'public service' as it is to questions of concentration and monopoly. Indeed, the BBC itself has turned to quantitative methods to demonstrate its 'net economic value' and has proposed a 'public value test' to justify the continuing relevance of public service broadcasting in a more unfavourable economic climate. According to a senior public policy adviser at the BBC, this emphasis on quantification is unprecedented:

> I think we are on a journey from where we were five years ago when the BBC said you couldn't measure anything. I think now with *Building Public Value* [BBC 2004] is the BBC's willingness to engage with two things more than we have ever done before. One is a measurement of how much value we are delivering, and the other is factoring into that measurement any positive or negative impact that we have had on the market.

Public service is now to be evaluated in terms of efficiency and economic impact, as well as its cultural relevance, using a range of increasingly, quantitative tools. The government's obsession with measuring has produced an 'audit culture' (Boyle 2002), in which 'evidence-based policy' is seen as intrinsically more impartial and reliable.

The obsession with evidence

The problem is that there is little reason to believe that a policy process based on data supplied by economists and lobbyists, and on 'scientific evidence' as opposed to personal belief, is necessarily guaranteed to be more effective. First, not all services are easily measured and the value to the public is not easily quantified. Will Davies argues that evidence-based approaches are unlikely to capture the qualities of public service institutions such as the BBC and that when 'measurement becomes too pervasive, qualitative and moral values are left out in the cold' (2005: 2). Second, there is no link between the provision of 'evidence' and the securing of impartiality. Indeed, at least one experienced British lobbyist rejects the possibility of a scientific, non-subjective approach to policymaking:

> You can take a purely fact-based approach to these things, an evidence-based approach. I don't think that such an approach really exists. I don't think there is an approach that exists without some kind of subjective view being taken, whether you call that political or not. People like to take the view that we can get the policymakers out of these kinds of areas and let competition law regulate it. But competition law is not some kind of purist theory. You are still making value judgments about what you think is the right level of competition in the marketplace.

This suggests a problem, not with empirical methods in general, but with the use of selective facts and subjective judgements. This empirical approach is designed theoretically to insulate the media policymaking and regulatory domains from the partisan politics and 'biased' opinions that surround them. The idea, however, that an evidence-based approach is necessarily free from bias or devoid of political interests is highly dubious. A perfect example of this was the revelation, in September 2006, that FCC officials had refused to distribute detailed reports that showed a link between increased media consolidation and decreased amounts of local news during its consideration three years earlier of whether to loosen media ownership rules (Associated Press 2006). There are, however, more routine pressures on the extent to which 'evidence-based' regulators are able to operate independently of politics. One policy insider, reflecting on Ofcom's radical plans for public service broadcasting (see chapter 7), praises the regulators at Ofcom 'for their analysis, their data gathering and the depth of knowledge that they have brought together', but then goes on to criticize them for having the tendency 'to throw a few think tank grenades into the discussion'. This happens because

> you have got a regulator that is led by intelligent and determined people who are keen to make their mark on public debate and also see themselves as players in the public debate, whereas in the past regulators saw their job as drier and more boring. Ofcom clearly don't want to be boring.

This demonstrates both the porous nature of the barrier between regulation and policymaking and the fact that regulatory institutions, despite their claims simply to be implementing government will, are active policy players that bring to the table their own political and ideological predisposi-tions. Indeed, politics permeates the regulatory field. For example, an offi-cial working inside the EC's Competition Directorate on Sky Television's control of Premier League football rights reflects on the fantasy of being totally impartial in the face of intense lobbying at the highest levels of UK government.

> There is a really strong school of thought that when we do our work that we are an independent competition authority, that we are objectively applying the law as best we can, we should sit in our room, write the paper and present our decision at the end. In an idea world, yes that is fantastic but in the real world it's just not as simple as that . . . even though I don't like it or agree with it, there are political realities to what we do and if we annoy enough people then we will get our wings clipped.

While not all evidence provided to policymakers is quantitative, it is still subject to these 'political realities'. The head of public policy for a large online company claims that 'we do use facts and rigorous intellectual argu-ments, but also common sense in our submissions, verbal or written, to government departments'. While some areas are more conducive to eco-nomic data,

> when you come to other areas that are more emotive, and I would guess maybe culture, child safety, law enforcement are more subjective areas where there is no right or wrong answer really, the balance is decided by politicians who are democratically elected. Really, they have to find that balance between competing interests.

Whether the subject is 'emotive' or 'rational', it seems therefore that the personal beliefs or political intuition of key policymakers play a significant role in determining the eventual shape of policy in a particular area. This illustrates Thomas Streeter's argument (1996) that media policymaking is not a scientific but an 'interpretative' activity, an ideological means of resolving differences and enforcing order. According to Streeter (1996: 117), 'underlying all the (very real) disagreements and debates is a rela-tively constant structure of expectations that limit discussion, not by coer-cion, but by way of the subtle but profound power of interpretation'. Those organizations that have the power to 'interpret' – for example, government agencies, regulators, think tanks and lobbyists – are then able to define the terms of policy debates and to stamp their imprint on to policy objectives. Streeter writes:

> Current policy discussions continue to be characterized by an artful nego-tiation of the tensions between cooperation and competition, between the perceived need for collective, particularly governmental efforts on behalf

of corporate industrial coordination and the principles of business autonomy. (1996: 310)

Academic input into the policymaking process

Meanwhile, the policymaking process continues to privilege quantitative
data and large-scale statistical evidence, a situation that threatens further
to disempower less well-resourced groups – who cannot afford major
economic analyses and large-scale surveys – and to hand the initiative to
'experts' with a direct line to policymakers. In the UK in particular, these
experts are likely to be not academics but specialist research agencies and
commercial polling organizations. Ofcom, for example, carried out major
research in its consultation on public service broadcasting and, while com-
missioning two out of six reports from academics in Phase 2 of its investi-
gation, turned to polling organizations MORI and ICM for quantitative
and qualitative research on the future of regional programming in its final
phase. Despite the vast amount of academic literature on the political significance, cultural importance and economic basis of public service broadcasting, academics ended up playing a relatively small role in these crucial
policy debates.

Why should the domination of empirical approaches necessarily contribute to the marginalization of academics in the policymaking process?
After all, there is no shortage of economists in university departments and
no lack of willingness to engage with 'scientific' methods. Indeed, in the
USA, many university-based economists and business specialists do still
contribute to the research phase, in particular, of media policymaking.
However, the grip of 'evidence-based' approaches in the context of some
hostility to 'abstract ideas' means that a significant constituency of more
critical and conceptually minded academics is likely to be excluded from
media policy circles. This drives home a wedge between empirical and
conceptual approaches, and leads to a situation where scholars, for reasons
of cost and commitment, are not as well placed as industry and government researchers to intervene in a process that is increasingly instrumental
and dominated by corporate interests.

This suggests another reason for the marginalization of academics in the
policy process: that there is no room for one of the defining features of the
job of an academic, to confront existing positions and to suggest alterna-
tives. The key to inclusion in the contemporary media policymaking process
is an ability to grasp *realpolitik* and to make a *practical* contribution to media
policy debates. A senior UK adviser to the government admits that while

some academics are still taken seriously, 'they have been practitioners, now involved in academia. Very practical people . . . Because *they engage with things as they are*, I think they have made a sterling contribution' (emphasis added). Measuring effectiveness in terms of an ability to stick to 'things as they are' presents a problem if you believe, as James Carey puts it, 'that scholarship, like many of the arts, flourishes when it stands in determined opposition to the established order' (Carey 1978: 440). This is not an excuse for deliberate abstraction and obscurantism, but recognition of the importance of the long tradition of academic criticism of existing arrangements and the formulation of proposals for alternative structures. These critiques are most likely to occur in contexts of broader political dissent and questioning – see, for example, the plans for the radical restructuring of British broadcasting and proposals for a fourth television channel in the UK in the 1970s, both of which were heavily influenced by the participation of leading media academics (see Freedman 2003a: 76–116). In recent years, 'academics have been marginalized' argues one involved in British policy debates, 'partly because we're almost all kicking against the trends. The only time you are taken seriously now is if you can say nice things about policies that are being proposed.' There are still opportunities for academics to intervene in the media policymaking process, but their chances of being listened to are hugely improved if they complement, rather than confront, existing political paradigms and policy approaches.

The public and the policymaking process

A common complaint, made by corporate lobbyists in particular, is that policymaking is skewed less by the abstractions of academics than by the whims of politicians and members of the public who start to interfere in the process, armed not with facts and data but with opinions and beliefs. 'It's frustrating', argues a lawyer for a well-known Washington, DC, legal firm, 'because when there is so much public and congressional involvement, you start to get away from dealing with the facts and reality and the real essence of policy and instead are dealing with trying to knock down a lot of myths and misperceptions out there.' The 2002 broadcast ownership debate, reflects another lobbyist, 'turned out to be emotional once it went to Congress . . . For those who had staked out their territory as being anti-deregulatory, the facts didn't matter.' According to this perspective, a logical procedure had become *illogical*; a rational argument *irrational*. Other lobbyists are simply nostalgic for a time when the public was more explicitly excluded from the policymaking arena:

It used to be with legislation and at the FCC you could get stuff done quietly and there wouldn't be anyone opposing to get it sort of done. It can't be done any more. And I'm not saying that was a good way to do things, but I think that we have now gone the other way, to the other extreme, where the average citizen has no idea of the substance, but they're told a way in and it tips the balance.

Those at the FCC involved in drawing up the liberalizing ownership rules are particularly bitter about the involvement of the public.

> X: We have this attachment to our television and we think we're expert because we spend so much time watching it, just as individuals . . . People feel they have a lot of expertise.
> Y: They feel like they understand the topic . . .
> X: They don't have the time or the information to engage in that [necessary] level of intricacy on this and that's why there is an expert agency to do this. And that's why these decisions aren't made by referenda.

This 'lack of expertise' effectively disenfranchised the hundreds of thousands of individuals who wrote to the FCC in protest at the prospect of increased consolidation.

> X: The vast majority of comments that said 'I'm against big media' are not helpful at all on the merits and don't add anything to the debate . . .
> Y: The difficulty in trying to use [those comments] is that we're looking for comments that are well supported in evidence . . .
> X: Agencies have to make decisions based on the facts and it's not terribly helpful to ask the average person 'what do you think of this?' because they will give you an overly simplistic answer. It's not their fault but they can't possibly know all the stuff that goes into making those decisions.

This is an extraordinary admission of failure of public policy: that when the public responds in unprecedented numbers, they are deemed to be 'unhelpful'. Pro-deregulation studies conducted for the FCC by a handful of economists proved to be more influential than the convictions of millions of citizens. Quantitative data supplied by economists, researchers and corporate lobbyists continues to be highly influential, gratefully received by policymakers and generally valued far higher than the 'irrational' and 'spontaneous' views of the public.

The privileging of highly selective empirical and evidence-based approaches to policymaking public opinion, fails both to depoliticize and to make any more objective the decision-making environment. Policymaking in a sphere of such cultural and political significance is bound to be highly political, and the fetishizing of 'scientific' data is one means of marginalizing the public from the public policy process while safeguarding it for the economists, lawyers and executives who are in a prime position to furnish the sort of information that policymakers are demanding.

Conclusion

This chapter has focused on some core challenges to pluralist principles of public policymaking: the extent to which it is competitive, accessible, transparent and scientific. It argues that, despite the growing number of 'stakeholders', there has not been a significant challenge to the power of a central policymaking core. Key decision-makers operate in close ideological conformity with the *broad* interests of one key constituency – that of business – in a way that structures the parameters of the debate, dictates what forms of participation are most effective and conditions the balance of power in the policy process. While a range of voices may be heard, there is little opportunity to question the assumptions about the desirability of market forces and 'consumer sovereignty' that increasingly dominate media policymaking. Public opinion is collected to lend support to predetermined policy objectives, but otherwise the process remains largely out of reach for members of the public and is therefore skewed by a fundamental imbalance in both resources and influence between public and private interests.

5

Media Ownership Policies

Does ownership matter?

In November 2006, Britain's largest pay-TV broadcaster, BSkyB, bought nearly 18 per cent of the country's largest commercial terrestrial broadcaster, ITV. The move was greeted with outrage in some quarters, further evidence of the growing influence of Rupert Murdoch over the British media. His News Corporation controls not only satellite operator BSkyB, but also owns four national newspapers with a combined share of one-third of total daily circulation, the networking site MySpace and a slew of publishing, film, television and newspaper interests across the world. Critics and rivals of Murdoch queued up to condemn the transaction. Virgin CEO Richard Branson, whose own plans to buy ITV were effectively scuppered by BSkyB's manoeuvre, accused Murdoch of being a 'threat to democracy' and called for the government to 'draw a line in the sand' over media ownership (quoted in Puttnam 2006). The film producer and Labour peer, David Puttnam, argued that what was at stake was 'the erosion of competition within the British media, and the consequences that has for British democracy' (Puttnam 2006). A former national newspaper editor described him as a 'predatory capitalist' and 'an object lesson in the dangers of concentrated cross-border power. Such power is always problematic because it is apt to reduce diversity, squeeze out the regional and local, and stifle dissent. When it occurs in the information industry, it threatens democracy' (Wilby 2006). Similar concerns were raised in the USA when Murdoch launched a bid in spring 2007 for the establishment icon the *Wall Street Journal*.

The idea that Rupert Murdoch is a 'threat to democracy' rests on the notion that media ownership *matters* and that, where it is concentrated, it represents an unacceptable challenge to pluralist principles of a diverse and competitive media system. Murdoch, argue his critics, is no ordinary media executive but one of the world's most influential individuals, an entrepreneur who has relied on his political connections to bypass existing rules, who has used his market power to shape the behaviour of other market players and who has been publicly associated for many years with a set of conservative and free-market ideological positions (Cassidy 2006). If ownership does *not* matter, to what extent is it significant that Murdoch's stated support for the invasion of Iraq in March 2003 was then repeated in the more than 175 newspaper titles owned by his News Corporation (see Greenslade 2003)? If ownership is *not* important, to what extent is it a concern that, according to a former media adviser to Tony Blair, '[n]o big decision could ever be made inside No 10 [Downing Street] without taking account of the likely reaction of three men' (Price 2006: 32), the Deputy Prime Minister, the Chancellor and Rupert Murdoch?

Ownership matters both because of the largely unaccountable political and economic power that accrues to those individuals and corporations with extensive media interests and because they are able to deploy their market power to act as influential cultural gatekeepers. This chapter considers policy approaches towards ownership and concentration in the light of recent initiatives in both the USA and the UK to liberalize media ownership rules. In 2003, the FCC proposed a sweeping number of changes (FCC 2003a) that included raising the national television cap (the proportion of the television audience reached by one broadcaster) from 35 per cent to 45 per cent, replacing the ban on newspaper/broadcast and radio/television cross-ownership with a flexible set of cross-media limits, and relaxing rules on local television ownership so that, in the biggest markets, one company could own three stations. While most of these proposals were frozen by federal judges the following year, the rules are once again under FCC review. In the UK, a consultation on media ownership rules (DCMS/DTI 2001) was followed by passage of the 2003 Communications Act that permits foreign companies to own terrestrial television, increases opportunities for radio and cross-media mergers and generally seeks to use competition law, rather than legislation focused on the media, in evaluating possible plurality concerns. The chapter first considers the FCC's liberalization proposals and then reflects on the importance of the issue of media ownership in the emergence and subsequent policymaking of New Labour.

The FCC and broadcast ownership rules

The politics of Michael Powell

The 1996 Telecommunications Act, presided over by the Clinton administration, increased the national television ownership cap to 35 per cent, relaxed some elements of telecoms and broadcast cross-ownership and allowed increasing concentration in radio markets. Overt hostility towards ownership rules accelerated, however, with the election of George W. Bush in 2000 and his appointment of Michael Powell as chair of the FCC in January 2001. Powell has impeccable Republican credentials – he is the son of former Secretary of State Colin Powell, and was a policy adviser to former Defense Secretary Dick Cheney and an anti-trust lawyer in the Department of Justice before being appointed as an FCC commissioner in 1997. Describing his politics as 'moderate, slightly right of center', he states that:

> I'm a big believer in individual entrepreneurship and innovation. I think American capitalism is the finest economic system ever invented. It has crushed – not beaten, *crushed* – every alternative deployed in the history of the world, and we should be proud of it instead of embarrassed by it. (Powell 2004a)

Powell also had powerful supporters in Congress. The then chairs of the two congressional committees with legislative oversight of the FCC, John McCain of the Senate Commerce Committee and Billy Tauzin, chair of the House Energy and Commerce Committee, both men with a track record of backing deregulatory measures for telecommunications and broadcasting, were 'enthusiastic supporters of Powell' (Albiniak 2001: 22). McCain publicly declared that Powell 'would make an excellent [FCC] chairman' (Albiniak 2000: 26), while Tauzin described him as 'the brightest light on the commission, the brightest mind' (McConnell 2000: 23) and declared that, under him, the FCC 'will become an agency that unleashes market forces' (Goodman 2001: E03). In 2000, the trade magazine *Broadcasting and Cable* wrote that 'Powell's deregulatory mantra has won him a lot of fans in the industry and among Capitol Hill Republicans (McConnell 2000: 23).

Powell signalled his intention to confront ownership rules within three months of his tenure at the FCC. In early 1998, he argued that it is 'indeed time to take a sober and realistic look at our broadcast ownership rules in light of the current competitive communications environment' (Powell 1998b). In 2000, he dissented from the FCC's reluctance to tackle the rules, condemning the refusal by other commissioners 'to fully consider the competitive landscape today and validate that these structural rules still serve their stated purposes' (Powell 2000). By 2001, soon after being appointed as chair, he announced plans to review the rules with a pretty clear deregulatory agenda: 'Validate the purpose of a rule in a modern context, or *eliminate it* . . . Resist regulatory intervention' (Goodman 2001: E03 – emphasis added), he argued to a congressional panel.

At one level, it may seem strange to appoint a figure with known deregulatory views to be in charge of overseeing and protecting broadcast diversity in the USA. After all, this is a figure with a background in anti-trust and a belief that consolidation is no bad thing. The USA, he argues (Powell 2004a), 'has got antitrust right. The presumption is business is OK. The presumption is mergers are not in and of themselves bad. People forget that monopoly isn't even illegal.' Instead, general anti-trust rules, not media-specific obligations, should be the default position to achieve the desired objectives of competition, diversity and localism: 'There may have been a time in which such objectives could not be achieved without regulatory intervention (*though I question it*). But, surely, these values are not incompatible with market forces, or market failures in the classic sense' (Powell 2000 – emphasis added). Despite his conviction that spectrum abundance now makes the rules even more redundant, he doubts that there was ever a genuine need to have special controls on media businesses as the market would naturally restore some sort of equilibrium.

At another level, however, Powell's open commitment to deregulatory policies meant that he was perfectly placed to re-regulate broadcast ownership at a time in which the media and telecommunications industries were assuming ever greater economic importance. Congress had mandated in Section 202h of the 1996 Telecommunications Act that ownership rules be reviewed every two years (later changed to four years) and senior figures in the White House and Congress had decided by 2000 that a more radical interpretation of this mandate was required in order to free up broadcast media markets for further acquisitions, mergers and restructuring. Section 202h, despite its anodyne phrasing (that the FCC 'shall repeal or modify any [ownership] regulation it determines to be no longer in the public interest'), was a Trojan horse for deregulatory interests and was actually conceived by lobbyists for News Corporation who were determined to keep liberalization of ownership rules on the political agenda (Mundy 2003). Powell interpreted 202h in precisely the way the lobbyists had hoped and senior Republicans had anticipated – as a mandate for deregulation – and launched a media ownership working group in October 2001 before announcing a full review of ownership rules the following September. The process culminated in June 2003 in a 3–2 decision (with the two Democrat commissioners voting against) to loosen ownership rules and sanction further cross-media ownership (see McChesney 2004: 252–97 for an extensive analysis of the review and the campaign against it).

In deciding on how to vote, Powell and his fellow Republicans accepted all the main arguments proposed by corporate advocates of liberalization.

First, they agreed with lobbyists that spectrum scarcity, the phenomenon that provided the historic justification for regulating broadcasting, had been largely abolished given the emergence of virtually limitless bandwidth. 'Given the overwhelming wealth of both broadcast and non-broadcast media options available today,' argued some of the largest American entertainment companies in a submission to the FCC, 'the factual underpinnings of the spectrum scarcity rationale of broadcast regulation . . . no longer are valid (*if they ever were*)' (Joint Commenters 2003: v – emphasis added). Second, they agreed with the claim made by many 'old media' companies that existing ownership rules were threatening profitability and therefore undermining the very existence of freely available broadcast outlets and quality newspapers. For example, CBS, a company that, in 2006, made $1.66 billion profit on nearly $14.5 billion worth of revenue (*Fortune* 2007), warned that ownership restrictions were putting 'at risk the rich American tradition of free, over-the-air broadcasting' (CBS 2006: 14).

Third, the FCC echoed industry lobbyists' arguments that ownership rules violated First Amendment freedoms.

> At issue [in the review] are bedrock principles of our republic: freedom of speech and the press, freedom to associate and to petition government, freedom to acquire and hold property in accordance with the law. Our Founding Fathers understood that government should not have the power to restrict speech without deeply compelling justifications. The public is ill-served when the government binds these sacred principles to regulatory rules of a bygone era. (Powell 2003b)

This statement of neo-liberal principles – concerning the protection of private property rights, defence of speech rights for corporations, and opposition to government intrusion into private economic decisions – was given extra weight by the final justification for liberalization: that traditional ownership rules were no longer necessary in the age of the internet. As Powell put it:

> the most striking difference between the world today and the world pre-remote [control] is that Americans now have access to a bottomless well of information called the Internet . . . The time has come to honestly and fairly examine the facts of the modern marketplace and build rules that reflect the digital world we live in today, not the bygone era of black-and-white television. (2003b)

In a striking example of technological determinism that confuses quantity with quality and exaggerates the diversity of online media consumption (see Turner 2004), Powell, along with many other liberalizers, insisted that the internet is an irrepressible source of media diversity that provides an innate rebuttal of the need for sustained ownership restrictions.

Measuring Diversity

The FCC, however, continued to acknowledge that viewpoint diversity – its desired policy objective – is 'fostered when there are multiple independently owned media outlets' (FCC 2003b: 4). The main way in which the FCC sought to manage the contradiction between increased diversity and reduced ownership controls was through a highly empirical analysis of diversity that focused on the number of sources in specific media markets more than the airing of different or 'antagonistic' voices that ought to compete in a true 'marketplace of ideas'. Concentration could then be identified quantitatively, much as in any other industry. Indeed, a senior FCC official, commenting on the empirical studies commissioned for the ownership review, compares the analysis of media concentration to scientific investigations of the risk posed by manufactured chemicals in the environment:

> If you wanted to know how many parts per billion of PCBs [polychlorinated biphenyls] should be in factory smoke, you would hope there would be some good research on the human health effects of PCBs and the point at which it becomes unsafe. *And in essence we're doing the same thing here.* These are predictive decisions. We have to decide at what point bad things start to happen . . . and the best way to do that is not to sit around and stick your finger in the air and hope you come up with some sort of answer but it's to look at facts and hope you come up with some sort of answer over time in different contexts and different factory scenarios and try to make predictions based on facts and nor just biases and beliefs. (Emphasis added)

The FCC's rules designed to maximize viewpoint diversity were based on a quantitative method of measuring diversity, a 'Diversity Index' (DI) based on Powell's preferred method: anti-trust analysis of the degree of concentration in any given market. This took into consideration the number of different media outlets (broadcast television, radio, newspaper and the internet) in a single market, and the number of companies (or 'voices') in that market, together with the weighting of each media sector in terms of consumer perception of their importance as a source of local news. The FCC's example of 'Anytown USA' was a market (FCC 2003b: 9–10) in which there are thirty-nine different media outlets, where one company owns two of the eight television stations and three of the twenty-six radio stations, and another company owns six of the twenty-six radio stations, where there are two separate daily papers and two separate internet providers. This produces a DI rating of 738, well below the threshold of 'moderate concentration' of 1,000, and far below the DI of 1,800 which constitutes a 'highly concentrated' market.

This is a highly unsatisfactory way of assessing diversity for a number of reasons, not least that it reduces the complexities of media diversity to a simple points system. First, market share is worked out simply in terms of the total number of outlets and not in terms of actual sales or ratings. This means that the market share of a community-owned or independent radio station with low audiences and minimal advertising is precisely the same as a commercial one with much larger audiences and more income. This immediately exaggerates the diversity of *real* markets where large radio groups such as Clear Channel will be able to use their resources and market power to exert far more influence over that locality than their 'competitors'. Second, the DI's quantitative methodology fails to assess the type of views that are actually expressed: there may be twenty-six separate radio stations but they may largely be playing the same tune or speaking in the same voice. Finally, and perhaps most importantly, the FCC's example is extremely unusual and therefore misleading: only a tiny number of cities in the USA have two separate daily newspapers, just as the existence of eighteen separate radio 'voices' in one area is also increasingly rare. It means ignoring markets like Mansfield, Ohio, where, in 2003, Clear Channel owned eleven out of the seventeen radio stations, or Albany, Georgia, where Cumulus owned eight of the fifteen stations (Dunbar and Pilhofer 2003). The 'fact' that much of the FCC's data and its reliance on a quantitatively measured 'Diversity Index' were later discredited by the Appeals Court – who argued that the index's methodology 'requires us to abandon both logic and reality' (*Prometheus* 2004: 68) – demonstrates the unreliability of exclusively empirical approaches. In summary, the index employed by the FCC is a means of defining diversity where *what* is being said is entirely irrelevant, where audience share and market power is ignored, and where only the number of people speaking and the form of speech is measured.

Given the fact that the FCC adopted such a restricted notion of diversity, accepted many of the arguments made by corporations about the *need* for liberalization, and fostered a view of the desirability of anti-trust rules as distinct from more sustained forms of regulation, it is not entirely surprising that there were only limited differences between the Commission and the industry during the 2002–3 review. The FCC rejected claims that local ownership rules were *totally* unnecessary because there was a financial incentive for broadcasters to maintain objectivity (2003a: 11) and dismissed the argument that the existence of any cross-ownership rule violated First Amendment principles of non-intervention in content issues, but otherwise it shared the corporate agenda. Indeed, some ferocious divisions took place *between* industry players over, for example, the size of the national ownership cap. Some of the largest corporations, like Fox, Viacom and NBC filed together as 'joint commenters' and clashed with medium-sized broadcasters represented by the NAB and the Network Affiliated Stations Alliance (NASA), described by one lobbyist for the joint commenters as hardly 'rocket scientists' but 'huge TV group owners', pretending to be 'little broadcasters', who did not want to see an increase in the cap.

The key division during the review was, therefore, not between regulator and industry, or between Republicans and Democrats (who, as a whole, remained fairly quiet about the issue), or between Senate and House, but between the FCC and the millions of members of the public who emailed, wrote and protested about the proposed liberalization of ownership rules, precisely the contributions dismissed by staff in the FCC's Media Bureau as 'unhelpful' because they were not supported by hard evidence (see chapter 4). It was the scale of the public response that 'opened' up the policy process and transformed media ownership into a major public issue. According to a Republican aide working for the Senate Commerce Committee at the time, Congress only started to take notice 'because of the public outcry'. Now that

> policymakers on the Hill have got engaged with the issues, there has been a shift from 'this is an issue not worth our time, we'll leave the FCC to make these decisions' to 'this is something we need to be engaged in.' Some even argue that it's partly because legislators are very affected by the media and whether they cover them [legislators] or not. In my opinion, it became a sexy issue once people became aware of it . . . Previously it had not been defined as sexy and had just been seen as a very boring and minute issue.

It had, however, always been a highly significant issue for senior figures in the White House. The same aide argues that media ownership is now a 'huge issue' both for the public and for the Republican administration:

> For this White House it is a tough issue because they have some active party loyals who had a lot at stake with this. And that's one of the reasons that the White House stayed out. But being pro-business, they were probably best pleased with the rules [revision] and that's why they didn't step

in and work [openly] with Congress to legislate. But behind the scenes, or so we're told, they had some of their supporters work within Congress to ensure these [liberalized] rules weren't overturned.

Despite congressional manoeuvrings, the rules were challenged by the Appeals Court in 2004 and were thrown back to the FCC, itself under a different chair, Kevin Martin. Another appointee of George W. Bush, Martin shares his predecessor's belief 'that a robust competitive market-place, not regulation, is ultimately the greatest protector of the public interest' (Martin 2006), and is equally dedicated to rolling back ownership rules. As long as neo-liberal politicians remain determined to curry favour with powerful media corporations and to reward their donors, and as long as sections of the public continue to challenge liberalization in the name of a more pluralistic media system, the battle over media ownership in the USA is likely to continue.

New Labour and media ownership

The evolution of New Labour's media ownership policy

If George W. Bush's White House has been at one remove from debates on ownership rules, the same cannot be said for New Labour. Acutely aware of the consequences of negative press coverage of Labour by titles like the *Sun* and the *Daily Mail* throughout the 1980s and early 1990s, Tony Blair was determined to secure a more harmonious relationship with media executives from the earliest days of the New Labour project. In particular, this involved striking up a close working relationship with Rupert Murdoch, most famously by flying to Australia in July 1995 to assure News Corporation executives that he would oppose the then Conservative government's plans to cap media ownership at a level that would prevent Murdoch from expanding in the UK (Freedman 2003a: 158). Blair was true to his word and, more than a year before winning office for the first time, New Labour figures were lobbying hard for looser controls on media ownership. 'My own preference', stated Labour's broadcasting spokesperson Lewis Moonie during the passage of the 1996 Broadcasting Act, 'is for complete deregulation . . . Cross media ownership is a good thing. The whole point is to ensure the creation of bigger companies that can compete abroad' (quoted in Prescott and Hellen 1996: 2). The result of this was that, in the only major debate that preceded the passing of the Act, 'the [Conservative] government found itself heavily pressured by the [Labour] opposition to be even more deregulatory than it intended'

(Goodwin 1998: 153; see Doyle 2002 for a full analysis of UK media owner-ship rules in the late 1990s).

The intellectual justification for this surprising turn of events was pro-vided by a high-profile research project into media regulation at the Labour-supporting Institute of Public Policy Research (IPPR). The research, eventually published as *New Media, New Policies* (Collins and Murroni 1996), was designed to signal a 'third way' in media policy, neither neo-liberal nor social democratic, that attacked the failure of both old left and new right for failing to 'balance the interests of producers and consumers of media and communications' (1996: 182). The book distinguishes between cross-ownership, not in itself a concern in the new world of digital conver-gence, and the more problematic phenomenon of concentrated owner-ship. However, even here, the authors insist that '[l]arge concentrated media organizations are not intrinsically undesirable. Large size tends to bring the resources required for comprehensive high quality reporting and the case of the BBC suggests that large organizations with a high share of media markets can serve the public interest' (1996: 75). What were required were robust competition laws, supplemented by relatively generous sector-specific limits on ownership. None of these policies would have presented Rupert Murdoch with a major headache, but the News Corporation boss would have been even more delighted by Tony Blair's promise, just before the 1997 election, not to introduce any legislation that would damage his business interests. 'It's not a question of Murdoch being too powerful. He's got a strong position and whatever authority of power he has needs to be exercised responsibly' (Blair 1997a: 12). As Freedman notes:

> In the five years since its last manifesto commitment to tackle media con-centration, Labour had transformed itself into the party *of* media concen-tration; its pledge to curb the power of Rupert Murdoch and News International had been rethought as a campaign to *court* the power of Rupert Murdoch and News International. (2003a: 170)

The endorsement of New Labour by the *Sun*, Britain's best-selling news-paper, in the 1997 election that swept Blair into office was ample reward for this strategy.

From this point on, New Labour identified competition rules as its pre-ferred mechanism for tackling issues of media concentration. In 1999, the government introduced a new Competition Commission to rule on matters concerning large mergers and acquisitions in an effort, the government claimed, to take the politics out of ownership debates. According to James Purnell, an adviser on media policy in the Number Ten Policy Unit, the primary tool for regulating media ownership would now be competition.

'As a government, we're very keen on effective competition policy – we've replaced the Competition Act which is as tough as any in the world and we'll apply those principles to the media (quoted in Freedman 2003a: 176). Depoliticizing media mergers, however, was far from straightforward, as the government found out early on when the then Trade and Industry Minister referred a proposed merger between two cable companies, NTL and Cable & Wireless Communications, to the Competition Commission against the advice of its own competition experts. Commentators noted that the referral was motivated less by concerns about a concentrated cable industry than by the likely reaction of cable's main competitor in the UK, Murdoch's BSkyB. The *Observer* concluded that the minister's actions 'opened the way for criticism that the Government's relationship with Rupert Murdoch . . . was more important than its aim of promoting competition' (Morgan 1999).

The government's first real indication that it was preparing to consider changes to media ownership rules came in its 2000 White Paper, *A New Future for Communications*, that confirmed that the government intended 'to create a new system for the regulation of media ownership which is appropriate to fast-changing, modern market conditions' (DTI/DCMS 2000: 36). Echoing Michael Powell's claim that increasing communicative 'abundance' justified deregulation and that spectrum scarcity concerns were no longer pressing, the White Paper argued that we live in a 'communications cornucopia', featuring 'dramatically increased quantities of images, information and data available to us from all over the world through a widening array of everyday devices and networks' (2000: 7), that virtually guaranteed some measure of pluralism and diversity thanks to the vigour of market forces and the roll-out of new technologies. The following year the government launched a consultation into media ownership rules (DCMS/DTI 2001) that attempted to strike a balance between the need for continuing safeguards on ownership concentration and a more liberalized environment for media mergers. On the one hand, it recognized that competition law 'cannot provide the certainty we need that a significant number of different media voices will continue to be heard or that prospective new entrants to the market will be able to add their voice' (2001: 8); on the other hand, it insisted that:

> we are committed to a deregulatory approach to media markets. From a commercial point of view, further liberalisation would benefit existing companies and potential new investors, providing for further consolidation, greater efficiency, more scope for investment, and a more significant international presence. (2001: 7)

The report proposed a biennial review of ownership rules along the lines of the FCC reviews (changed in the 2003 Communications Act to ensure one review at least every three years), suggested some liberalization of television and radio ownership rules, and confirmed that the government would keep the existing ban on foreign ownership of broadcasters. However, in the most controversial area of cross-media ownership, it concluded that it could scrap, retain or reformulate the current rules (2001: 34), a rather obvious assertion that satisfied no one. Critics of liberalization condemned the pro-deregulatory tone of the consultation, while the industry attacked government for further prevaricating over the issue of cross-media ownership. 'It seems the government is reluctant to grasp the issue because on the one hand it's paranoid about upsetting Murdoch,' argued a senior broadcaster in the *Guardian*, 'and it doesn't want to offend the non-Murdoch community on the other' (quoted in Wells et al. 2001). Instead of taking a firm decision either way, the proposals were put out to further consultation in anticipation of a more sustained piece of legislation to be tabled the following year.

Media ownership in the 2003 Communications Act

Any confusion about New Labour's loyalties and its attitude towards ownership and diversity were put to rest with the introduction of the draft communications bill in May 2002 that, in the words of its two lead authors, involved 'substantial liberalisation' within individual media markets and a reduction of cross-media ownership rules (Hewitt and Jowell 2002). This included the removal of the 15 per cent cap on television audience share, the abolition of restrictions on the ownership of more than one national radio licence and the easing of rules that prevented multiple commercial radio ownership. Culture Secretary Tessa Jowell boasted to Parliament that 'these changes are deregulatory. We will depend more on competition and on competition law exercised by a sector-specific regulator. Ownership regulations will disappear or be reduced. Self-regulation will be extended wherever possible' (HoC Debates, 7 May 2002: col. 35).

Two clauses were particularly controversial: first, the decision to permit the acquisition of Channel Five by a newspaper group, a move that could facilitate Rupert Murdoch's move into terrestrial broadcasting, and, second, the decision to lift the ban on foreign ownership of UK broadcasting. The view, expressed only six months earlier, that without 'reciprocal arrangements with other nations that would allow our own companies to expand into their markets, we do not feel we could justify lifting our ban' (DCMS/

DTI 2001: 18), had somehow changed into a determination that '[w]e will abolish all rules on foreign ownership, to secure the investment and skills that a more open market offers' (Hewitt and Jowell 2002). According to Matthew Horsman, a media analyst at Investec Securities, the shift went 'well beyond what anyone expected, particularly given the signals that government has been making about safeguarding plurality. There is huge commercial logic to this but it is surprising it has come from a Labour government' (quoted in Wells and Cassy 2002). Given that neither of these decisions had featured in the media ownership consultation paper, many people speculated that 'intense lobbying from Mr Murdoch's acolytes' (Wells and Wray 2002) and other transnational media companies had contributed to this change of heart.

Government insiders, less surprisingly, insist that these decisions were taken on the basis of industrial logic. One of the central participants in the debate acknowledges that the proposal to allow foreign ownership of broadcasting did not exist in the first draft of the bill but claims that its insertion was merely 'a case of taking a decision based on first principles', given that there was 'no intellectual justification' for retaining the ban. The reason that it was kept secret in the run-up to the publication of the draft bill was simply that it would have deflected attention away from the core concerns of the bill and would have fed the media's obsession with Rupert Murdoch's impact on government policy. 'The important thing to establish was that we wouldn't let fictions that exist in the minds of journalists define the legislative content.' According to Bill Bush, then special adviser to the culture secretary, the prime minister 'didn't follow the political case. He said he was persuaded by the technical case . . . there was no heat from Number Ten whatsoever' (Bush 2005). A Downing Street policy adviser concurs that the decision to liberalize ownership rules was taken on purely economic grounds: it was

> a decision based on global issues on the direction of the media industry, rather than public policy imperatives . . . the drafting of a piece of legislation like that is driven by what the global industry looks like and what the national industry looks like. We don't make policy in a vacuum, we make it in response to global trends.

This revelation that media ownership policy is taken on strictly economic, rather than public – i.e. social – policy grounds is interesting in itself and demonstrates New Labour's focus on maximizing the profitability of British media in the world market above more local concerns of diversity and accountability. However, it does little to ward off suspicion that the formulation of ownership policy is linked to political considerations. This suspicion was strengthened by the publication of documents showing that BSkyB lobbyists met with Downing Street officials six times during the passage of the communications bill in 2003, seeking (and gaining) assurances, amongst other things, that plurality concerns could not be used to block mergers if they met existing ownership rules and that there was not going to be a U-turn on the new Channel Five ownership policy. According to the *Guardian*, the files reveal 'how the media tycoon Rupert Murdoch wields extensive lobbying clout over the Blair government' (Leigh and Evans 2005). For Granville Williams of the Campaign for Press and Broadcasting Freedom, the documents demonstrate 'the uncomfortable truth . . . that the main proposals and changes in terms of media ownership [in the 2003 Communications Act] were achieved through the corporate lobbying of groups like News International, Carlton/Granada and the commercial radio industry' (Williams 2005a).

It is not the case that there was complete harmony between corporate interests and the government over the liberalization of media ownership laws at the time. News International, for example, criticized the retention of *any* cross-ownership limits, describing them as 'arbitrary thresholds' that 'punish success and cannot take account of the rapid changes that are occurring in the industry and the new forms of competition that media companies face' (News International 2002: 4). Trinity Mirror, one of the UK's largest newspaper publishers, also argued that the reforms 'do not go far enough in liberalizing cross-media ownership restrictions . . . and that [a] percentage restriction on cross-media ownership . . . would be entirely subjective in detail' (Trinity Mirror 2002). Given that Trinity Mirror and News International were the two companies most directly affected by maintaining the cross-ownership restrictions, their reservations were hardly surprising.

A more sustained level of opposition to the government's liberalization plans was centred on campaigners who objected, in particular, to the government's privileging of consumer over citizen interests in the activities of the new communications regulator, Ofcom. Led by Lord Puttnam inside and the organization Public Voice outside Parliament, they attempted to force the government to ensure that Ofcom would address non-economic as well as economic objectives in its supervision of communications markets. Livingstone et al. (2006) note the linguistic shifts during the passage of the bill, where initial references to 'customers' and 'consumers' in Ofcom's remit were, after much argument, replaced in the legislation by references to both 'citizens' and 'consumers', a change then ignored by Ofcom in its mission statement. Livingstone et al. (2006: 22) identify a 'double elision in the interpretation of its [Ofcom's] general duties: it conjoins citizens and consumers as the citizen-consumer; and it foregrounds competition as the primary instrument to further both consumer and citizen interests. This positions Ofcom primarily as an economic regulator.' This also explains why, in its first review of ownership rules, Ofcom suggested that, while there was no need for change at this stage, 'further deregulation should be considered' in the areas of local radio provision, digital radio multiplexes and local cross-media ownership (Ofcom 2006a: 5). Ofcom's deregulatory zeal is further illustrated by its description of the FCC's sweeping proposals for changes to US broadcast ownership rules, dismissed by Appeals Court judges as poorly conceived and opposed by literally millions of Americans, as only 'modest proposals for liberalisation' (2006a: 14).

The biggest argument concerning media ownership during the passage of the 2003 Communications Act focused on Lord Puttnam's demand for a public interest plurality test to examine major media mergers. Puttnam denied that this was specifically designed to prevent the further expansion of Rupert Murdoch and insisted instead that it was proprietor-neutral and 'a move towards making the Berlusconi-isation of British democracy an impossibility' (HoL Debates, 2 July 2003: col. 911). Despite the rather innocuous wording of Lord Puttnam's amendment – that media mergers should be partly assessed on the extent to which they facilitated 'a plurality of media owners committed to a balanced and impartial presentation of news and to a balanced presentation of comment' (2003: col. 908) – the government initially resisted it. Heritage minister Lord McIntosh argued in favour of concentration that 'more [companies] is not always better' (2003: col. 913) and that a plurality test might politicize broadcasting (by requiring news programmes to incorporate 'comment') and introduce 'content regulation into newspapers' (2003: col. 912). (The Tribune Company had made the latter argument in its opposition to ownership restrictions in the USA, a claim dismissed even by the FCC). However, faced with sustained and cross-party opposition, the government caved in and agreed to the introduction of a media public interest test in the case of large mergers, mostly involving newspapers and broadcasters.

The problem is that such a test is unlikely to be robust enough to withstand pressure from either politicians or astute media barons. The test requires the secretary of state to judge whether there are sufficient public interest considerations arising from a particular merger to recommend further action. Noting that politicians can be swayed by a range of interests, the commentator Roy Greenslade argues that 'despite all attempts to improve the regulatory regime and to make the process as objective as possible, the subjective element remains of paramount importance' (2004: 6). It will not be easy to insulate decisions made on the basis of protecting pluralism and diversity from the instrumental considerations that arise from government's determination to avoid, wherever possible, antagonizing powerful media owners. Even the welcome announcement of an inquiry into BSkyB's acquisition of a 17.9 per cent stake in ITV is unlikely to herald a meaningful shift in the government's attitude towards media ownership. Rupert Murdoch, moreover, 'will continue to do what he has always done: to weaken his rivals, not by producing better quality content, still less by developing original TV programmes or innovative films, but by exploiting his dominant market position' (Wilby 2006). Without a fundamentally different attitude by government towards media concentration, the public interest test is doomed to be a lightweight tool in the face of aggressive liberalization.

Tony Blair's Downing Street has been at the heart of moves since 1997 to dissipate the impact of media ownership restrictions in an attempt, at least initially, to prove New Labour's pro-market credentials and to win support from influential media owners. It has combined promises to stimulate competition and protect diversity with a conception of media pluralism that fetishizes scale, rewards expansion and undermines traditional controls on concentration. It has proved to be not only susceptible to industry lobbying for fewer ownership rules, but also a willing accomplice in initiatives to free up media markets, increase possibilities for inward investment and enhance opportunities for domestic profitability – all of this carried out, somewhat ironically, in the name of promoting diversity and pluralism.

Conclusion

The issues highlighted by pluralists – of the need for democracy to have robust competition, multiple sources of information, a plethora of media outlets, and a free range of voices and opinions – have been taken up and hegemonized by neo-liberal actors in the USA and the UK, seeking to define and realize these objectives in market terms and through market transactions. Recent reviews of media ownership policies in both countries have been predicated on a limited number of technological, economic and political arguments, often proposed by corporate interests, that make a strategy of ownership liberalization intrinsically desirable and ultimately necessary. Yet the liberalization of ownership rules is likely to contribute to a situation marked not by heterogeneity and diversity, but by restricted competition, oligopolistic markets and political consensus. Media ownership is by no means the sole explanatory factor of media performance and the existence of media ownership rules are not at all sufficient to ensure genuine competition and diversity, but they are an important first step in challenging concentrated and unaccountable formations of media power. Their undoing by neo-liberal governments is of serious concern.

6

Media Content Policies

Content is by far the most contentious area of media policy activity but it is also, in theory, the least exposed to conscious public policy actions. In contrast to questions of ownership, licensing and intellectual property rights where the state is seen to have a legitimate role, modern liberal democratic governments repeatedly declare their unwillingness to legislate on what types of content are, or are not, permissible. Just as censorship is seen as one of the hallmarks of authoritarian regimes, non-intervention into the minutiae of daily decisions of what to publish or broadcast is seen as a defining characteristic of pluralist government that facilitates – as long as it is legal – the distribution of both popular and unpopular, mainstream and marginal, compliant and critical ideas.

This norm bears little relation to reality, where media content is subject to a barrage of both formal and informal pressure from governments, judges, political parties, pressure groups and corporations, all of them seeking to maximize the amount of material to which they are sympathetic and minimize material which they consider damaging. Ed Baker (2002: 116–21) argues that there are three types of policy response to 'good' and 'bad' content (defined as material that produces, respectively, positive and negative externalities, for example education and edification on the one hand and ignorance or greed on the other). The first consists of subsidies designed to produce 'good' material that, according to Baker, is under-provided by market forces. Perhaps the best example of this is the case of public service broadcasting that we discuss in the next chapter. The second response concerns the use of structural interventions like anti-trust and ownership rules (assessed in the previous chapter) that 'encourage the allocation of decision-making control over content creation to people with commitments to quality rather than merely to the bottom line' (2002: 120). The third response is to restrict or suppress 'bad' content, i.e. material that is perceived by policy actors to be politically or socially undesirable. This chapter focuses on the latter form of 'negative policy' – in many ways the most problematic approach for liberal democratic regimes – and, after examining existing mechanisms of and justifications for content regulation, assesses policy responses to 'obscene', 'indecent' and 'critical' content in the first few years of the twenty-first century. Unusually, these examples concern instances where there is substantial conflict, rather than accommodation, between government and industry and therefore offer up a particularly relevant analysis of the strength of pluralist perspectives on contemporary policy.

Content policies in liberal democracies

If media ownership policies are characterized by the degree of government intervention and the number of different rules applied, liberal democratic theory would seem to suggest, especially in opposition to the censorious instincts of authoritarian governments, that non-intervention is the norm when it comes to media content policies. Prior restraint, in particular, would seem incompatible with the commitments to freedom and independence which, as we saw in chapter 3, are foundational principles of pluralist media policy environments. Section 326 of the 1934 Communications Act makes this plain in relation to broadcasting in the USA:

> Nothing in this act shall be understood or construed to give the [Federal Communications] Commission the power of censorship over the radio communications or signals transmitted by any radio station, and no regulation or condition shall be promulgated or fixed by the Commission which shall interfere with the right of free speech by means of radio communication.

The situation with regard to the press appears to be equally clear. In response to the conclusions of a parliamentary committee report in 2003 that proposed some degree of statutory regulation, the British government firmly rejected the idea of any special controls on the press.

> The Government strongly believes that a free press is vital to the health of our democracy. There should be no laws that specifically seek to restrict that freedom and Government should not seek to intervene in any way in what a newspaper or magazine chooses to publish. (DCMS 2003: 1)

Yet two weeks before stepping down as prime minister, Tony Blair – having spent thirteen years as Labour leader courting the support of the popular press – delivered a speech that attacked British newspapers for behaving like 'feral beasts, just tearing people and reputations to bits' and warned that the 'regulatory framework at some point will need revision' (Blair 2007).

This points to a dilemma for pluralists in relation to the regulation of media content: the need to weigh commitments to free speech, epitomized by the First Amendment and Millian principles, alongside the state's responsibility to protect the 'public interest'. Responding to the (very infrequent) critical press coverage of the 'war on terror', George W. Bush notes that:

> A free society is where people feel free without retribution to speak. A good society is one where information flows to the people. We're of the people. On the other hand, there's some information which could damage our ability to collect information, and that's where the real rub has been from my perspective. (Bush 2005)

There is, he concludes, a 'delicate balance' between freedom and control. In the UK, for example, the Ofcom Broadcasting Code that sets out the rules on acceptable broadcast content, also makes it clear that there are necessary limits to free speech:

> Freedom of expression is at the heart of any democratic state. It is an essential right to hold opinions and receive and impart information and ideas. Broadcasting and freedom of expression are intrinsically linked. However, with such rights come duties and responsibilities. (Ofcom 2005: 1)

Rules are required that recognize the right to free speech while, at the same time, 'robustly protecting those too young to exercise fully informed choices for themselves' (2005: 1) or minimizing the degree of harm and offence to general audiences.

The idea that liberal democratic governments are reluctant, by their very nature, to intervene in questions of media content is further undermined by the plethora of generalist laws that surround the media concerning, for example, defamation, data protection, contempt of court and copyright. Without a constitutional guarantee of free speech, the British media are particularly vulnerable to legal restrictions. Indeed, according to Julian Petley (1999: 143), there are 'some 50 pieces of legislation that restrict media freedom', including the Obscene Publications Act, Police and Criminal Evidence Act, the Terrorism Act, the Public Records Act and, perhaps most notoriously of all, the Official Secrets Act (OSA). Originally passed in 1911 to counter the alleged threat of German spies, the OSA rules any unauthorized communication or receipt of official information to be a criminal offence. It is so all-embracing that it covers not just military and security information but even the most minor details of government and civil service conduct. For Petley (1999: 148), the increased use of these various forms of prior restraint suggests that 'freedom of expression is rather more heavily regulated and circumscribed in Britain than might at first appear'.

The USA is by no means an unregulated paradise and has its own espionage and security laws that impinge on media freedom, but it is nevertheless true that the First Amendment has historically offered at least some protection to journalists and broadcasters from formal government and judicial intrusion. Libel, for example, is far harder to prove in the USA where, according to Joseph Turow (1999: 67), 'concern for the First Amendment takes precedence over libel laws as they relate to the media'. Even in issues concerning national security, where the Executive has done its best to keep military information secret, the Supreme Court has shown occasional willingness to rule in favour of publication. This happened most famously in the case of the 'Pentagon Papers', classified Defense Department documents analysing American involvement in the Vietnam War that were published by the *New York Times*, where the Court 'absolved the media, ruling that the government had been overly cautious in classifying the information as top secret' (Graber 2002: 74). The introduction of freedom of information legislation as early as 1967 has further aided journalists in monitoring government activities. Indeed, in an overwhelmingly commercial system, it may be the case that, at times, the main source of pressure on media content is not necessarily government but concentrated private media ownership that seeks ratings success and advertiser support at the expense of the pursuit of critical or minority perspectives. As Robert McChesney puts it, the ' "market" can be a most effective censor' (2004: 225). However, recent narrow and corporate-friendly interpretations of the First Amendment (described in chapter 3), combined with an administration engaged in an indefinite 'war on terror', have contributed to a situation in which government now appears to be increasingly prepared to limit the rights of reporters and to restrict media freedom – a claim we examine in more detail later in this chapter.

While newspapers and magazines are subject only to general legislation, broadcast content – with its wide availability and social influence – is treated rather differently. Britain, for example, has detailed rules expressed in the Ofcom Broadcasting Code and BBC Producers' Guidelines on everything from impartiality, balance, accuracy, swearing and the representation of sex and violence to demonstrations of exorcism and precautions surrounding the broadcasting of flashing lights affecting viewers with photosensitive epilepsy (Ofcom 2005: 19). Political advertising remains banned and the UK is a signatory to the European Commission's 'Television without Frontiers' directive (EC 1989) that places further restrictions on the scheduling and content of advertisements, dictating that a majority of mainly drama and documentary programming should be reserved for content of European origin. US broadcasting, despite the First Amendment and Section 326 of the Communications Act, is also subject to limited content rules, most obviously in the areas of obscenity and indecency (that we deal with in the next section) and children's programming. The Children's Television Act of 1990 mandates, for example, that stations must offer a minimum of three hours per week of 'core programming' and limits commercials to ten and a half minutes per hour on weekends and twelve minutes per hour on weekdays (Title 47, *US Code*, Ch. 5, § 303a).

For some industry voices, statutory regulation is, by its very nature, incompatible with a modern market democracy. Sir Christopher Meyer, the chairman of the Press Complaints Commission, predicts that 'one of these days the State will get out of the business of regulating content on television and radio; and that an expanded system of self-regulation will cover all forms of content delivery' (2006: 32). This assertion is given further impetus by the UK government's support for new instruments of 'co-regulation', whereby regulators and industries work in partnership to devise rules and supervise conduct. Self- and co-regulation have also been championed because of the rapid development of the internet as a media platform that is not easily subject to existing regulatory provisions. A clear distinction has now been made between material that is generally dissemi- nated and that which is 'sought out', in other words between linear and non-linear, 'push' and 'pull' technologies. Representatives of the latter industries (ISPs, online content producers and advertisers) are calling for modest self-regulatory structures in order, they claim, to stimulate innova- tion and creativity and to maintain the diversity of the online world. According to the UK Broadband Stakeholder Group, '[n]ew audio-visual content services, made possible through innovation in digital technology and the internet, should be given time to evolve and develop rather than being shackled by premature and unnecessary regulation [sic] intervention by the EU' (quoted in Williams 2005b: 4). During discussions in 2005–6 about whether to expand the terms of the Television without Frontiers directive (TWF) to non-linear services, this argument was repeated most forcefully by the British government, who feared that 'the extension of scope will create huge new regulatory burdens, expensive and hard or impossible to enforce . . . We shouldn't put restrictions in place to inhibit growth and innovation' (Woodward 2006: 28).

Some industry figures take this argument much further and insist that any proposed distinction between 'strong' regulation of linear services and 'light touch' regulation of non-linear services is increasingly undesirable and untenable because of the challenges posed by digital technologies. Reflecting, during the TWF negotiations, on whether online audio-visual content should be regulated in the same way as television or whether television content regulation should increasingly be deregulated along the lines of the internet, James Murdoch, CEO of BSkyB, declared that 'the first option is for the birds' and that '[o]ver time, lessening of TV content regulation is inevitable' (Murdoch 2005). For Murdoch, the inevitable pluralism and diversity of a multimedia environment galvanized by the power of the internet justifies the virtual abolition of public intervention into and regulation of audio-visual content.

> A totally new approach which recognizes the new on-demand world we live in is badly needed . . . there is a long way to go before consumers enjoy the sovereignty that is their right. We don't need more controls to achieve that. We need a bonfire of controls. Then commerce will be free to drive our culture forward to the real Golden Age of broadcasting. For me, it can't come soon enough. (Murdoch 2005)

This is a pure – and fairly extreme – account of a neo-liberal approach to content regulation that associates the market with dynamism and equates regulation with stagnation and oppression. How do we then explain contrasting approaches to content regulation undertaken by market-friendly governments that adopt a totally different perspective on the role of government, first in relation to questions of broadcast obscenity and indecency in the USA, and then in relation to issues of national security in both the USA and the UK?

A war on indecency?

On 19 January 2003, the rock singer Bono was heard to utter the words 'this is really, really fucking brilliant' (or 'this is fucking great') during NBC's live transmission of the Golden Globes Award. The FCC, the agency charged by Congress with overseeing programme content, received 234 complaints – the vast majority from individuals associated with a conservative pressure group, the Parents Television Council (PTC) (FCC 2003c: 1) – arguing that such language was indecent and a violation of federal law. Bono's words, and the FCC orders that followed, signalled the beginning of a sustained assault in the USA by government and regulators on the broadcasting of 'bad language' and the depiction of sex and nudity that resulted in millions of dollars of fines and the emergence of a climate of self-censorship on the part of American broadcasters. That the same events did *not* take place in the UK reveals much both about the residual permissiveness of public broadcasting culture in Britain and about the political influence of conservative ideas and 'family values' on key parts of the American political system.

US law appears to be quite clear on the issue of broadcast indecency. Section 1464 of title 18 of the US Code states that '[w]hoever utters any obscene, indecent, or profane language by means of radio communication shall be fined under this title or imprisoned not more than two years, or both'. The FCC adheres to the Supreme Court's definition of obscenity as material that 'appeals to the prurient interest', depicts sexual conduct in an offensive way and has no significant artistic or literary merit (FCC 2005). While obscene material is not entitled to First Amendment protection and thus may not be broadcast at any time, indecent content – defined as 'sexual or excretory material that does not rise to the level of obscenity' (FCC 2005) – does have constitutional protection as long as it is transmitted in the 'safe harbor' hours between 10 p.m. and 6 a.m. The FCC often justifies its intervention into content matters with reference to the celebrated Supreme Court case, *FCC v. Pacifica Foundation (FCC* 1978), that ruled that comedian George Carlin's *Seven Words You Can Never Say on Television*, broadcast on Pacifica Radio in 1973, was indeed indecent (the relevant words being shit, piss, fuck, cunt, cocksucker, motherfucker and tits, several of which have been the object of recent FCC actions). According to Justice Breyer, the existence of free-speech rights for broadcasters does not automatically give them the right to cause harm: 'Patently offensive, indecent material presented over the airwaves confronts the citizen, not only in public, but also in the privacy of the home, where the individual's right to be left alone plainly outweighs the First Amendment rights of an intruder' (1978: 26).

Yet how does one differentiate between material that is indecent or decent and between material that is obscene or merely shocking? In an attempt further to clarify its definition of indecency, the FCC emphasizes the importance of *context* in two ways: first, in terms of the wider culture so that indecent material must be 'patently offensive as measured by contemporary community standards' (FCC 2006b: 5); second, by contextual analysis of the programme itself, for example, the degree of graphic-ness involved, the extent to which the offensive images or words are fleeting or repeated and whether the material aims deliberately to titillate or shock the audience. 'In examining these three factors,' the Commission concludes, 'we must weigh and balance them on a case-by-case basis' (2006b: 5). Such refinements, however, do little to offset the plainly subjective assessments of precisely what constitutes 'contemporary community standards', what makes a programme *'patently* offensive' and whether a broadcaster's intention is deliberately to 'titillate or shock'.

These debates have been at the centre of the many indecency cases that the FCC has considered since 2003. Indeed, Bono's words at the 2003 Golden Globes were found initially not to be indecent. The head of the FCC's enforcement bureau ruled in October 2003 that the word ' "fucking" may be crude and offensive, but, in the context presented here, did not describe sexual or excretory organs or activities' and that 'fleeting and isolated remarks of this nature do not warrant Commission action' (FCC 2003c: 3). Lobbied heavily by the PTC, FCC commissioners then overturned this decision and, in March 2004, issued another order that concluded that the ' "F-Word" is one of the most vulgar, graphic and explicit descriptions of sexual activity in the English language. Its use *invariably* invokes a coarse sexual image' (FCC 2004a: 5 – emphasis added). Retreating from previous precedent that a single or fleeting use of the 'F-Word' could not be considered indecent, and ignoring the FCC's own advice that there are *no* words 'that are always unlawful' (FCC 2005), the commissioners warned broadcasters that 'they will be subject to potential enforcement for *any* broadcast of the "F-Word" or a variation thereof' (2004a: 8 – emphasis added). The order is not simply threatening in its warning to broadcasters about any future infringements of indecency rules, but extraordinarily polite in its determination to refer to the 'F-Word' throughout (as opposed to the use of 'fucking' in the original order), as if a more demure atmosphere was sweeping through Washington, DC.

Further evidence of a new climate was provided by the Commission's (and, to a certain extent, the public's) reaction to two further transgressions that took place in the months before its order on the Golden Globes. In December 2003, referring to her show *The Simple Life*, Nicole Richie asked the audience at the Billboard Music Awards – aired live by Fox – whether they had 'ever tried to get cow shit out of a Prada bag? It's not so fucking simple' (quoted in Huck 2006: 2). Two months later, in front of a television audience of some 100 hundred million people, the singers Janet Jackson and Justin Timberlake took part in a half-time segment during the Superbowl 'that concluded with Mr. Timberlake's removal of a portion of Ms. Jackson's bustier, exposing her breast to the camera' (FCC 2004b: 2). Buoyed by the 542,000 complaints received by the Commission and unsympathetic to the claim by broadcaster CBS that the fleeting exposure of a nipple in a live performance was beyond the network's control, the FCC fined Viacom (owner of CBS) $550,000, the maximum $27,500 fine for each CBS affiliate that had aired the Superbowl.

> Viacom betrayed its trust, not only to the FCC arising from its obligation to operate its stations in the public interest and in a manner consistent with the Commission's rules, but to each parent who reasonably assumed that the national broadcast of a major sporting event on a Sunday evening would not contain offensive sexual material unsuitable for children, the very class of viewers that the Commission's indecency rule was designed to protect. (FCC 2004b: 13)

The fines started to stack up during 2004. The FCC penalized Fox nearly $1.2 million for featuring an episode of the reality programme *Married by America* in which bachelors were seen licking whipped cream off strippers; it fined Clear Channel $495,000 for a Howard Stern radio show that featured explicit sexual references and then fined the *Elliot in the Morning* radio show $247,500 for broadcasting a detailed interview about the attractions of a particular porn star. As the Center for Public Integrity noted at the time, 'thanks to broader applications of its powers to regulate indecent broadcasting' (Dunbar 2005), the FCC was able to levy record fines – some $7.9 million according to the *Wall Street Journal* (Schatz 2005) – far more in one single year than in the previous ten years combined. The high point of penalties (or low point of broadcast behaviour depending on your perspective) came in March 2006 when the FCC fined CBS $3.6 million for showing a 'sexual situation' (a teen orgy with, however, no images of nudity) in its programme *Without a Trace*.

Why did indecency become a major issue?

What was the reason for this increasing focus on indecency? Was it simply that broadcasters started behaving badly in 2004 or that audiences suddenly started noticing? After all, Howard Stern had offended audiences throughout the 1990s and he continued to broadcast on free-to-air radio until 2004 when Clear Channel, strong political supporters of George W. Bush, eventually sacked him in order to pre-empt any further punishment. The FCC have even acknowledged (2004a: 5) that musicians had used the 'F-Word' several times during awards ceremonies in previous years. For some, the growth in broadcast sex and violence is directly linked to the rapid consolidation of the media industry. According to Bob McChesney and Ben Scott of the media activist group Free Press, 'big media companies are risk-averse and market-sensitive, homogenizing and replicating low-cost, high-ratings content in a race to the bottom' (McChesney and Scott 2005). Democrat

FCC commissioner Michael Copps concurs that as 'media conglomerates grow ever larger and station control moves farther away from the local community, community standards seem to count for less when programming decisions are made' (quoted in FCC 2006c: 23), leading to an increasingly alienated and embittered public.

Yet the dominant voices raised against 'indecency' and 'obscenity' back in 2004 were not those of left-wing critics of corporate media domination but of conservatives who saw television and radio's growing 'coarseness' and diminution of 'family values' as evidence of the 'liberal' domination of American broadcasting. This feeling was organized on the ground by groups like the Parents Television Council, but was echoed inside Congress by a growing consensus that something had to be done to tackle broadcast indecency. By March 2004, versions of a 'Broadcast Decency Enforcement Act' had passed through Senate and House committees, proposing to increase the maximum penalty for indecency violations from $27,500 to $500,000. While these initiatives were cross-party, there was little doubt, as *Business Week* pointed out, that '[m]uch of the agitation is coming from the Right, which sees the public airwaves as a key battleground in the culture wars . . . No pol wants to appear soft on smut in an election year' (Yang 2004).

Partisan politics did intervene in the end as the legislation was dropped just before the presidential election when the Democratic Senator Byron Dorgan attached an amendment blocking the FCC's proposed relaxation of media ownership rules (see chapter 5) to the clauses on indecency. By linking the issue of media consolidation and broadcast indecency, Dorgan stood apart from the other high-profile sponsors of indecency legislation, Republicans Fred Upton and Sam Brownback, both of them firm supporters of broadcast ownership deregulation. Caught between their horror of indecency and their links to the media and telecommunications industries, they exemplify the contradictions of the neo-conservative world-view. Brownback demonstrated his split loyalties in comments to a Senate hearing on media ownership in January 2003:

> I will not support efforts to use our mutual and legitimate concerns over indecency or increased coarseness in our society as a ruse to push forward damaging regulatory competition policies, such as national ownership limitations in the radio market, or restraints on converged ownership between various forms of media. (Quoted in Frank 2006: 281)

As Frank notes, '[f]aced with a choice between protecting corporate profits and actually doing something about the open cultural sewer he has spent his career deploring, Brownback chose the former . . . The free-market system is inviolable' (2006: 75).

George W. Bush's re-election in November 2004 gave confidence to those seeking harsher indecency penalties. Following a CNN exit poll that revealed that 22 per cent of the electorate said that 'moral values' mattered most to them (more than terrorism at 19 per cent, the economy at 20 per cent and health care at 18 per cent) (CNN 2004), politicians and regulators seized the opportunity to demonstrate their pro-family credentials. The *New York Times'* Frank Rich pointed out that, despite evidence that 'moral values' were of less importance to voters in 2004 than in either 2000 or 1996, 'opportunistic ayatollahs on the right have been working overtime to inflate this nonmandate into a landslide by ginning up cultural controversies that might induce censorship by a compliant FCC and, failing that, self-censorship by TV networks' (Rich 2004a). In further evidence of a growing moral crusade, Attorney General Alberto Gonzales warned that 'aggressive prosecution' of obscenity cases would join the 'war on terror', violent crime and human trafficking as top priorities for the Justice Department in 2005 (Eggerton 2005a). James Sensenbrenner, chair of the House Judiciary Committee, told industry executives later that year that he was actually in favour of criminalizing indecency violations: 'People who are in flagrant disregard should face a criminal process rather than a regulator process. That is the way to go. Aim the cannon specifically at the people committing the offenses, rather than the blunderbuss approach that gets the good actors' (quoted in Boliek 2005).

At the FCC, a new chairman, Kevin Martin, a former White House aide to George W. Bush, was intensifying his campaign against indecency. Martin launched a campaign to extend indecency regulations to cable and satellite channels that were not subject to such restrictions. Addressing a Senate hearing on indecency in November 2005, Martin warned that if 'cable and satellite operators continue to refuse to offer parents more tools such as family friendly programming packages, basic indecency and profanity restrictions may be a viable alternative that should be considered' (Martin 2005: 11). *Salon* magazine reported that Martin met regularly with evangelical activists, seeking their support and promising to 'change the television landscape' (Scherer 2005). In the summer of 2005, Martin even appointed Penny Nance, the founder of the Kids First Coalition, 'a group that fights abortion, cloning and indecency in the name of "pro-child, pro-family public policy" ' (Scherer 2005) as an adviser to the FCC on indecency issues.

Bush himself combined support for further indecency legislation (backing Martin's proposal to extend regulations to cable and satellite) with a celebration of consumer sovereignty as an effective form of self-regulation. Demonstrating a neo-conservative concern with family values as well as a neo-liberal emphasis on market discipline, he told newspaper editors:

> Look, we're a free society. The marketplace makes decisions. If you don't like something, don't watch it. And, presumably, advertising dollars will wither and the show will go off the air, but I have no problems with [statutory] standards being set to help parents make good decisions. (Quoted in Eggerton 2005b)

In June 2006, complaining that broadcasters had 'too often pushed the bounds of decency' and that people 'expected the government to do something about it' (quoted in Baker 2006), Bush signed into law the revived Broadcast Decency Enforcement Act, massively increasing indecency fines. The *Washington Post* noted that, with mid-term elections around the corner, the White House 'decided to showcase the signing of the . . . Act at a time when Bush and Republican congressional allies are trying to reassure disaffected conservative supporters that they remain committed to conservative causes' (Baker 2006).

Not everyone agrees that indecency is a battleground that ought to be dominated by conservatives. Indeed, Democratic commissioner and anti-consolidation campaigner Michael Copps has been one of the most zealous activists in pressing for higher fines and attempting to strengthen indecency regulations. For example, it was Copps 'who in 2003, writing to the PTC, gave the FCC an "F" for indecency enforcement. And it was Copps who told the *Washington Times* last year that steamy daytime soap operas could become a potential target in an FCC indecency crackdown' (Boehlert 2005a). Perhaps not surprisingly, the Parents Television Council has congratulated both Martin and Copps for their committed stand on indecency: 'Both of them have been beacons of light [on] this issue' (quoted in Boehlert 2005a).

Indecency, however, is a very problematic basis on which to conduct an argument for progressive media reform. This is partly because it is an area traditionally monopolized by conservative voices with a moral agenda concerning the promulgation of family values and the representation of 'traditional' (i.e. heterosexual and pro-marriage) norms. In this situation, the definition of terms like obscenity and indecency – already notoriously imprecise – lies in the hands of those more interested in issues of nudity and language rather than, for example, the 'obscenity' of poverty, inequality and war. But it can also be explained by the fact that well-intentioned attempts to tie indecency to growing conglomeration have failed because, as we have already seen, cultural conservatives are easily able to combine their horror of promiscuous corporate content with firm support for corporate concentration.

Far from the White House and FCC campaigns against indecency and obscenity actually challenging the corporate 'race to the bottom', they have simply confused broadcasters about what is and is not permissible. In the FCC's 'omnibus order' of March 2006 (FCC 2006b) that examined dozens of alleged infringements between 2002 and 2005, commissioners agreed, amongst other findings, that pixellating nudity and bleeping out swear words did not constitute an adequate defence against indecency; that Nicole Richie's single reference to 'bullshit' in the 2003 Billboard Awards was indeed indecent; and that, despite their own emphasis on the importance of context, references to 'fuck' and 'shit' by real-life blues musicians in a Martin Scorsese documentary on the history of the blues were also indecent. They condemned the use by detectives in *NYPD Blue* of the word 'bullshit' as a 'vulgar reference to the product of excretory activity', concluding that it was therefore 'patently offensive' (2006b: 38) (as if New York City policemen should be role models for linguistic civility), while also arguing (2006b: 37) that the terms 'dick' and dickhead', used in the same programme, 'are not sufficiently vulgar, explicit, or graphic descriptions of sexual organs or activities to support a finding of patent offensiveness' (see Rintouls 2006 for an excellent analysis of the inconsistency of the FCC's indecency decisions).

The chilling of speech

Yet the most severe consequence of this indecency campaign is not the baffling application of the rules, nor the inconvenience to broadcasters, but its contribution to a 'chilling' of free speech that is just as likely to suppress imaginative and creative material as it is to remove crude and genuinely offensive material from the airwaves. Fearful of reprisals and fines from the FCC, broadcasters have repeatedly edited or refused to show, in particular, war-related programmes. For example, mindful of the FCC's Golden Globes ruling in March 2004 (that ruled the 'F-Word' as indecent), sixty-six ABC affiliates declined to broadcast *Saving Private Ryan* in November 2004 because of its depiction of violence and use of swearing. In February 2005, PBS decided to distribute both a 'clean' and a 'raw' version of a *Frontline* documentary on the Iraq War. 'Stations that want the unedited version . . . will be required to pre-record it and to sign a waiver indemnifying PBS against damages of fines they might incur because of the broadcast' (McLeary 2005). In October 2006, PBS executives decided that a scene in a *Frontline* documentary, *Return of the Taliban*, where Canadian soldiers use the word 'fuck', was not worth the risk of keeping in. 'It's a really sorry state of affairs if we're Disney-fying combat,' commented its producer, while *Frontline's* executive editor added that 'what I fear, really, is that we're on the verge of making some of our best material less forceful, less powerful' (quoted in Dana 2006). Such caution is particularly damaging in the context of the need to encourage critical reflection on the legitimacy (or even decency) of war given American involvement in conflicts in both Iraq and Afghanistan. As Frank Rich warned in the *New York Times*, the whole episode concerns

> the presentation of war at a time when we are fighting one. That some of the companies whose stations refused to broadcast *Saving Private Ryan* also own major American newspapers in cities as various as Providence and Atlanta leaves you wondering what other kind of self-censorship will be practiced next. If these media outlets are afraid to show a graphic Holly-wood treatment of a 60-year-old war starring the beloved Tom Hanks because the feds might fine them, toy with their licences or deny them permission to expand their empires, might they defensively soften their news divisions' efforts to present the graphic truth of an ongoing war? (Rich 2004b)

It is hard to feel too much sympathy for the corporations in these debates. Having presided over a highly sensationalist and cost-effective diet of violence, sex, gossip and scandal – the sort of programming that McChesney (2000) refers to as the product of 'hyper-commercialism' – and having shown little regard for localism and diversity in their pressure for reduced ownership restrictions, broadcasters and producers are not in a particularly strong position to boast of a 'moral high ground'. Indeed, any regret they may express about the poor quality of their content is mostly driven by financial considerations about the consequences of being accused of indecency. According to a senior Washington, DC, lobbyist for one of the companies most heavily targeted by the FCC:

> We don't enjoy getting fined . . . It's not our goal at all. And we don't like to have a little black mark against our licences either because it's licence renewal time, the cycle has begun and we have to file licence renewals for our television and radio stations . . . We don't go out and try to do it. You put on what you think is the most appropriate content for your audience. Sometimes we slip up. I mean sometimes we have no idea what is going to happen.

An editorial in the trade magazine *Broadcasting and Cable* accused the indus-try of remaining silent in the face of tougher indecency legislation simply because they feared that by raising their voices they would invite even tougher action and larger fines. These days, it concluded, 'silence is deafening and dangerous' (*Broadcasting and Cable* 2006). More often than not, however, executives simply do not feel the need to justify the quality of their programming as long as it delivers profits for their shareholders. In a high-profile speech attacking the FCC's crackdown on indecency, Viacom chairman Sumner Redstone provided a revealing perception of his own company's programming when we he argued that 'the price of freedom of religion, or of speech, or of the press, is that we must put up with a good deal of rubbish'. He quickly added that as a 'responsible media executive, and more importantly a parent and grandparent, I have no intention of pushing rubbish, but I defend others' freedom to create what some, including me, might not like' (quoted in Eggerton 2006). The perception of media corporations as 'pushers of rubbish' with voracious appetites for expansion is likely to undermine their attempts to be seen as brave warriors for freedom of speech and democratic values.

And yet, it would be just as short-sighted to credit the FCC with honourable motives in tackling indecency or to exaggerate their mandate. While it may be true that significant numbers of people did complain about the Janet Jackson episode during the Superbowl, many other accusations of indecency have been launched by just a handful of activists. Jeff Jarvis, a blogger for *BuzzMachine*, discovered via a freedom of information request that the FCC's fine of $1.2 million against Fox for a sexually suggestive (but not explicit) edition of its reality programme *Married by America* was triggered not by the 159 complaints originally cited by the Commission, but by *three* concerned citizens (Jarvis 2004). The crucial point is that while several million complaints about the liberalization of media ownership rules were dismissed by the FCC's Media Bureau on the basis that they were biased (see chapter 4), it only took three letters to trigger decisive agency action over indecency. According to actor Richard Dreyfuss, whose PBS programme *Cop Shop* was edited to pre-empt a response by the FCC, the motivations behind the current preoccupation with obscenity are profoundly illiberal and heavily politicized:

> It is inescapably censorship under guidelines imposed after the fact by those who are in temporary political power, and so it should be treated as what it is – a real-world moral and ethical battle with grimly wrongheaded, un-American types who play pick and choose when they define our freedoms of speech and religion as it fits their particular political needs. (Quoted in Goodman 2004)

The fact that Congress has now asked the FCC to consider ways of regulating TV violence suggests that this 'moral battle' is likely to continue.

A war on journalists?

Accusations of censorship are more common when it comes to the analysis of government information policy regimes. In an age of increasingly 'mediated politics' (Bennett and Entman 2001), governments are likely to deploy a range of methods to control information flows, from gentle techniques of news management to more brutal forms of overt suppression. This is particularly applicable to governments engaged in military conflict. As noted earlier in the chapter, George W. Bush's assertion that there is a 'delicate balance' between free speech and security rights points to an ongoing struggle in the USA and the UK between the need to facilitate the free flow of information in the name of democracy and the obligation to curb speech rights in order to wage the most effective 'war on terror'. 'And I gotta tell you', argued the president in June 2005, warning journalists not to publish details of US security-related matters, 'after having gone through 9/11, my bias, my slant is toward making damn sure that we can get all the information we want to get, without tipping the enemy' (Bush 2005).

To what extent can government's relationship with broadcasters and reporters, and its determination not only to gain the best 'slant' on events but to attempt to define what events are legitimate areas of journalistic inquiry, be considered as media policy proper? Robert Entman argues that, although 'the government heavily influences or, in many cases, determines the information that most Americans receive via the news media' (2003: 462), 'government *policy and law* have relatively little direct impact on the information that appears or does not appear in the news' as opposed to government officials who have 'very much to do with media content' (2003: 463). If, however, we take an expansive view of media policy that acknowledges the importance of informal as well as formal, legal mechanisms used by public authorities to 'shape, or try to shape, the structures and practices of the media' – Garnham's definition of media policy (1998: 210) that we cited in chapter 1 – then the increasingly systematic attempts by government to influence news content can be said to fall into the domain of media policy.

One of the most obvious ways in which recent British and American governments have sought to control news agendas and win favourable coverage of their policies has been through their extensive use of political public relations and news management techniques, analysed in detail in political communications rather than media policy literature (see, for example, Jones 2000 on the UK; Fritz et al. 2004 on the USA). However, the relentless manner in which these strategies have been applied suggests that techniques of 'spin' and 'branding', no longer optional add-ons to but core components of contemporary political life, are increasingly connected to government's wider vision of the role of the media. The suggestion by New Labour special adviser Jo Moore in an email sent on 9/11 that 'this would be a good day to get out anything we want to bury' (quoted in Stanyer 2002: 383) indicates an approach to government in which media agenda-setting is a policy priority. It was an entirely logical, though utterly cynical, statement to make in a government that has enormously expanded its communications operations in order to deal more effectively with the media.

The Bush administration is guilty of equally crude attempts to manipulate the news agenda, for example, by issuing a directive on the eve of the Iraq war banning the taking of pictures of coffins returning from the war (Milbank 2003: 23), or by its distribution of 'video news releases' to local television stations, one of which concerned a government anti-drug initiative that contained 'a "suggested live intro" for news anchors to read, interviews with Washington officials and a closing similar to a typical broadcast news sign-off' (Cooper and Steinberg 2005). In January 2005, it emerged that members of the Bush Cabinet had hired three commentators to promote government programmes in the media without their articles revealing that they were on the government payroll (Boehlert 2005b). It was therefore no surprise when a report in *USA Today* showed that the Bush administration spent $250 million on contracts with major public relations firms between 2001 and 2004, more than double what Bill Clinton – hardly a novice in public relations himself – had spent in his second term in office (Drinkard 2005). These efforts at news management were not confined to the domestic front. When Defense Secretary Donald Rumsfeld boasted that the US military 'has sought non-traditional means to provide accurate information to the Iraqi people in the face of an aggressive campaign of disinformation' (Rumsfeld 2006), what he meant was that his department had 'paid Iraqi newspapers to carry positive news about U.S. efforts in Iraq' without identifying itself as the source of the stories (White and Graham 2005). These initiatives exemplify what Andrew Calabrese (2005: 163) has described as a government propaganda campaign 'to rebuild confidence in "Brand America"'.

The impact of the 'war on terror'

The British and American governments have influenced news coverage in another – and more formal – way. For both George W. Bush and Tony Blair, the events of 9/11 and the subsequent unleashing of the 'war on terror' justified the passage of legislation that they argued was necessary to protect their national security interests. The USA Patriot Act (passed in October 2001) and the UK Terrorism Acts of 2001 and 2006 contain measures that hand more power to the authorities and that restrict civil liberties (in terms of facilitating extra surveillance measures together with the rights to intercept private communication and to detain terrorist suspects for longer periods of time). They also have a direct impact on the work of journalists.

Section 215 of the Patriot Act, for example, allows the FBI to seek a secret court order 'requiring the production of "any tangible thing" . . . from anyone for investigations involving foreign intelligence or international terrorism. The person or business receiving the order cannot tell anyone that the FBI sought or obtained the "tangible things"' (RCFP 2005: 46). The Reporters Committee for Freedom of the Press warns that journalists should be 'concerned' about certain provisions of the Act that abolish the need for proof of 'probable cause' and so make 'statutory protections for newsrooms almost irrelevant when it comes to terrorism investigations' (2005: 45). Section 2 of the British 2006 Terrorism Act criminalizes the 'glorification' and 'justification' of terrorism in such a way that legitimate journalistic attempts to uncover the motivations behind terrorist attacks can now be seen as 'encouraging terrorism' and are therefore highly risky. Reflecting on another clause in the legislation that forbids anyone (including journalists) from knowingly visiting a terrorist training camp, John Simpson, the BBC's world affairs editor, argues that it will be 'much harder to defend society better against terrorism if we prevent journalists from finding out the precise nature of the threat against us' (Simpson 2006). While there is little evidence thus far about the extent to which newsrooms have been searched and investigative journalists jailed for 'glorifying' terrorism, there is no doubt that such measures contribute to what a senior lobbyist for the Newspaper Association of America refers to as 'a chilling effect on reporters doing their job'.

Of course, it is not only the imposition of new pieces of legislation but a restrictive interpretation of existing laws that is placing additional burdens on the news media. As we have already noted, there is no shortage of instruments available in the UK to suppress the disclosure of information related to national security. What was notable about New Labour in its earliest incarnation (before it took office), was its promise to end the British 'culture of secrecy' through reform of the Official Secrets Act (OSA), the introduction of freedom of information legislation and a human rights act. However, by 2000, Freedom of Expression campaigners' Article 19 had already noted that despite 'the unacceptability of attempting to chill free expression by criminalizing journalists carrying out their job of investigating alleged government wrongdoings, the Labour government currently in power has displayed an increased willingness to deploy [the] OSA' (Article 19 2000). The pursuit of the 'war on terror' has only accelerated this trend. Far from proposing to abolish or reduce the scope of the OSA, the Labour government is planning to strengthen it. In February 2004, charges brought under the OSA against Katherine Gunn, a translator at the Government Communications Headquarters who leaked classified information showing that the USA had planned to bug the phones and emails of UN security council members in the lead-up to the Iraq war, were dropped. Number Ten's official response was that 'given the disappointing outcome of the case, it was only common sense to review the working of the OSA' (PMOS 2004). True to their word, ministers announced plans to 'increase the severity of gagging orders already in existence' under the OSA and to scrap the 'duress of circumstance' defence that was successfully used by Ms. Gun (Rayment 2006).

The same clampdown on secrecy is evident in the government's recent plans to reform the Freedom of Information Act that it had, to its credit, introduced in 2005. Although this had been littered with exemptions since its introduction (most controversially of all in relation to the formulation of government policy), the legislation signalled a minimal commitment to openness and transparency. However, as soon as it became clear that the Act was popular with journalists trying to uncover uncomfortable facts about the government, proposals were drafted that would lead to many fewer requests being granted (DCA 2006). Tony Blair himself argued that there was a clear financial consideration to open government: 'what's important to realize is this generates an awful lot of work for government and it's important there is some sort of cost benefit relationship to it' (quoted in Newspaper Society 2006). The Campaign for Freedom of Information (CFOI) responded by pointing out that the proposed savings of £11.8 million were insignificant in comparison to another official report that showed the government could save some £660 million 'by getting a better deal on its office supplies' (CFOI 2006).

A similar squeeze on freedom of information has occurred in the USA in recent years. One month after 9/11, Attorney General John Ashcroft issued a directive to agency heads encouraging them to 'deny access more often to public records if a claim of invasion of privacy or a claim of breach of national security can be alleged' (RCFP 2005: 1). Figures released in 2004 showed that decisions to classify information concerning national security increased 50 per cent between 2001 and 2003, in contrast to the average for the five years from 1996, and that the total number of classifications increased by 25 per cent in 2003 alone (Committee on Government Reform Minority Office 2004). In February 2006, the *New York Times* revealed the existence of a secret plan to *re-classify* thousands of intelligence-related documents, a process that speeded up after 9/11. According to intelligence historians quoted in the article, 'it is part of a marked trend towards greater secrecy under the Bush administration, which has increased the pace of classifying documents, slowed declassification and discouraged the release of some material of the Freedom of Information Act' (Shane 2006).

The 'decertification' of the media

There is a further way in which the Bush and Blair governments have sought to intervene in news content: through regular confrontations with journalists and organizations with whom they disagree. The last few years have seen, at times, the virtual breakdown of relations between the British government and the BBC, and between the Bush administration and several of the country's leading newspapers, including the *New York Times* and the *Washington Post*. A liberal pluralist perspective on government-media relations argues that this should be an inherently antagonistic relationship and that the job of the news media is to hold the executive to account, even in times of war when government is at its most sensitive to criticism. A media system that is popular with government is one that is not doing its job; neither is a government that does not attempt to win the most positive coverage of its activities. Not surprisingly, 'bad blood' between senior politicians and the news media is nothing new. Consider, for example, the very hostile atmosphere that existed between the BBC and Labour Prime Minister Harold Wilson for most of the 1960s and 1970s and which, according to Freedman (2003a: 48), partially influenced his approach to wider questions of BBC funding and expansion. Yet the venom reserved by the Bush and Blair administrations for parts of the news media suggests new levels of mutual antipathy that may have significant repercussions on the media's ability to report on politics in the public interest.

New Labour has long had a tempestuous relationship with the BBC. The communications strategy of Tony Blair's former press secretary and communications director, Alastair Campbell, involved attempts to 'spin' positive coverage and then to complain fiercely when this did not achieve the desired results. When the BBC failed to reproduce faithfully the government's narrative of the 'war on terror', Campbell grew increasingly irritated and 'singled out' the BBC for its reporting of the war (Stanyer 2002: 382). According to the then director general of the BBC, Greg Dyke (2005a: 253): 'For Alastair Campbell and his team in the Downing Street press office our refusal to report what they wanted us to do, in the way they wanted us to, made us a target even before the war itself began.' Indeed, despite being preoccupied with details concerning the imminent invasion of Iraq, Prime Minister Blair found time to write to Dyke complaining that BBC coverage contained too much editorializing and too little support for British and American plans to invade Iraq and remove Saddam Hussein.

> I believe, and I am not alone in believing, that you have not got the balance right between support and dissent; between news and comment; between the voices of the Iraqi regime and the voices of Iraqi dissidents; or between the diplomatic support we have, and diplomatic opposition. (Quoted in Dyke 2005a: 254)

Even though senior BBC editorial staff were prevented from attending the enormous anti-war demonstration in London on 15 February 2003 (the largest ever in Britain's history) and even though a Cardiff University study (Lewis 2003) found that BBC coverage of the war was amongst the most sympathetic to the government, 'the complaints from Campbell never stopped' (Dyke 2005a: 257).

The situation deteriorated after one of its journalists, Andrew Gilligan, accused the government of 'sexing up' stories about the risks posed by Saddam Hussein to British interests. When the BBC refused to apologize and withdraw the allegations, it was told that 'the BBC would now have the full force of the Government's PR machine thrown at it' (2005: 278). In July 2003, the source of the original story, the government scientist Dr David Kelly, was 'outed' by the government and subsequently committed suicide, triggering an inquiry into the affair led by Lord Hutton. Published in January 2004, the Hutton Report totally exonerated the government and accused the BBC of serious flaws in its editorial practices. Although the report's findings were widely condemned (a *Guardian* poll [Watt 2004] found that three times as many people trusted the BBC to tell the truth in comparison to the government), within twenty-four hours the chairman and the director-general of the BBC had resigned – both departures seen by many as the victims of a Downing Street vendetta against the corporation likely to have serious consequences for the future independence of BBC newsgathering. According to Georgina Born, there is clear evidence, post-Hutton, of 'timidity', 'editorial caution' and a 'BBC more prone to censorship' (Born 2004: 464–5) as the corporation seeks to come to terms with the implications of the Hutton Report.

New Labour's 'war against the BBC' (Ashley 2003: 13) has coincided with an equally hostile campaign by the Bush administration against sections of the media, most notably the print press who have, at times, been willing to criticize Bush's policies, especially on Iraq. This has involved, for example, the criminal prosecution of several journalists, among them Judith Miller of the *New York Times*, for failing to reveal confidential sources, the favouring of local television journalists who are more likely to reproduce administration statements than their national press counterparts, and the Attorney General John Ashcroft's freezing out of the press from his Patriot Act tour following 9/11 (Alterman 2005). These moves add up to what journalism commentator Jay Rosen has called the 'de-certification' of the press (Rosen 2004).

Far from promoting the First Amendment rights of reporters, senior administration officials have instead been threatening journalists for publishing 'unpatriotic' information. Bush himself warned in January 2006 that '[w]e must remember there is a difference between responsible and irresponsible debate – and it's even more important to conduct this debate responsibly when American troops are risking their lives overseas' (quoted in Parry 2006). When journalists from the *New York Times* and *Washington Post* won Pulitzer Prizes in 2006 for hard-hitting investigative pieces on the CIA's 'secret prisons' in Europe and the National Security Agency's domestic surveillance programme, former White House official William Bennett argued on national radio that they belonged in jail and not at an awards ceremony (Carr 2006). Attorney General Alberto Gonzales added that he was considering the possibility of prosecuting journalists for publishing classified information, whatever the motivations. 'We have an obligation to enforce the law and to prosecute those who engage in criminal activity' (quoted in Liptak 2006). Not to be outdone, the House Permanent Select Committee on Intelligence convened a hearing in May 2006 to explore whether a new law was needed to tackle the problem of leaking, where its chairman Pete Hoekstra condemned the 'detrimental effect that their [the media's] actions can and do have on national security' (Hoekstra 2006: 4).

Both governments justify their attacks by denouncing journalists' cynicism, accusing them of promoting the idea that 'all politicians are liars', and arguing they have had a corrosive effect on contemporary politics. While elected politicians are ultimately subject to the discipline of voters, journalists face no such accountability. Pre-empting some of the criticisms made by John Lloyd in his critique of a powerful, irresponsible and partisan media (Lloyd 2004), then Labour Party chairman Charles Clarke argued back in 2002 that the BBC's flagship *Today* programme (that had done so much to antagonize the government) was dominated by 'matters of minor significance rather than tackling the real issues of concern [and] obsessed with process, personalities and gossip and spin' (quoted in Stanyer 2003: 312). Bush administration officials have repeated this picture in relation to some of the most influential national newspapers: that they are out of touch with the concerns of ordinary people and locked into a fascination with the personalities that inhabit life 'inside the beltway'. As one Bush insider explained to the 'elite' press: 'Let me clue you in. We don't care. You see, you're outnumbered two to one by folks in the big, wide middle of America, busy working people who don't read the *New York Times* or *Washington Post* or the *LA Times*' (quoted in Alterman 2005). Calls by senior politicians for a more substantive approach to politics and a focus on the key issues that affect the majority of citizens would be easier to believe if either administration had taken steps to open up information channels and to avoid spin, measures which palpably neither government has taken.

Although antipathy between government and media is hardly a recent phenomenon, there appears to be something distinctive about the recent attacks on the news media. While previous conflicts have often focused on a single reporter, broadcaster or newspaper, these attacks are aimed at the institution of investigative and independent journalism itself. If journalists cannot be relied upon to act 'responsibly', in other words to adopt a more acquiescent attitude towards government, then the traditional liberal view of journalism as a 'fourth estate' can no longer be taken for granted. According to White House chief of staff Andrew Card, the media 'don't represent the public any more than other people do. In our democracy, the people who represent the public stood for election . . . I don't believe you have a check-and-balance function' (quoted in Auletta 2004). A resolution passed in 2006 by a leading US association for media and journalism academics argues that the Bush administration 'has engaged in a number of practices and has enacted a series of severe and extraordinary policies that attack the press specifically and by extension, democracy itself' (AEJMC

2006). According to Jay Rosen (2005), the Bush administration has introduced a new 'post press' policy where the press are now seen to represent only themselves:

> There's a difference between going around the press in an effort to avoid troublesome questions, and trying to unseat the idea that these people, professional journalists assigned to cover politics, have a legitimate role to play in our politics. [In excluding the press from his Patriot Act tour, attorney general John] Ashcroft was out to unseat that idea about the traditional press. He wanted it out of the picture of how you battle for the public opinion. (Rosen 2005)

These measures – of news management, moves towards secrecy and attacks on journalism – have little in common with the rhetoric of a pluralist commitment to robust debate based on First Amendment or Millian principles. Instead, they illustrate a revealing contradiction between the British and American governments' stated commitment to free and open competition in the market and their determination to stifle opposition and to intervene in the 'marketplace of ideas'. However, to what extent can these activities be related to media policy in the ways in which it is commonly defined? We have argued that the increasingly systematic use by those at the heart of government of a range of techniques that are designed to influence media content constitutes a highly significant example of 'informal' media policy, in the sense that they provide a means by which those in power attempt to impose their perspectives and discipline on media systems. Furthermore, while it is hard to say definitively that these forms of 'content intervention' have any kind of predictable impact on the development of systems of media regulation, it would be equally difficult to argue that media policy questions can be insulated from the context of government–media relations. For example, while the British government has firmly denied any link between the issues raised in the Hutton Report and its attitude towards Charter renewal, it is not entirely fanciful to suggest that 'the enduring sense of resentment against the BBC, and specifically the *Today* programme, which still simmers just below the surface within some parts of the Labour Government' (Barnett 2006a: 61), was completely irrelevant in relation to decisions about the future of the licence fee. Similarly, it would be hard to disprove Greg Dyke's assertion that one of the reasons why US broadcasters were largely 'cheerleaders' for American involvement in the Iraq war was because, in the face of the administration's onslaught against its critics, they were reluctant to 'upset the Bush administration' at a time when they were pursuing changes to the ownership rules (Dyke 2005a: 322). Either way, these examples illustrate, once again, the political nature of the context in which actors confront each other in the development of media policy.

Conclusion

Despite the existence of First Amendment and Millian arguments for freedom of expression and non-intervention in the editorial process, media content is subject to multiple forms of policy action. This is far from surprising given the attention paid to content by politicians and the public in contrast to other, often more technical, media policy issues. Dozens of generalist laws and formal systems of statutory regulation surround the production of media material but the impact of the internet, combined with the dominance of neo-liberal visions of market discipline, has led to a situation in which sections of the media industry are increasingly questioning the need for content policies in the first place. However, the attempts by US policymakers, influenced by conservative ideas, to tackle obscenity and indecency as well as the measures taken by the Bush and Blair administrations to control information flows as part of their involvement in the 'war on terror' demonstrate the highly politicized nature of media policy formation. This applies both to the development of formal instruments of media content regulation and to the use of more informal procedures to shape media content. Pro-market governments seem to be quite prepared to advocate economic liberalism, to resort to forms of authoritarian populism and, at the same time, to use their power to lean on broadcasters and journalists – behaviour that points to a more fundamental contradiction about the interventionist role of the neo-liberal state. Furthermore, the conflicts that do take place between government and media organizations reveal not a pluralist paradise of fair but competitive jockeying for position, but a private battle between rival centres of political and corporate power to dominate our contemporary media landscape.

7

The Disciplining of Public Broadcasting

In media systems dominated by for-profit organizations whose main concern is to maximize readerships, ratings and revenues, public and non-commercial media have an especially important role to play. They are seen as essential to the creation of pluralist media environments in which multiple forms of finance, ownership and content are more likely to facilitate diversity and stimulate meaningful competition. Public broadcasting, in particular, is a crucial example of the 'corrective surgery' that, it was argued in chapter 1, is necessary to compensate for the tendency of markets to under-serve minority audiences and to produce powerful private monopolies or oligopolies in the media value chain. Yet public broadcasting is not merely the medicine that it is sometimes necessary to take to counter the ills of commercial television and radio. It refers, in many ways, to a different kind of cultural institution with its own vision of broadcasting based on contrasting values and commitments. While there are many versions of what is ultimately a philosophy rather than a particular channel or set of programmes (see Blumler 1991), there are nevertheless some core normative principles common to different conceptions of the public broadcasting 'idea'.

First, public broadcasting is based on the rejection of 'the market definition of broadcasting as the delivery of a set of distinct commodities to consumers rather than as the establishment of a communicative relationship' (Garnham 1994: 18). Public broadcasting's main goal is not to sell audiences to advertisers or subscription broadcasters but to engage viewers and listeners in a dialogue about public life. Broadcasting, according to this view, should facilitate public conversation and not private transactions. Second, this involves the characterization of its audiences as rational citizens with a broad range of interests and needs that must be met irrespective of their purchasing power, geographical location or social position. Third, public broadcasting attempts to foster, independently of government and vested interests, what Scannell and Cardiff (1990: 277) describe as a 'shared public life', the 'we-feeling' of membership of national or regional communities that may be counterposed to the 'I-feeling' engendered through the free market's emphasis on individual consumer preferences. Fourth, public broadcasting is marked by its 'structure of ambition' (Tracey 1998: 18), a progressive instinct whereby broadcast services with a commitment to quality and creativity can contribute to a process of social amelioration and illumination as well as enjoyment. Finally, through achieving all of the above, public broadcasting is seen as a profoundly democratic phenomenon and as a key means through which public opinion is realized and cemented. Acknowledging Habermas's emphasis on the idea of a public sphere and communicative rationality, Scannell (1989: 136) describes public broadcasting 'as a public good that has unobtrusively contributed to the democratization of everyday life'.

There have been, of course, many valuable critiques of the actual performance of specific public broadcasters, frequently from those on the left who are profoundly uncomfortable with the paternalism and conservative ideological frameworks of public broadcasters (see, for example, Chakravartty and Sarikakis 2006: 88; Curtis 1984; Glasgow University Media Group 1976; McChesney 2004: 245–6). Today, however, the most influential attacks emanate not from the left but from pro-market advocates (e.g. B. Cox 2004; Elstein 2004) who see the existing arrangements for public broadcasting as both undesirable and unsustainable given contemporary technological, social and political developments. In a digital era in which increasing numbers of savvy consumers are able to choose from hundreds of channels that reflect a wide array of consumer interests and backgrounds, critics are quick to argue that there are now few remaining justifications for public funding, mixed programming and statutory content obligations.

This chapter examines whether these attacks on the rationale for public broadcasting have been echoed by the British and American governments in recent years and focuses, in particular, on policies concerning the BBC in the UK and, to a lesser extent, those concerning Public Broadcasting Service (PBS) television and National Public Radio (NPR) in the USA. While the relationships between government and public broadcaster in these two cases are obviously political – how could it be otherwise given the fact that public broadcasting is the result of purposeful and systematic interventions into wider media markets? – it is nevertheless worth considering how the different political complexions of the two governments map on to their policies for public broadcasting. Of course, there are also crucial differences between the broadcasters themselves: the BBC plays a hugely influential role in British public life and is the most dominant broadcaster in the country in comparison to the rather marginal role played by PBS and NPR in the USA. The point, however, is that how public broadcasting is organized reveals much about the *broader* priorities and interests of a particular society. As Tracey puts it:

> the definition of policies for national [public] broadcasting systems is neces-
> sarily suggestive of a definition of policies for the character of a whole
> society. They capture the sets of choices and preferences which colour all
> the imperatives, ambitions and institutions which constitute in the most
> literal sense a social order. (1998: 39–40)

In examining the Labour government's approach to BBC charter renewal, and the Bush administration's funding and governance plans for public broadcasting, this chapter should further illuminate the imperatives and ambitions that dominate elite political life in the contemporary UK and USA.

A public service for all: New Labour and the BBC

If New Labour's neo-liberal instincts are exemplified by the deregulatory ownership measures contained in the 2003 Communications Act and by its creation of a new regulator, Ofcom, whose responsibility is above all to facilitate a thriving communications *market*, its approach to the BBC can be seen to suggest a different set of political priorities. The government sanctioned a relatively generous, above-inflation pay rise for the corpora-tion during the period 2000/1–2006/7 and has continued to back the idea of a licence fee. Hesmondhalgh, however, argues (2005: 103) that the 'truth is more complicated' in that for every act of kindness, there follows a more punitive measure from the government: licence fee rises are followed by demands for increased financial stringency; support for the independence of the BBC is complemented by systematic complaints about anti-government coverage; justification of the need for non-commercial output is superseded by an insistence that it steps up its commercial enterprises. For Hesmondhalgh, this is another sign of New Labour's 'hybridity' (2005: 106); for others, it is evidence of a more 'fundamental contradiction between Labour's predilection for market solutions and its professed aim of upholding PSB [public service broadcasting] as a vibrant sector' (Hardy 2004: 101).

Let us consider these contrasting perspectives in the light of the government's proposals for the future of the BBC as contained in its White Paper, *A Public Service for All: The BBC in the Digital Age* (DCMS 2006). The White Paper was required by the impending need to renew the BBC's

Royal Charter and was shaped by a number of contextual factors and arguments:

1. *Technological:* The declining audiences for terrestrial television, the popularity of pay television, the government's commitment to analogue switch-off, and the more general changes in media consumption with the rise of web-based, mobile and other digital platforms have transformed the wider media environment. Claims concerning the end of spectrum scarcity and an increase in diversity in a multi-channel system have led the government to reconsider the need for an institution designed to compensate for the shortcomings of commercial broadcasting and for a monopoly licence fee in a situation in which BBC's audience share is likely to fragment.

2. *Economic:* The declining value of the existing analogue spectrum, together with the migration of audiences to online media and the resulting loss in advertising revenue, has undermined what Ofcom (2004: 6) calls 'the historical compact' underlying public service broadcasting in the UK: the willingness of commercial broadcasters to provide public service programming in return for valuable broadcast licences. If commercial broadcasters are relieved of their public service responsibilities, this will lead to a situation in which the BBC will be the only provider of PSB, undermining the pluralism and vitality of the PSB environment and reducing the incentive for the BBC to be creative and forward-thinking as it will 'no longer face competition for quality' (2004: 6).

3. *Political:* Charter Review was 'overshadowed' (Collins 2006: 15) by the bruising encounter between the government and the BBC over the corporation's coverage of the Iraq war that led to the eventual removal of director general Greg Dyke in January 2004 (discussed in chapter 6). Decisions about the BBC's future were made in the context of 'serious challenges to the BBC's legitimacy' (2006: 15) that followed from the publication of the Hutton Report.

4. *Commercial:* There has been a sustained campaign of lobbying by the BBC's commercial competitors who are determined to limit the corporation's scope of action. Organizations like the British Internet Publishers' Alliance, who have protested vociferously against the BBC's new media activities (see BIPA [2003]), and News International who, through both its newspapers and its lobbyists, has repeatedly railed against licence fee increases on the basis that they give the BBC 'an unfair advantage in developing new markets' (Hinsliff, 2006), have directed enormous resources in

the last few years towards interventions in the policymaking process. Alarmed by the BBC's energetic entry into new media markets, its commercial competitors increasingly argue that it must confine its activities to areas of market failure, in other words to programmes and services that the for-profit sector has little interest in providing.

Senior commercial broadcasters regularly accuse the BBC of a range of sins: the deputy chairman of Channel Four calls it a 'cultural tyranny' (B. Cox 2004: 64); a very influential lobbyist at Number Ten describes it as 'a phenomenally effective political organization' that deploys 'the most effective public relations machine that I have ever seen. For a completely biased news service, it has managed to persuade people that it is objective'; former Channel Five chief executive David Elstein argues that 'its original rationale and its funding mechanism are relics from a bygone age. So the BBC casts around for a new rationale, and clings to its funding mechanism like a drowning man to a leaking life-vest' (2004: 14). According to Richard Eyre, former head of ITV, the whole model of public service broadcasting is obsolete: 'it will soon be dead because it relies on an active broadcaster and a passive viewer . . . Public Service Broadcasting will soon be dead for lack of definition (Eyre 1999). The former chief executive of Channel Four, Michael Jackson, concurs that the PSB idea is no longer relevant: 'Public service broadcasting is a battle-standard we no longer need to rally to . . . It's become the pointless ju-ju stick of British broadcasting . . . Let's be candid, the term public service broadcasting is now drained of all purpose and meaning' (quoted in Clarke 2001).

5. Regulatory: Ofcom has played a key role in setting out an agenda for both public service broadcasting in general and the BBC in particular in the multi-channel age. Although the regulation and performance of the BBC is largely outside of its remit, Ofcom launched in 2004 a detailed, three-part review that evaluated the funding and future of PSB and the BBC. Its Phase 2 report (Ofcom 2004) insists that the BBC 'should remain the cornerstone of public service TV broadcasting' (2004: 8), but also proposes that:

- The money available to PSB should not be increased (2004: 6), effectively leading to cuts in revenue.
- Any plans for new services 'should be subject to a rigorous independent evaluation to ensure that they add public value and would not unduly displace commercial activities' (2004: 9).
- The licence fee should be maintained but 'limited subscription services' introduced to find future activities (2004: 9).

- The corporation should 'take a leading role in the UK plans for digital switchover' (2004: 9).
- More use should be made of independent producers in the provision of PSB programmes (2004: 13).
- A new 'public service publisher' (PSP) should be considered to facilitate plurality of PSB delivery with a fund open to competitive tender by all broadcasters (2004: 13–15). Ofcom has since reiterated its desire to see the principle of 'contestability' introduced in relation to PSB funding so that rival suppliers can be financed out of existing PSB revenues to secure 'effective competition for quality' (Ofcom 2007: 5). The implications of this 'top-slicing' of licence fee funds is, of course, potentially very serious for the BBC as it seeks to meet the challenge of digital switchover and a new broadcast climate.

Many of these points were echoed in the report (Burns 2004) published by the independent panel chaired by Lord Burns, chairman of the Abbey National Bank, that was set up by the DCMS to advise on Charter review. Burns' report dovetails with Ofcom's proposals concerning the advantages of contestability, accepts industry arguments about the need to scale down public service obligations for commercial broadcasters and for the BBC not to compete in popular genres (like 'makeover' programmes and some game shows), and acknowledges (but does not challenge) the resentment aimed at the BBC from its commercial rivals. Above all, the report agrees 'with Ofcom that the lesson of history is that plurality and competition are an important aspect of PSB provision if we are to see continuing innovation, fresh ideas and value for money' (2004: 10), a claim dismissed by one media commentator – on the evidence of many high-quality BBC programmes that emerged and flourished without the incentive of competition – as 'an erroneous theory that is spreading like bindweed' (Bell 2005a: 5).

These various arguments, including what Karel Williams et al. (2006: 5) describe as the 'collective "monstering" of the BBC', set the tone for the legislative process which saw, first, the emergence of a Green Paper in 2005 and then the eventual publication of the White Paper in March 2006 (DCMS 2006). The Secretary of State for Culture, Media and Sport, Tessa Jowell, introduced the document to parliament with a ringing endorsement of the value of the BBC as a 'driving force to enrich our public realm. It is the embodiment of the public realm as one of those places that brings people together as equals' (HoC Debates 14 March 2006: col. 1311). Jowell confirmed the BBC as the 'cornerstone' (col. 1312) of PSB and guaranteed the future of the licence fee until at least 2016. The White Paper maps out an expansive definition of the 'purposes' and 'characteristics' of the BBC – including its role in '[s]ustaining citizenship and civil society' and '[p]romoting education and learning' (DCMS 2006: 3) – and assigns it the critical role of acting as a 'trusted guide' during the process of 'building Digital Britain' (2006: 4). Labour's support for both the mission and the continued funding of the BBC could not have been made clearer. Yet, within the seventy-six pages of the White Paper, are a series of claims, demands and prescriptions that seek to change the balance of forces within British broadcasting in such a way as to undermine the BBC's position as a confident, independent and non-commercial public broadcaster.

First, there is the almost parodic use of the 'new planetary vulgate' identified by Bourdieu and Wacquant (2001) as a hallmark of neo-liberalism. The report is littered with references to flexibility, dynamism, innovation, novelty, creativity, diversity, transparency, efficiency and competition. Perhaps it is not possible to formulate media policy in the twenty-first century without using these phrases but the regularity of their use leads to the impression that, without the proposed reforms, the BBC (like all public institutions) is likely to collapse into the opposite of these highly desirable states: stagnation, rigidity, bureaucracy, uniformity and so on.

More significant is the premise on which the White Paper is based: that the future of the BBC is tied fundamentally to the prospects of its com-mercial rivals. True, there are two other overarching objectives of Charter renewal – to ensure that the BBC keeps up with technological change and 'to reconnect the BBC with the citizens it serves' (DCMS 2006: 2) – but both of these missions are subject to the more profound need to develop 'a new relationship with the rest of the broadcasting landscape' (Jowell 2006: 8). In a speech to industry executives, shortly after the publication of the White Paper, Jowell made it quite clear that the government's desire to see the BBC as a continuing cultural and technological force depends on the vitality of the larger UK media sector. She argued that:

> A complex and competitive market exists in today's world and we are clear that that market, in order to maximize choice for licence fee payers, must also continue to prosper. To achieve the right balance, there's a need to provide certainty and assurance to the [commercial] industry. (2006:9)

All the specific changes and reforms outlined in the White Paper are subject, therefore, to this reconceptualization of the BBC's role: that it can no longer operate as a cultural institution in its own right and with its own logic and values, but that both its existence and its daily operations are to be judged *primarily* in relation to the impact it has on the wider media market.

The crucial point here is that that impact is assumed by the government to be *negative*. First, there is no empirical data to prove that the BBC has damaged investment and profitability in the British media market. Even Ofcom has admitted that 'we do not have sufficient evidence to prove or disprove the existence of overall crowding-out efficiency losses from the public funding of the BBC in aggregate' (Ofcom 2004: 45). Second, and more importantly, even if there was some evidence of 'crowding out', why should the commercial sector be protected from this given that, for example, the government has failed to protect the BBC (and licence fee payers) when it is regularly 'crowded out' of Premier League soccer rights by a Sky broadcaster equipped to pay vastly over the odds in order to secure and maintain its subscription base? Tessa Jowell, in her foreword to the White Paper, actually recognizes that commercial and public service broadcasters do not naturally share the same orientations and that PSB is, at its core, an intervention *into* market practices: 'The notion of broadcasting as a public service and not just an industry like any other was born in Britain, as was the notion of health provision for all' (DCMS 2006: 2). Yet how much do we hear of the government complaining about the National Health Service 'crowding out' private health providers and threatening to cancel operations if they are seen to have a negative impact on the profits of private health providers? (Given the government's determination to embed market forces inside health care (Leys 2001: 165–210), perhaps this is not too far away.)

Individual details of the White Paper need, therefore, to be evaluated in the light of the government's commitment to rebalancing the relationship between the activities of the BBC and the requirements of its commercial rivals. We will consider six key recommendations that illustrate this process: the government's proposals for service licences, public value tests, tougher competition regulation, the promotion of digital, increased use of independent producers and the abolition of the board of governors and its replacement by a Trust (references are to sections of the White Paper (DCMS 2006)).

Service licences

In the light of the commercial sector's systematic lobbying to restrict the scope of the activities of public broadcasters (see ACT et al. 2004), the mere definition of public service is highly politically charged. According to Karol Jakubowicz (2004: 20), the campaign against PSB operators 'usually begins with a demand for a clear definition of PSB'. What this really means is that:

> Public Service Broadcasters should not do anything the commercial sector wants to do, it should not offer content, use technologies or draw on sources of funding which the commercial sector wants for itself. The real objective, therefore, is to produce a formulation which could be used to halt any change or evolution of public service broadcasting since any new development not expressly covered by this definition could be challenged and reversed. (2004: 20)

In 2003 and 2004, pressed by the BBC's commercial rivals, the government commissioned reviews of the corporation's online, digital television and digital radio services, all of which evaluated the impact of the BBC's entrance into new media markets in an attempt to redefine and 'reframe the public service role of the BBC in the convergence era' (Klontzas 2006: 6). This desire further to distinguish the BBC from its 'competition' is reflected in the White Paper's imposition of new 'purposes' and 'characteristics', a move rationalized in rather ominous terms:

> In a world where there is more choice than ever in TV and radio, it is vital that the BBC is able to justify the privilege of the licence fee. So it must be completely transparent about its objectives and about how it will be measured in meeting them. (DCMS 2006: 3)

Concretely, in order to give the rest of the industry 'greater clarity and certainty about the BBC's activities' (5.1.2), the White Paper requires BBC managers to draw up licences that will outline the main characteristics of every channel, station or service run by the BBC. This is likely to consist of a set of promises to users about the aims and objectives of the service, as well as information on access, target audience and delivery. The service must be justified not only in terms of how it connects to the BBC's new set of purposes, but also how it impacts on the wider market (5.2.4). The case study given in the White Paper concerns Radios 1 and 2, the subject of many recent complaints by commercial radio groups who have argued that these stations are not distinctive enough and are unfairly dominating specific market segments. Assessment of the extent to which individual services meet the terms of their licences is likely to be conducted internally but, as Tom O'Malley (2006) points out, it is impossible to rule out Ofcom taking on this role and applying its pro-market perspective to these finely balanced judgements.

There is little reason to believe that service licences will contribute to an increased sense of focus and purpose and far more reason to expect that they may yield 'clear indicators' (5.2.1) for commercial rivals to exploit in their claims of unfair competition. Indeed, the White Paper notes that '[w]e have received further helpful evidence from the commercial radio sector, which underlined the importance of getting service licences right' (5.2.1). The question is: right for whom? Prominent media commentator Steven Barnett, who is broadly sympathetic to the White Paper, warns that, in this context, service licences may undermine the government's stated aim for the BBC to be flexible in its relationship to audiences. 'The real danger,' he argues (Barnett 2006b: 25), 'is that under pressure from the commercial sector those service licences become straitjackets which actually prevent the BBC from adapting its programme strategies and its operational decisions to ensure that it does indeed remain central to British cultural life.' Service licences, therefore, may be both counterproductive for the BBC and a stick to be used by its commercial competitors who wish to prevent the corporation from moving into potentially profitable new areas of media activity.

Public value tests

All new services and any major changes to existing services will now be subject to a test that will weigh up the 'public value' of the proposed change 'against its impact on the market, including both commercial and not-for-profit concerns' (5.3.3). A crucial part of this will be the 'market impact assessments' carried out by Ofcom in the case of new services and the BBC Trust in relation to changes to existing services, although even here the methodology must be agreed in advance with Ofcom. This represents, according to the experienced broadcasting analyst Steve Hewlett, 'unprecedented external oversight of BBC activity' (Hewlett 2006).

The idea of evaluating the 'value' of a broadcasting service sounds harmless enough and, indeed, the way in which the BBC talks about it in its *Building Public Value* document (BBC 2004) in terms of the civic, educational, social and political benefits that the BBC may bring to its audiences, appears to be substantially positive. Public value, however, is not a neutral concept but an idea first developed by Harvard professor Mark Moore in his 1995 book *Creating Public Value* (Moore 1995) that 'revolutionised thinking about how public managers should go about their business and assess the efficiency of their work' (Harkin 2005). The concept was seized upon in a Cabinet Office strategy unit paper that used it as an 'analytical framework' (Kelly et al. 2002) for the government's reform of the public sector which, through its private finance schemes and performance indicators, sought to develop a new market-laden ethos for the delivery of public services. The real agenda of a 'public value' approach is made clear in the paper: 'as UK experience in prisons, employment and welfare services has shown, the combination of strong public sector institutions and competition from private and non-profit organizations achieves the best balance of accountability, innovation and efficiency' (2002: 5).

Why should this approach not be applied to broadcasting services? First, because the subjective judgements on value will be made by the instruments and personnel of Ofcom, an organization poorly equipped for such a task. Second, as James Harkin points out, because 'public value cannot be measured quantitatively without lapsing into absurdity and is, therefore, of much more limited use than the theory of value that is used to analyse the market economy' (Harkin 2005). It is, therefore, very likely that the proposed market impact assessments and public value tests will generate enormous amounts of data – the 'evidence-based' approach favoured by Ofcom – that are far better suited to an understanding of broadcasting as a straightforward economic, rather than a complex social and cultural, practice. It is the kind of data that is likely to be used in the review the government has now promised in the next five years to consider the possibility of 'contestability' ('top-slicing' of the licence fee), a key driver of public value, according to Kelly et al. (2002: 5). Public value tests that 'at first look like a small technical detail . . . might well turn out to be a key feature of the new governance regime at the BBC' (Hewlett 2006), and are a clear sign of Ofcom's influence on the future of the BBC and its inscription into a new, market rationality.

New forms of competition regulation

The government is so determined to ensure that the BBC does not unfairly distort the market for broadcasting in the UK that it insists, in the White Paper, on a new series of competition rules to add to those to which it is already subject. It is therefore requiring the corporation to develop a 'new fair trading regime' that will cover all its services, both commercial and public (6.1.10), and is imposing *ex ante* regulatory codes to supplement the existing *ex post* rules. While the new BBC Trust will enforce the rules, it will be 'required to take account of Ofcom's views in deciding which areas should be covered and in formulating the codes themselves' (6.1.13). Areas such as cross-promotion, exclusivity contracts and the use of proprietary distribution technologies will now be subject to an extra layer of competition regulation in order to 'put in place the right relationship between the BBC and rest of the market' (6.1.3).

Why is the government imposing restrictions that are beyond those faced by commercial broadcasters? The answer is surely related to the fact that 'Ofcom and the OFT [Office of Fair Trading] are concerned that their existing *ex post* competition powers are insufficient to regulate the BBC' (6.1.6) and that this concern must have been made clear to these bodies by a host of commercial rivals to the BBC. It is yet further evidence, not simply of Ofcom's ability to shape the behaviour of the BBC and of the government's willingness to accommodate commercial concerns, but of New Labour's desire to *correct* the 'distortion' caused by the fact that the BBC is the creation of deliberate public intervention in the market.

The promotion of digital

The White Paper instructs the BBC to act as a key driver of the digital revolution: making its programmes available on digital platforms, stimulating the take-up of digital technologies and leading audiences into a digital future. In particular, as we discuss in the next chapter, this means assisting the preparation of analogue switch-off, scheduled to take place between 2008 and 2012, and indeed taking 'a leading role in making digital switchover happen' (4.3.1). This will involve practical measures to extend the digital network, to publicize the mechanics of switchover itself and both to set up and pay for 'schemes to ensure that the most vulnerable households are not left behind' (4.3.7), including the provision of free set-top boxes for the elderly and selected other groups.

At one level, this is hardly a contentious proposal. The BBC has long showed willingness to push digital broadcasting – it was a key driver behind the success of DAB (digital audio broadcasting), has launched a slew of new digital television and radio channels in recent years and has helped to popularize digital television with its investment in the Freeview system. The White Paper's proposals, however, go beyond a simple acknowledgement of the BBC's role in stimulating digital take-up to include a heavily prescriptive demand that it *lead* audiences into a digital future. This, notes commentator Steve Hewlett (2007: 3), compromises perceptions of the BBC's independence: 'It is pretty clear that the corporation is now regarded in some important parts of Whitehall as just another government department, with its licence fee a ready source of cash to support a variety of policy objectives.' Klontzas (2006: 2) agrees that the BBC is increasingly a 'policy delivery mechanism' and notes the tension in policy discourse between the 'market distortion potential of the BBC [discussed earlier in this chapter], and the proactive role it is invited to play in promoting digitalization' (2006: 6). For Georgina Born, this contradiction demonstrates 'the incoherence of neo-liberal policy in this area' (2004: 498): while the government relies on the BBC to develop and popularize new services, when it does this successfully it is criticized by the commercial sector and hemmed in by the government. 'The BBC cannot win: commercialise and compete, but not too well, while the government behaves towards the corporation as a hectoring nanny' (2004: 498). What is especially revealing is that it is the BBC – and not the private sector – that is expected to shoulder the responsibility for digital switchover, despite the benefits that are likely to accrue in the future for many commercial broadcasters and content providers.

Independent production quotas

The White Paper insists that a further 25 per cent of the BBC's television output should be open to external producers, supplementing the existing 25 per cent independent production quota. In fairness, this is not the government's idea – the BBC first developed the idea of what it calls a 'window of creative competition' (WOCC) in order to discipline its own workforce and to impress the government of its commitment to stimulating the base of British television production. The government, however, is even more determined to secure a 'plurality of content providers' (8.2.4) that will introduce further competition into the sector, and sees independent producers as precisely the embodiments of creativity, innovation and flexibility that epitomize a dynamic and growing industry.

This is to idealize a sector based as much on casualization, massive insecurity and, often, low pay as it is on entrepreneurial flair and creativity. It also sustains the myth that the independent sector is a hub of small but energetic grass-roots players and not a rapidly consolidating area of the British media. Faulkner et al. (2006: 29) note that governments have encouraged independent production for the last thirty years

> on the assumption that breaking up the vertically integrated bureaucratic monoliths and encouraging independent producers will liberate creativity. Unintentionally and unexpectedly, it has created a new kind of corporate in the form of the financially motivated super indie which is beholden to the capital market and a new kind of producer/owner with opportunities to sell up and become rich through an ownership stake. The independent production company therefore does not so much liberate the creative producer as enmesh the producer/owner in new financial instrumentalities, which, on current programming evidence, generates as much chintz as it does art.

Tom O'Malley (2006) asks whether the WOCC is likely to undermine the BBC's own skills base and what impact 'this weakening of the skills base will have on creativity and innovation', characteristics highlighted by the White Paper as crucial for the future of the BBC. 'Perhaps', he reflects, 'the government should have commissioned its own impact assessment in this area before agreeing so readily to the idea of the "Window".' The fact that the government has also agreed to a 25 per cent independent production quota for BBC Online signals its desire to see the entrepreneurial mentality of the independent sector extended throughout the wider media environment.

BBC governance

The White Paper abolishes the board of governors and puts in its place a Trust, whose main responsibility is to act as the champion of licence fee payers, and an executive board, that assumes responsibility for managerial control of the Corporation. This shift is designed to avoid the conflicts present in the governors' role of simultaneously representing public and management interests. Few will disagree with the idea of a Trust that fights energetically on behalf of the public and stands up to commercial or government interference. Nor could anyone disagree with the government's insistence that both Trust and Board will have 'an unprecedented obligation to openness and transparency' (9.2.1). The problem is that there is no detailed discussion as to how either objective will be facilitated. Indeed, far from the public having a mechanism with which to influence the Trust's agenda or to access minutes of Trust meetings (something that would have been in the public interest during the tussle between Greg Dyke and the governors in 2004), the White Paper makes it clear that this proposed openness amounts to licence fee payers knowing 'which part of the organization is responsible for addressing their concerns' (9.5.1). The best the White Paper can offer licence fee payers in terms of the accountability of Trust members is that it will 'publish its arrangements for doing business' (9.3.8), a rather unfortunate turn of phrase.

More disturbing, however, is the likely composition of the Trust and its ability to confront threats to the BBC's independence. While the results of the public consultation showed that there was support for Trust members to be 'drawn from a range of backgrounds and professional experience' (9.3.3), the White Paper proposes a rather narrower definition of those who can represent the public interest: people who have experience in the broadcasting and media industries (including new media); competition; the financial, legal, corporate or regulatory aspects of running large organizations; managing a large property portfolio; expertise in the areas covered by the BBC's public purposes, including international affairs; and in delivering the accountability of such organisations to their stakeholders. (9.3.6)

In the context of the White Paper's attempt to tie public service broadcasting to the interests of the rest of the broadcasting world, there is a strong possibility that we could see a Trust populated, not with fearless fighters for licence fee payers and the public interest, but with executives from the media and other industries who see their role in representing the BBC *as part of and in relation to the wider commercial UK media environment*.

The licence fee settlement of January 2007

The proof of the government's commitment to a flourishing BBC, however, lies not simply with policy prescriptions but with the licence fee level it is willing to sanction. In January 2007, ten months after the publication of the White Paper, the government rejected the BBC's bid for an increase of 1.8 per cent above inflation and awarded it instead a below-inflation rise that, according to director general Mark Thompson, would leave 'a gap of around £2bn over the next six years between what we believed we needed to deliver our vision and what will actually be available' (quoted in Gibson 2007: 6). While the *Daily Mail* (19 January 2007) opined that 'viewers and listeners [are] entitled to feel deeply sceptical about its pleas of poverty' and suggested that this was still a generous settlement, other competitors, like the British Internet Publishers' Association, were simply grateful that the BBC was 'finally being reined in' (quoted in Kiss 2006).

Many commentators blamed the negotiating tactics of Mark Thompson – who had originally pressed for a 2.3 per cent rise before bowing to political pressure and revising it downwards – in asking for a substantial increase at a moment when the Treasury was declaring a freeze on spending in the public sector. However, both the level of the licence fee and the manner in which it was reached reveal much about the ambivalent attitude held by the government towards the BBC.

First, having mapped out an activist role for the BBC in relation to digital switchover, the settlement is unlikely to provide the corporation with all the money it needs fully to promote and help implement the move to digital as well as to maintain an audience share that justifies its grip on the licence fee. The government's ring-fencing of £600m within the settlement to promote digital simply means that other budgets will have to be trimmed, undermining its own demand for the BBC to deliver the new 'purposes' set out in its proposals for the corporation. 'This is a genuinely disappointing settlement,' argued one commentator. 'It is not enough to fund the vision of the BBC the Government itself set out in its White Paper' (quoted in Luckhurst 2007). This is far from an oversight on the part of the government given that the settlement is predicated on efficiency savings to be undertaken by the BBC. This was highlighted in Secretary of State Tessa Jowell's parliamentary statement on the deal, a speech littered with the language of fiscal sobriety: 'the new BBC trust must ensure that licence fee payers get the best possible value for [their] investment. We expect the trust to ensure efficiency in the BBC . . . we believe that the BBC can realize up to 3 per cent cash-releasing savings annually from 2008' (HoC Debates, 18 January 2007: col. 933).

Second, having guaranteed the licence fee until at least 2016, the government seems to have accepted Ofcom's argument that the BBC should no longer have a monopoly on licence fee revenue in the future. While the White Paper had hinted at this – promising a review that would consider the possibility of distributing public money 'more widely beyond the BBC' (DCMS 2006: 63) – Jowell revealed to parliament 'that we may require the BBC to contribute to the first six years of Channel 4's switchover costs' (HoC Debates, 18 January 2007: col. 934). The provision of a purportedly generous award was, therefore, simultaneously accompanied by the unprecedented requirement for the BBC to subsidize another broadcaster without any apparent consideration of why this burden should not be shared amongst all the broadcasters set to benefit from digital switchover. Indeed, one leading opponent of the licence fee, David Elstein, noted astutely that the most significant part of the settlement was 'the precedent set by the government earmarking a chunk of income, £600m, for digital switchover, that is not for BBC content purposes' (quoted in Brown 2007: 3) – a potential precedent for 'top-slicing' the licence fee as recommended by Ofcom and others.

Finally, the settlement reveals the profoundly political nature of the decision-making process concerning the licence fee. While Tessa Jowell sought to depersonalize the issue, most commentators identified the imprint of then Chancellor Gordon Brown in both the below-inflation rise and the decision to break the link with inflation, a measure that was introduced in 1988 in an effort, ironically, to depoliticize the issue of BBC finances. According to one Labour special adviser, the 2007 settlement was the clear result of power struggles within government.

Tessa [Jowell] is a featherweight with no future. This was Gordon's revenge. The BBC has never had a go at Brown. He was untouched by Hutton. But he is a philistine. He ought to bend his public spending rules for the BBC, but he can't see that it is a special case. Currying favour with Rupert Murdoch is more important – and this is what this licence fee settlement is really all about. (Quoted in Luckhurst 2007)

Whether this is true or not, the uncertainty that surrounded the eventual resolution of the licence fee award confounded promises made by civil servants and special advisers that the process was 'relentlessly open' and that 'when we get to the point when the government is publishing conclusions, that everybody will be able to see the evidence and the process that has led to those conclusions'. According to one observer, 'the machinations of the negotiation have instead been conducted in a manner which would embarrass Machiavelli' (Bell 2007: 4); another journalist comments that, despite the government's claims to have increased transparency in the policymaking field, the licence fee negotiations highlight 'the way in which years of debate still boil down to discussions between a handful of individuals behind closed doors over a period of a few weeks' (Gibson 2007: 3). Once more, the secrecy, leaks and turf wars that dominated the process do little to suggest either a pluralist model of policymaking or long-term confidence in the future of the licence fee.

The Bush administration and public broadcasting

If New Labour's relationship with the BBC can be described as, at best, ambivalent, George W. Bush's approach to public broadcasting in the USA demonstrates few such ambiguities. The White House's recent dealings with the Corporation for Public Broadcasting (CPB), the organization set up by Congress to promote and fund non-commercial television and radio, reveals a partisanship and instrumentality that challenges the very existence of independent, public broadcasting. Bush, of course, is hardly the first politician to seek to interfere with the administration of the CPB. In 1967, Lyndon Johnson appointed Frank Pace Jnr, a former army secretary and CEO of defence company General Dynamics, as the first chairman of the CPB. One of Pace's first decisions was to commission research on how public broadcasting might be used to deal with riot control. According to broadcasting historian Eric Barnouw (1990: 399), the 'President's support [for public broadcasting] had created vast expectations among supporters of noncommercial television. Now they wondered if it was being hugged to death.' In 1972, Nixon's White House vetoed the authorization by Congress of $155 million for the CPB and instructed the corporation to adopt a more local and narrowly 'educational' perspective. William Hoynes (1994: 3) notes that 'Nixon's call for a return to the "bedrock of localism," as the administration put it, was a cover for the more political problems the administration had with the system', in particular over accusations of liberal bias.

According to Hoynes (1994: 7–11), there are two further assumptions that underlie the conservative critique of American public broadcasting: first, that non-commercial broadcasting is an affront to the market principles that ensure the most efficient organization of media markets and, second, that the choice facilitated by pay television has undermined the need for publicly funded channels. These assumptions, dismissed by Hoynes as resting on 'ideological constructions rather than simple facts' (1994: 10), are particularly powerful at a time when the combination of the hegemony of neo-liberal ideas and the pace of technological transformation is threatening to engulf public broadcasting in a 'perfect storm'. The fact that the Bush administration's interventions are the latest in a long history of partisan interference into the funding and programming of non-commercial broadcasting does not suggest that its future can easily be guaranteed.

Attacks on the Corporation for Public Broadcasting

There are three main elements of neo-conservative policy towards public broadcasting: the repeated accusations of liberal bias, the hyper-politicization of the CPB and the ongoing attempts to cut public funding of PBS and NPR. The first two strategies are best exemplified by the record of former chairman Kenneth Tomlinson, previously the head of the government's Voice of America service in the Reagan administration and a close associate of Karl Rove, a senior adviser in George W. Bush's White House. Tomlinson was actually appointed to the board by Bill Clinton in 2000 but promoted to chair by Bush in 2003, where, in the words of one prominent neo-conservative columnist, Robert Novak (2005), his mission was 'to reduce the ideological imbalance in public broadcasting'. According to the *New York Times*, Tomlinson had a long record of criticizing public television programmes 'as too liberal overall' and claimed that 'at PBS headquarters there is a tone deafness to issues of tone and balance' (quoted in Labaton et al. 2005). Tomlinson set about restoring equilibrium to PBS by immediately complaining to Pat Mitchell, the chief executive of PBS, that the programme

Now, hosted by administration critic Bill Moyers, 'does not contain anything approaching the balance the law requires for public broadcasting' (quoted in Labaton et al. 2005). He then paid a consultant, without the knowledge of the rest of the CPB board, to monitor the political affiliations of guests on *Now* (as well as on other programmes) who were categorized as, for example, 'pro-' or 'anti-Bush', 'pro-' or 'anti-administration', 'pro-' or 'anti-Tom Delay' (referring to the then House majority leader). In a further attempt to correct liberal bias and address what he claimed to be the scarcity of conservative voices on the airwaves, Tomlinson encouraged PBS to adopt *The Journal Editorial Report*, a programme featuring members of the editorial board of the business-oriented *Wall Street Journal*. Asked at a Senate subcommittee hearing on PSB funding whether this represented a clear example of conservative advocacy, Tomlinson replied 'yes, yes . . . I certainly thought it was a good idea. And I thought it was an important idea because of the importance of having balance in current affairs broadcasting' (quoted in PBS 2005). Ironically, Tomlinson suppressed the results of a poll (carried out by a Republican polling firm at around this time) that showed that both PBS and NPR had an 80 per cent favourable rating and that a clear majority (55 per cent) of PBS viewers found it to be more 'fair and balanced' than all its other rivals (Ireland 2005).

Appointments to the CPB showed further evidence of Republican partisanship. In March 2005, Tomlinson hired a White House official, the director of the Office of Global Communications, Mary Catherine Andrews, to draft the guiding principles for the two new ombudsmen chosen by Tomlinson to monitor political content on PBS and NPR. Andrews's insistence that 'I was careful not to work on the project during office hours during my last days at the White House' (quoted in Labaton et al. 2005) was of little consolation to those arguing that this appointment provided more evidence of the declining independence of the CPB. Three months later, Tomlinson's preferred candidate, Patricia Harrison, a former co-chair of the Republican National Committee, was picked to be the new president and chief executive of the corporation. Following her appointment, Harrison then hired three officers from the State Department, including two from the Public Affairs and Public Diplomacy section with responsibility for government propaganda, to senior posts at the CPB.

Tomlinson eventually paid the price for his largely unaccountable and highly partisan attempts to implant conservative values inside the CPB and, by extension, to the programmes aired on public television and radio. A report by Inspector General Kenneth Konz (2005) concluded that Tomlinson had violated provisions of the 1967 Public Broadcasting Act by dealing directly with the creators of *The Journal Editorial Report* and by using 'political tests' to recruit Harrison to the corporation. The report also found that he was mainly responsible for creating an organizational environment that allowed senior CPB executives 'to operate without appropriate checks and balances' (2005: ii). Although Tomlinson resigned immediately after learning about the report's findings, he was unapologetic and accused Konz (rather disingenuously) of opting 'for politics over good judgment', repeating that his objective all along had been to 'help bring balance and objectivity in public broadcasting' (quoted in 2005, Appendix C: 2). One line of enquiry that was missing from Konz's report, however, was the involvement of the White House. This may partly be explained by the fact that Konz was 'not permitted to interview White House person-nel' (Konz 2005: 2) and partly because evidence linking the administration to Tomlinson may have been contained in a 'separate investigative report' that was submitted 'to the Board for their disposition' (2005: 2), but never published. Indeed, despite Tomlinson's repeated insistence that the administration had no influence on the running of the CPB, emails revealing that he had 'pursued policies and the appointment of executives at the behest of the White House' were leaked by a disgruntled CPB official to NPR in June 2005 (Folkenflik 2005).

The White House shows no signs of encouraging a less partisan approach to the governance of public broadcasting given its appointment of another conservative figure, comedy writer and commercial television producer Warren Bell, to the CPB board during the congressional recess in December 2006. Bell's nomination had initially been stalled by the Senate Commerce Committee, due to concerns about his lack of public broadcasting experience and his close identification with conservative ideas. A regular contributor to the neo-conservative *National Review*, Bell describes himself as 'thoroughly conservative in ways that strike horror into the hearts of my Hollywood colleagues. I support a woman's right to choose what movie we should see but not that other one. I am on the Right in every way' (Bell 2005a). Equally disturbing – in terms of his viability as a champion of public broadcasting – is his uncertainty as to why he was nominated to the position in the first place given his self-declared preference for commercial sports radio over NPR. According to White House spokesman Tony Fratto, however, Bell's experience in network television made him an ideal candidate for the position: 'He has innovative ideas on making public television *more competitive with mainstream media* and expressed a very strong commitment to improving CPB (quoted in Gold 2006a – emphasis added).

This appointment might suggest a determination on the part of the administration to simultaneously politicize *and* commercialize PBS and NPR. Rather than seeking, as the British government has done, to restrict the scope of public broadcasting in order to placate its commercial competitors, the White House might want to foster a more populist approach to public broadcasting in the hope that it would curb critical coverage of the administration. However, it is more likely that Bell's appointment was motivated simply by his ideological views rather than his commercial experience, particularly because many Republicans continue to doubt the need for public broadcasting in a multi-channel age. According to Representative Ernest Istook of Oklahoma: 'We do not need a nationwide subsidy . . . to reach a few targeted households' now that it is getting 'harder and harder to distinguish public TV from the rest of broadcasting because other broadcasters, a great many, carry the same type of programs today, and each year public broadcasting looks more and more like other networks' (*Cong. Rec.* 23 June 2005: H5023). The *New York Times* may well be correct, therefore, to suggest that administration supporters:

> have a larger agenda – to 'hollow out' public broadcasting and fill it with programming that suits their political agenda. And if public broadcasting becomes too political to suit all but the most loyal Republicans or too boring in the name of balance, that could mean the slow death of such broadcasting, which could have been the goal all along. (*New York Times* 2005)

Cuts in the funding of US public broadcasting

This complements the third dimension of current White House policy towards public broadcasting: its regular attempts to cut federal funding for the CPB. In June 2005, the House Appropriations Committee voted to cut a quarter of the $400 million budget for public television and radio, a move that 'went significantly beyond those requested by the White House' (Labaton et al. 2005). Republicans argued that this was necessary to tackle growing deficits, and sketched out a picture of a bloated CPB redistributing money from the needy to the privileged consumers of public broadcasting. One conservative commentator revealed that the median income for NPR listeners was nearly $90,000: 'these are people who could clearly afford to pay for NPR themselves. But they must figure why should they do that when liberals in Congress are willing to soak the taxpayers for a subsidy' (Kincaid 2005). Representative Ginny

Brown-Waite of Florida contributed to the congressional debate on the cuts by announcing (*Cong. Rec.* 23 June 2005: H5041) that, thanks to merchandising and marketing rights, 'Big Bird [from the PBS programme *Sesame Street*] is a billionaire' and insisting that 'Big Bird is strong enough to fly on his own. If we cannot get this billionaire off the public trough, than I ask how can we ever hope to cut spending.' This argument was not enough to convince all her fellow Republicans, eighty-seven of whom joined with Democrats, following a vociferous public campaign, to vote down the cuts and restore funding to the CPB (and neither was it supported by the Government Accountability Office which published a report [GAO 2007] denying the existence of large reserves that could offset federal funding if it was withdrawn).

Undeterred by this defeat, the administration returned the following year to press for cuts of $157 million, a move that was, once again, beaten back by the determined opposition of viewers and listeners. In February 2007, George W. Bush launched yet another assault on the funding of public broadcasting with proposals to cut nearly 25 per cent of the entire CPB budget in a move that would, according to a senior figure from the CPB, 'mean the end of our ability to support some of the most treasured educational children's series and primetime icons to which CPB funding contributes' (quoted in Teinowitz 2007). Given that President Bush agreed at the same time to *increase* the budget for US international broadcasting by 3.8 per cent, allowing the administration to improve the propaganda services to the Middle East, the Horn of Africa and Cuba that it argues is 'pivotal to promoting freedom and democracy and enhancing understanding in key regions' (BBG 2007), domestic audiences are entitled to doubt that the cuts are motivated by budgetary concerns alone.

Is there a future for non-commercial broadcasting in the USA? Administration supporters argue that the recent attacks on public broadcasters were merely justified by the need to address the problem of liberal bias; proponents of public broadcasting such as the Association of Public Television Stations argue that 'the Administration is charging ahead in laying the foundation for the elimination of public broadcasting in America' (quoted in Free Press 2007). Whichever perspective is more accurate, there is little doubt that recent events have undermined the ability of public broadcasting to offer independent, high quality, non-commercial programming. The prospects of reduced federal funding (that currently provides approximately 15 per cent of the revenue for public television (GAO 2007: 28)) is forcing broadcasters increasingly to turn to other sources of income, in particular merchandising tie-ins, sponsorship and branding. According to PBS president Paula Kerger:

> We just have to be really careful about anything that is really obtrusive or smacks of too much commercialism. But at the end of the day, most people understand that we need to do some amount of corporate under-writing in order to support the work we're doing. (Quoted in Gold 2006b)

Deals with McDonalds, the cable giant Comcast, Disney and the super-market chain Albertsons are justified by the need 'to tap into new revenue streams' (Gold 2006b), a new form of dependence that is likely to reinforce a culture of caution and an atmosphere of fear.

> Not only fear that there won't be enough, but also the fear of offending the funder, whether it be the public, corporations, foundations, or govern-ment; of saying or doing something that will prompt the hand that feeds to shut off the nourishment or meddle with and censor programming. That, in turn, leads to what may be the worst kind of censorship: self-censorship, a preemptive, self-inflicted blow to stave off the clenched fist of the funder. (Winship 2007)

If public broadcasting is to survive in the USA, it must fend off the hostility of government as well as the lure of the market in order to renew itself as a credible, and even popular, alternative to mainstream media.

Conclusion

The policies of both the Blair and the Bush administrations concerning public broadcasting tell us something significant about the ways in which neo-liberal governments seek to discipline public institutions. Despite the Labour government's vocal enthusiasm for the principle of PSB and for the BBC as a public service institution, the underlying objective of the government's White Paper on the BBC is to enshrine the corporation in market logic. Borrowing heavily from Ofcom's recommendations, it sees the BBC not as an autonomous proponent of public service values but as an organization that is part of an increasingly competitive, marketized environment and needs regulating according to that logic. Bearing in mind that the BBC has already made many concessions to market reforms – with its operation of an 'internal market' in the 1990s and sell-offs and redundan-cies in the following decade – it may seem strange that the corporation is being treated to such harsh medicine. It is even more mysterious why the White House should be so concerned by the performance of a broadcasting system that is fairly marginal to mainstream American political debate. Indeed, the Bush administration's instinct towards public broadcasting has been less to do with discipline and more to do with punishment: for being too 'liberal' and 'non-commercial' in a highly profit-driven media environment. Both cases, however, illuminate a key point about neo-liberalization: that *all* areas of public provision, irrespective of their record or their popularity, are vulnerable to political interference and restructuring (although not necessarily privatized or broken up), and are forced to adapt to and internalize market-friendly practices.

8

The Politics of Digital

Why digital?

Author: Why are we so committed to a digital future?
Downing Street policy adviser: [laughs] What take a step back to 1999 or earlier? [pause] I think it's a fair question and one the government will ultimately have to answer when it decides to switch off the analogue signal, so it's not a stupid question and it's one we should all ask.

Interview, November 2004

James Purnell, broadcasting minister: The key question about [digital] switchover is not *whether* it's going to happen . . . The key questions are really: *how* is it going to happen and *when* is it going to happen.

Evidence to House of Commons Select Committee on Culture,
Media and Sport, December 2005

The impact of digitization has been felt throughout the media. Digital-led convergence has facilitated new markets, new business models, new services and new modes of production and consumption just as it has also, as we have already seen, contributed to pressure to liberalize ownership rules, to reduce content regulation and to re-evaluate the justification for public service broadcasting. Now, governments across the world are preparing to switch off analogue television signals and to usher in a radical new era marked, they promise, by abundance, interactivity and high quality. The USA is due to shut down analogue transmissions in February 2009, while the UK has earmarked 2008–12 as the designated timetable for switchover. Yet analogue shutdown is an enormously complex, costly and controversial project that has, thus far, stimulated remarkably little public debate. Legislatures, specialist committees, industry bodies and pressure groups have had extensive discussions about the procedures and implications of switchover, but rarely has the fundamental question of *why digital?* been asked of or fully answered by those leading the transition. Just because digitalization is possible does not make it intrinsically desirable, nor is the path to a digital future a predictable one. For one leading British commentator on media policy, some basic issues remain unresolved:

> Who thought we must go through this massive process to convert to digital and why? Was is the Treasury because they saw pots of money? Was it commercial interests because they saw a way of marginalizing the BBC? Was it a policy wonk from Downing Street who thought 'here is my chance to expand my territory'?

This section attempts to unravel some of these issues and to clarify the different motivations behind the transition to digital television (DTV). It does not attempt to outline the various approaches adopted by governments to stimulate DTV (see Brown and Picard 2004; Colombo and Vittadini 2006; Galperin 2004; Hart 2004 for extensive accounts) or to assess the detailed strategies for switchover itself (see Adda and Ottaviani 2005; Iosifidis 2006), but rather to focus on the often shifting justifications provided for the embrace of DTV. This involves counterposing the often 'pluralist, functionalist or administrative' perspectives on technological change adopted by the proponents of switchover with a 'critical problematic approach' in which the exercise and pursuit of power is seen as central (Corcoran 2006: 9). It must be emphasized that this does not in any way suggest some sort of Luddite opposition to digital and an associated desire to return to only a handful of channels, but simply the wish to identify some of the conflicts and interests that lie behind the promotion of a digital future.

The origins of digital television policy

The turn to digital television occurred at the time when the British and American governments were extolling the virtues of a 'multimedia revolution' that was facilitating the possibility of an 'information society' that both countries aspired to build. This was most famously expressed in the speech by then Vice-President Al Gore to the International Telecommunications Union (ITU) in March 1994. Gore's comments focused on his vision of a 'global information infrastructure', more commonly referred to as an 'information superhighway', a series of digital networks that would revolutionize existing communication structures. Gore had used his commitment to the superhighway as a central part of his electoral campaign two years earlier to present himself (and his presidential running mate Bill Clinton) as the forward-looking, cutting-edge candidates best placed to take control of a 'new economy'. In his speech to the ITU, Gore spelled out the principles that would underpin the construction of a digital superhighway that would give the USA tremendous economic advantages: the need for private investment, the promotion of competition, the creation of flexible regulation, the provision of open access and the guarantee of universal service (Gore 1994).

These principles underpinned the passage of the 1996 Telecommunications Act that provided digital television with its first legislative framework. Following heavy lobbying by commercial broadcasters, the Act sanctioned the giveaway of digital spectrum, worth anything from $40 billion to $100 billion, to existing terrestrial broadcasters on the basis that they would promise to start up digital transmissions in the ensuing years and to release their analogue spectrum back to the government who would then be able to auction it off. Even some free-market supporters reacted to this spectrum gift with fury: conservative columnist William Safire described it as 'corporate theft', while leading senators John McCain and Bob Dole dubbed it, respectively, as a 'scam' and as 'corporate welfare' (quoted in McChesney 2000: 152). Despite (or perhaps because of) this, then FCC chair Reed Hundt (1996) celebrated the agreement of a single DTV standard as a victory for market forces in particular: 'Our goal has been to trust the market, not government, to define the digital television of the future. Today's agreement . . . eliminates needless government regulation on technical issues better left to the marketplace to decide.'

Digital television, however, was initially conceptualized in far more ambitious terms than simply a boost for government coffers or a new source of revenue for the electronics industry. Vice-President Gore was asked by President Clinton to chair a committee examining public service responsibilities for digital broadcasters on the basis that the airwaves would continue to be 'a forum not just for entertainment, but for education, enlightenment and civic debate' (Gore 1997). In his first presentation to the group, Gore claimed that television was going through

> the greatest transformation in is history, one that is truly bigger than the shift from black and white to colour – the move from analog to digital broadcasting. It's like the difference between a one-man band and a symphony . . . digital broadcasting will be more dynamic and more flexible; more competitive and more interactive – and potentially much more responsive to the needs and interests of the American people. (Gore 1997)

The committee's report, published the following year, stressed that DTV would massively improve picture and sound quality, facilitate high-definition television (HDTV) (a technology policy objective since the

1980s), and also provide a range of new interactive and premium services that would benefit consumers (Advisory Committee 1998: xii–xiii). On similar lines, the powerful Senate Commerce Committee chairman John McCain argued that DTV would 'provide Americans with an array of services unavailable from conventional television broadcasting: crystal-clear pictures and sound, interactivity, and internet-based services. Rather than merely *watching* television, we can *participate* in television' (McCain 1998). Digital television, therefore, was pursued by commercial interests (for example, the consumer electronics and software industries as well as broadcasters), promoted by governments eager to associate themselves with the dividends of an 'information revolution', portrayed as a boost to the performance of citizenship, and publicized as a huge step forward for the quality and interactivity of the broadcast experience.

Many elements of this approach were echoed in British government attitude towards digital television in the 1990s. This was in itself influenced by the work of the European Commission's 'high level group on the information society', founded in order to assess the opportunities for European producers in an information age. Its report, *Europe and the Global Information Society* (known as the Bangemann Report) (EC 1994) took as its starting point the desirability of building a European information society in which the 'key issue for the emergence of new markets is the need for a new regulatory environment allowing full competition. This will be a prerequisite for mobilizing the private capital necessary for innovation, growth and development' (EC 1994). Driven by a desire to overcome the disparity with the USA in PC penetration rates and to secure a competitive edge through the expansion of an information services sector, the report proposed an industrial vision – with some additional non-market applications – based on the rapid deployment of market forces in the information and communication technologies industries, and made recommendations concerning deregulation that were eerily similar to Gore's plans for the superhighway. This view of the roll-out of digital technologies simultaneously enabling and requiring market liberalization was expressed in the British Conservative government's proposals for the loosening of media ownership rules and the provisions for digital terrestrial television that were eventually inscribed into the 1996 Broadcasting Act. In particular, its plans for DTV (see Goodwin 1998: 149–54) were justified by the promise of a communications revolution that would benefit commercial interests and facilitate an expansion of broadcast outlets. 'For many people', the government went on to argue (DNH 1995b: 1), 'it will provide their first experience of the full potential of the information superhighways. It will provide significant opportunities for the British manufacturing and programme production industries.'

The government's proposals for DTV were firmly welcomed by New Labour whose broadcasting spokesperson, Lewis Moonie, confirmed that '[w]e have no quarrel with the Government inasmuch as we want digital television to get going, as everyone else does' (HoC Debates, 16 April 1996: col. 605). This was hardly a surprise given New Labour's vigorous enthusiasm for a digital future that had seen the publication of a consultation paper, *Communicating Britain's Future* (Labour Party 1995), based on extensive discussions with leading communications companies, including News International, BT, Microsoft and the BBC, that proposed the construction of a digital superhighway to be financed by the private sector but to be designed in partnership with government. Once in office, and buoyed by the take-up of the new digital television services that demonstrated to some the efficacy of market mechanisms in popularizing DTV, Labour sought to develop an approach to analogue switch-off based on a combination of economic objectives (for example, the value of analogue spectrum and the benefits of DTV for British manufacturing) and lofty ideals. In September 1999, Culture Secretary Chris Smith announced the principles behind switchover – of affordability, access and availability – and insisted that viewers' interests must come first if a switchover deadline of 2010 was to be achieved. 'This revolution is not just about the young and trendy. It is about everyone – because all parts of our society can and should benefit' (quoted in BBC 1999). He was even more expansive in his statement to parliament later that year. While DTV would benefit everyone:

> In particular, people with disabilities could benefit from the new and sophisticated services that digital television offers. There is too often an assumption that digital television is of interest only to those who want a greater choice of programmes. It brings many other advantages. For example, it can bring better signing services for deaf people. Through the links with interactivity, it can enable the home delivery services for housebound people. It can help to provide community information and welfare advice for people who face disadvantage and difficulty. (HoC Debates, 29 October 1999: col. 1210)

Indeed, the government was so confident about the popularity and potential of DTV that it included a commitment to switch from analogue to digital in its manifesto for the 2001 general election – a rather unlikely pledge given that governments rarely campaign on services they plan to *withdraw*, but certainly a sign of the Blair administration's determination to secure a 'digital nation' (Labour Party 2001: 11).

While there were some significant contrasts between the two countries' approaches to DTV (not least in the obvious differences between their respective broadcasting ecologies and political cultures, and in the emphasis placed on the social benefits of digital in the UK and the value of HDTV in the USA), by the beginning of the twenty-first century the British and American governments were pursuing *broadly* similar strategies in relation to DTV. They both saw DTV as a key component of the 'information' and 'knowledge' economies they were eager to build; they shared a view of DTV as a potential driver of broadband and other interactive services; they agreed that DTV would increase the quality and flexibility of the viewing experience; market forces, in the view of both administrations, were to be decisive in setting standards and providing services with government set to play only a limited 'steering' role; both of them emphasized the value of the analogue spectrum to be released to government after switchover; and both of them agreed that digital innovations required and facilitated the liberalization of existing regulatory structures. As Murdock and Golding noted at the time:

> the completion of convergence would be measured by the arrival of open infrastructures and multifunction consumer equipment. Because governments have come to accept that this state of affairs is self-evidently desirable and universally beneficial and to regard increases in taxation and public intervention as against the political spirit of the time, corporate advocates have little difficulty in arguing that capitalizing on convergence requires a further relaxation of the constraints on their freedom of action. (1999: 120)

Promises of a digital broadcast nirvana, therefore, coincided with and relied on a process of relentless marketization (and indeed wider deregulation) that was reshaping the media systems of the UK and the USA as they entered a new millennium.

Plans for digital switchover

By 2002 nirvana was still some distance away. The problem was that the market had, thus far, failed to deliver the secure growth in digital services and take-up by households that would guarantee the initial government deadlines for analogue shut-down: by the end of 2006 in the USA and 2010 in the UK. The situation was particularly acute in the USA where only 23 per cent of commercial broadcasters had met their promise, made following the spectrum giveaway in 1996, to be transmitting digitally by May 2002. Digital transition, according to Senate Commerce Committee chairman John McCain, 'has been a grave disappointment for American consumers. It is nothing short of a spectrum heist for American taxpayers' (*Cong. Rec.*, 1 May 2002: S3583). In the UK, digital television was far more advanced, with some 35 per cent of households accessing digital services by the end of 2001, largely thanks to the mass conversion to digital of BSkyB's analogue satellite customers (Aroldo et al. 2006: 209). However, an increasing number of reports indicated that there existed a significant minority of people who had little interest in switching, with one poll showing that 32 per cent of people 'would not want digital TV' at all and that 66 per cent of people who had not switched had 'not even considered getting digital TV' (quoted in BBC 2001). The government's determination to secure a 2010 switch-off suffered a further setback when, in March 2002, the only digital terrestrial television (DTT) operator, ITV Digital (formerly OnDigital) – the centre-piece of the government's desire to be 'platform neutral' – collapsed, unable to compete with the competitive presence of BSkyB. 'Having determined a transition to DTV,' argues Georgina Born (2004: 493), 'the government became alarmed by the scale of resistance and the consequent political dangers of being seen to impose it.'

The response by both the US and the UK governments to these problems was to accelerate their preparations for switchover but also to adopt a more instrumental discourse about the advantages of DTV and the necessity of switchover. In the USA in particular, earlier promises about DTV's capacity to stimulate civic debate, to provide community information and to serve diverse interests – issues that were raised in the Gore Commission and then not taken up by the FCC – were replaced by a set of concerns that mirrored the market preoccupations of the Bush administration. The British government, on the other hand, continued to talk about DTV's capacity to offer citizens 'the opportunity to engage with government in a new way, through a device they already trust and feel comfortable with – their television' (Cabinet Office 2003: 17). It remains to be seen whether initiatives like the government's DTV channel UK Online Interactive are more likely to function as mechanisms for government publicity than as agents of meaningful public interaction, and there is certainly little evidence thus far that DTV projects will be able to overcome structural issues of exclusion and inequality (see Gunter 2004). Indeed, while the internet is now seen as the more appropriate instrument for facilitating social and political renewal, there has been, as Born puts it (2006: 39), 'something of a conceptual lock-down in the way digitisation is framed'. The advantages of DTV and the justification for switchover are increasingly focused around economistic frames of *consumer choice, industrial gain, market efficiency* and *technological inevitability*.

Digital choice

According to a policy adviser to Tony Blair, the 'one overriding motivation' for switchover concerns 'choice for viewers'. The capacity of DTV to provide audiences with more choice is a fundamental part of its appeal and is based on the claim that digital broadcasting facilitates a 'communications cornucopia' in which all tastes will be catered for and no minority will be left unfulfilled. First, this is an argument about multi-channel broadcasting in general and not DTV in particular – analogue cable and satellite services long ago broke the grip of the major networks and undermined the impact of spectrum scarcity. Second, the claim is based on a rather narrow understanding of choice that equates the increase in the number of media outlets with an increase in diversity and neglects the argument that 'the expansion of choice is always *pre-structured* by the conditions of competition' (Curran 2002: 230). A digital broadcast environment dominated by existing voices and organized along commercial lines is likely to serve unequal consumers and reproduce well-established patterns of concentration and influence. Third, even this restricted understanding of choice is being further reduced to denoting (in the USA) a choice between high-definition or standard-definition television and (in the UK) a choice of which digital platforms to sign up to. According to one of the civil servants responsible for implementing digital policy, facilitating 'access and choice' (Zeff 2005: 8) is the first reason for switchover. As only 75 per cent of the country have access to DTT signals – a figure that will continue until the analogue spectrum is released – switchover is justified by the government's determination that 'as far as possible, people have a choice of platforms' (2005: 8–9). For the Downing Street policy adviser quoted above, 'switchover is motivated by the fact that 25 per cent of the country can't get DTT' – a statement that does little to tie DTV to a more expansive notion of choice.

Consumers are also set to gain from an increased choice of new mobile and wireless broadband services that will be stimulated by the freeing up of analogue spectrum. Interestingly, leading proponents of digitization deliberately use the language of 'freedom' to describe and rationalize the appeal of digital technologies and the value of switchover. For Ed Richards, former Downing Street media policy adviser and latterly Ofcom CEO, digital convergence involves 'a gentle, gradual, evolving, historic act of liberation. The liberation of consumers, viewers, listeners, to determine their own viewing, their own listening, their own schedule, their own compilations, their own content and even their own services' (Richards 2005). 'The liberation of [analogue] spectrum,' according to John McCain, 'will unleash a multitude of new commercial wireless services . . . By facilitating more broadband deployment and competition, freeing the spectrum would allow us to rely more heavily on the market, rather than government, to regulate telecommunications' (McCain 2004).

Industrial benefits

The equation of consumer choice with the expansion of market opportunities and market freedoms is echoed in the frequent invocations of the economic benefits of DTV. This refers to more than the mere value to government of the analogue spectrum soon to be auctioned off (as important as this is). Many governments are now focused on the need to position their economies to take advantage of the rise of 'new markets for our creative industries' in 'the third industrial revolution' (Jowell 2006), and see developments like DTV as part of a strategic response to the challenges of globalization (and the growth of China and India as major economic players). A policy adviser to the prime minister is particularly pragmatic about the opportunities presented by DTV to the economic health of the UK:

> The machinations of [our DTV] policy, beneath the philosophical level [concerning choice] is driven firstly by our industrial ambition to retain this world leadership thing that we have got . . . It's about being a country that is warm and receptive to all kinds of different content creators, digital technology innovators . . . It's the classic cluster approach. What we are saying is that we want to create an environment that is as welcoming as we possibly can so these clusters can start up, be it in Dundee or wherever. So the underpinning of the philosophical objective is this industrial perspective.

This perspective draws on claims concerning the value of 'creativity' and 'innovation' in an 'information society' that have been heavily critiqued by, for example, Garnham (2005) and Webster (2006) as being ahistorical and ideological, although it is admirably honest, at least, in its assessment of the industrial motives that underpin DTV policy. The FCC's Ken Feree is equally blunt about the advantages to industry of naming a firm date for switchover: 'the certainty of 2009 would provide benefits to those that have a stake in an orderly transition, including broadcasters, public safety authorities [post-9/11 the possibility of using the 'liberated' analogue spectrum for homeland security purposes is often near the top of the switchover agenda in the USA], advanced wireless service providers, consumer electronics manufacturers and retailers' (Feree 2004). No wonder that when the transition date was announced, the head of industry group the High Tech DTV Coalition welcomed it as 'just about the best Christmas present that I can think of coming to the tech sector from the public policy process' (quoted in Broache 2005).

The efficiency of digital

This emphasis on the industrial benefits of DTV helps to explain the largely sympathetic attitude that policymakers have adopted towards commercial broadcasters in the transition to digital. Consider the issue of efficiency. Alongside the much-repeated statement that DTV is far superior to its analogue counterpart because digital compression allows for the more efficient use of spectrum and thus creates the possibility of many more channels and creative possibilities, one of the main justifications for switchover given by the UK government is that '[s]imulcasting in both analogue and digital is inefficient for broadcasters' (Zeff 2005: 9). The same concern for the financial health of broadcasters is demonstrated by the FCC's assertion that a firm switchover date is necessary as broadcasters need to know 'precisely how long they will be required to run side-by-side analog and digital facilities and can make budget and maintenance decisions accordingly' (Feree 2004). Indeed, having donated extremely valuable digital spectrum to existing broadcasters, neither government has shown much appetite for *requiring* commercial broadcasters to provide digital transmission and digital programming, or for penalizing them when they have fallen short of their promises. Even John McCain's threat in 2002 to reclaim the spectrum given to broadcasters if they failed to speed up their preparations for switchover was tempered by his insistence that 'I continue to be a firm believer in market forces' (*Cong. Rec.* 1 May 2002: S3585) and that, therefore, voluntary proposals were far more desirable than taking statutory measures that would punish the commercial sector.

Digital inevitability

What is most curious is that this gentle approach has not been applied to the general public on whom digital switchover is to be imposed. The one choice the public are *not* being given is whether analogue transmission should continue. In anticipation of the potential public fury that could result from analogue shutdown, one of the most powerful motivations that policymakers have given for the public to commit to digital is that, quite simply, digital is the future and there is no way of stopping it: 'Switchover is happening and it is inevitable,' said broadcasting minister James Purnell when pressed on the motivations for the UK government's DTV policy (quoted in House of Commons 2006b: Ev235). Former FCC chairman Michael Powell embodies this narrative of technological inevitability in his response to critics of the DTV transition:

> The cold truth, however, is that we have no choice – not just because Congress has mandated it (which is reason enough) but because the trends in technology and the forces of change will ultimately demand it of any provider that hopes to be relevant in the digital future. (Powell 2002)

Aside from the fact that an abstract entity like 'the forces of change' is not in a position to demand anything of anyone, Powell's implication is clear: there is a political and technological momentum to switchover policy that cannot be reversed. Any remaining critical voices in this situation are likely to find themselves irrelevant both to the ongoing debates and to the digital future, a point acknowledged by one British media reporter: 'Everybody has got so used to the idea of switchover that much of the industry has stopped questioning what the point of the policy is, while journalists have become bored' (Sabbagh 2006). This fatalism is common to many deterministic accounts of technological change that paint all developments – silent to sound movies, black and white to colour television, vinyl to CD – as following an internal, almost organic, logic. It is an effective, highly ideological, way of naturalizing change, marginalizing discussion of possible alternative paths of development and masking the interests that lie behind the chosen technological innovation (see Williams 1974 for an influential critique of technological determinism).

The immediate task, therefore, for the coalition of interests involved in implementing DTV policy is, as the body charged with informing British viewers about switchover puts it, to convince the public that 'ensuring that all households are able to benefit from digital television by switching off analogue terrestrial transmissions is a *natural progression* and *the way of the future*' (Digital UK 2005 – emphasis added). Indeed, recent official publicity in the USA and the UK reduces the complex issues that surround what is an extremely controversial policy into three simple reasons for analogue switch-off in each country.

- DTV broadcast technology is 'more flexible and efficient'
- It will facilitate HDTV and 'multicasting'
- It will release valuable spectrum that can be used for the emergency services

(FCC 2006d)

- Switchover is 'fairer' as it will allow more people to access DTT
- DTV is more 'efficient' and will provide more channels and new services
- Switchover will 'ensure the UK continues as a world leader in broadcasting'

(Digital UK 2006).

Switchover, according to these perspectives, is an unproblematic and unambiguously positive process.

Digital switchover as a political project

The intention of this section has not been to evaluate the success of the precise arrangements that the UK and the US governments have made for digital transition, but to consider some of the contrasting motivations for and justifications of switchover. As we move towards the day of reckoning, it is worth confronting some of the claims made by digital proponents about the switchover process. First, it is not at all clear that this has been the consumer-led process governments have claimed it to be. In her announcement of the date of analogue shut-down, Culture Minister Tessa Jowell emphasized the 'immense opportunities switchover will bring for viewers, who in the overwhelming majority *are demanding it*' (Jowell 2005 – emphasis added). While it is true that by the end of 2005 some 73 per cent of British households had signed up to DTV (Ofcom 2006b: 171), there is less evidence that the British public was 'demanding' switchover. Millions of BSkyB satellite subscribers had already been switched to digital while millions more took advantage of the non-subscription 'Freeview' service, launched by a consortium led by the BBC after the collapse of ITV Digital, in anticipation of switch-off. Opinion polls, meanwhile, continue to demonstrate a significant minority who show little interest in DTV: while there is only a very small number of viewers who have indicated that they will *not* switch, some 63 per cent of non-digital households report that they are happy with current television provision with 73 per cent saying that they have no immediate plans to convert (Ofcom 2006b: 253–4). There is even less evidence of popular demand for switchover in the USA where, at the end of 2005, digital penetration stood at only 53 per cent of households (2006b: 187) and where, according to one poll in January 2007, 61 per cent of Americans 'had no idea the transition was taking place' (quoted in Hearn 2007). Switchover, reflects media commentator Emily Bell (2005c: 5), 'may perhaps be the first and last example of a technological change led by the legislature rather than the consumer'.

If the DTV transition has not been consumer-led, neither has it been market-led. The sluggish response to the challenge of digital by US broadcasters (despite the generosity of the gift to them of digital spectrum), together with the fact that the US government felt compelled to legislate that all new television sets must contain digital tuners after 2007, suggests a reluctance on the part of commercial interests to *lead* the transition. The situation is even more marked in the UK where the government has repeatedly turned to the BBC – a non-market enterprise – to boost the prospects for DTV. The BBC has been a key driver of DTV through its coordination of Freeview and its heavy investment in a range of digital television and radio services (investment that, as we have already noted, has been attacked by the commercial sector on whom few requirements for digital innovation have been made). The instruction by government in its 2006 white paper (DCMS 2006) that the BBC should play a leading role in switchover – through building the digital infrastructure, promoting the transition and even financially assisting Channel Four in its preparations for switchover – is perhaps the final irony in seeing DTV roll-out as evidence of the dynamism of the market.

Indeed, neither government has sought to hide their deep involvement in the transition to digital. Culture Minister Tessa Jowell (2005) acknowledges switchover policy as an example of 'government intervention', while former FCC chair Michael Powell talks of the 'government–industry partnership' that helped to 'break the log-jam that was the DTV transition' (Powell 2004b). Far from analogue switch-off developing on an organic or market-oriented basis, it has often required decisive government activity in order to drive it forwards – proposals to subsidize the costs of transition ($1.5 billion has been made available in the USA and £800 million in the UK) in order to ensure maximum roll-out of DTV are just the latest examples of this interventionist stance. Digital switchover is a clear example of coercive, determined, political government.

This explains why it has been criticized by different parts of the political spectrum. Those on the pro-market right see it as evidence of 'big' government and of the stifling of free-market instincts. In 1998, John McCain warned of the dangers of government 'micromanaging' the switchover process (although this did not stop him from later calling on government to accelerate the transition in order to hand over analogue spectrum to the emergency services as soon as possible, to avoid a repeat of the tragedy of Hurricane Katrina (see McCain 2005)). In the UK, commercial broadcaster David Elstein has long argued against the forced adoption of DTT and has attacked government policy as being 'politicised from the outset' (2002: 1), motivated by a hostility towards Rupert Murdoch's BSkyB and a desire to protect the already pampered BBC (a rather strange claim given the government's many run-ins with the BBC and its desire *not* to antagonize Rupert Murdoch whenever possible). From the left, consumer groups and media reform organizations have attacked switchover policy for placing unfair burdens on consumers and for fostering greater amounts of privatization given that much of the analogue spectrum is almost certainly bound to be sold to the highest bidder (see, for example, Consumers Union 2005).

The claim that the DTV transition is a political project does not mean that it refers to the *same* political project in both countries. Galperin (2004) and Hart (2004) are right to emphasize the different political and institutional contexts that have led to the accentuation of many different problems facing the USA and the UK governments at any one time. Indeed, one of the conceptual faults of the British approach to DTV is to assume an overarching desire for multi-channel television modelled on the American system that justifies the imposition of analogue switch-off. While terrestrial viewing has fragmented in the USA, over 70 per cent of all British viewing continues to be dominated by the five terrestrial networks, some seventeen years after the introduction of pay-television and eight years after the first digital services – a figure that drops to the still rather impressive level of 57 per cent in multi-channel homes (Ofcom 2006b: 233).

Despite these differences, however, there is little doubt that key policymakers in both countries share the same underlying assumptions about the desirability of DTV and the need for switchover: that they represent an essential ingredient of their industrial policy perspectives as they seek to answer the challenges of globalization and increased international competition. As Hernan Galperin argues:

> the transition to digital TV is much more than a tale of technological innovation. It is a story about large-scale changes in the normative models as well as the institutions that shape television as an economic and social force – and, ultimately, about the politics of the information society. (2004: 4)

Both governments have relied on similar arguments to rationalize an extremely complex and controversial initiative – a project whose costs and benefits remain unclear, as even the British parliamentary select committee examining analogue switch-off acknowledged in their conclusion that the 'narrow economic case for switchover is inconclusive' (House of Commons 2006a: 24). They have adopted largely economistic discourses that stress the 'efficiency', 'value' and 'choice' enabled by DTV, although these objectives have been defined in restricted terms that reflect market, rather than broader social and cultural, preoccupations. Perhaps this is because the discussion of the need for and benefits of DTV has been confined to select policymaking circles and not subject to wider public debate and referendum. While it is true that regulatory bodies like Ofcom and the FCC have carried out extensive surveys about the public's attitude towards DTV and switchover, the question of whether to switch off the analogue spectrum has never really been in doubt. Faced with such a fait accompli, the nature of that public consultation is immediately limited. Indeed, one of the key industry figures charged with planning for switchover in the UK admits that the policy has been:

> perfectly well discussed in very small areas by very few people. But for most people, it's just another technical change which is why there hasn't been a row and why they aren't that interested in discussing it. We don't know and we can't be sure. The fact that it is our telly [means that] we may be kidding ourselves and that is enormously significant.

Perhaps the imposition of DTV is the 'right' thing to do and an example of proactive and responsible government in shaping the future of its citizens. The problem is that, even if this is the case, the USA and the UK governments have failed to engage their citizens in the kind of conversation that is supposed to be the hallmark of pluralist democracy and democratic politics. Instead they have resorted to an element of compulsion and a series of assertions that even some of the greatest advocates of DTV find problematic. Greg Dyke, the former director general of the BBC and champion of its new digital channels and services, admitted to a moment of doubt about the whole DTV project when he remembered all the arguments he had used to press for switchover.

> Banal arguments like digital is good for us, it's progress (and we can't let my mum stand in the way of progress), and just think how expensive it would be for the likes of the BBC, ITV and Channels Four and Five if they had to continue broadcasting in both analogue and digital?
>
> Suddenly I was back as a switchover supporter, a digital loyalist – but for a brief second I was nearly lost to the cause. (Dyke 2005b)

It remains to be seen whether whole populations can be won to the cause and, more importantly, why they should be.

The 'problem' of piracy

Digital television, it must be stressed, is only one part of the American and British governments' determination to build an 'information society', along with other initiatives concerning, for example, the roll-out of broadband, the deployment of wireless and mobile technologies and, above all, the exploitation of intellectual property (IP). The figures quoted in chapter 1 show that the 'creative' and 'copyright' industries – whose main asset is their control of IP – make a significant contribution (of between 6 and 8 per cent) to the gross domestic products of the USA and the UK. In such a situation, it is hardly surprising to hear the British government claim that 'the greatest threat to the future sustainability and growth of the . . . creative industries is the theft of their intellectual property' (Patent Office et al. 2005: 1). This theft refers to the 'piracy' facilitated by the emergence of digital technologies that enable far greater levels of unauthorized copying and distribution, and that threaten the existing revenue streams and property relations inside the media industries. According to the British government, over £4.5 billion was lost to IP piracy in 2003 alone (2005: 1).

The argument is most often applied to the recorded music industry where, according to its international trade association, the IFPI (2006: 4), one-third of all CDs bought around the world are thought to be digitally produced illegal copies with a value in 2005 of $4.5 billion, approximately 20 per cent of total market value. The situation, however, has been particularly exacerbated by the internet where the rapid growth of peer-to-peer (P2P) networking services (like BitTorrent, Morpheus and Kazaa) that allow for the illicit downloading of tracks, together with the 'burning' of CDs and the 'ripping' of music files, has been blamed by industry executives for the 23 per cent decline in global CD sales between 2000 and 2006 (Adegoke 2007). The argument that these unlicensed activities are costing the industry billions of dollars in lost sales and hurting artists through reduced royalty payments was put most forcefully in the early days of P2P by Michael Greene, CEO of the National Academy of Recording Arts and Sciences, in his opening address to the 2002 Grammy Awards.

> No question the most insidious virus in our midst is the illegal downloading of music on the Net. It goes by many names and its apologists offer a myriad of excuses. This illegal file-sharing and ripping of music files is pervasive, out of control and oh so criminal. Many of the nominees here tonight, especially the new, less established artists, are in danger of being marginalized out of our business. Ripping is stealing their livelihood one

digital file at a time, leaving their musical dreams hopelessly snared in this World Wide Web of theft and indifference. (Quoted in Freedman 2003b: 179)

The next section examines the extent to which policymakers have tended to share this definition of P2P as digital theft, and considers the main strategic policy responses to the issue of piracy. It assesses the extent to which there has been a similar 'government–industry partnership' over copyright as the one we saw develop in relation to digital switchover and finally analyses the motivations behind and consequences of the predominant political responses to P2P.

Confronting digital piracy

For government and corporate interests, copyright is the key foundation on which any profitable enterprise in the 'creative industries' is based. The music industry, for example, is built not on the creativity of musicians and producers but, as a UK government report puts it, on 'copyright and its success is dependent on the value attached to music by end consumers and intermediate business users' (DCMS 2000: 25). While the internet lowers distribution costs and enables new services, it also disrupts existing copyright structures through its disintermediating potential – its capacity to bypass traditional gatekeepers and open up new distributive possibilities. 'For the copyright industries,' argued Senate Judiciary Committee chairman Patrick Leahy at a 2001 hearing on the impact of the internet on copyright, 'to paraphrase a classic phrase: It is the best of times, it is the worst of times; it is the age of wisdom, it is the age of foolishness' (Leahy 2001). He was referring in particular to the growing phenomenon of unlicensed downloading that was threatening to degrade the value of music by refusing to abide by established copyright regimes and to undermine the viability of existing business models of recorded music. Concerned by the dangers posed by the internet and the diminishing respect for corporate ownership that much P2P activity symbolized, the major recording labels 'had to become more aggressive. They had to reconstitute some structure of property rights in cyberspace and some means – either technical or legal – of defining pirates and stopping them' (Spar 2001: 350).

The first task was to conceptualize unauthorized downloading, burning and ripping as theft by arguing that intellectual property needs to be treated in precisely the same way as any other form of property. 'Theft is theft,' argued Mitch Bainwol, CEO of the Recording Industry of America (RIAA) in the Supreme Court case against P2P service Grokster.

> Whether physical or intellectual, in a store or over the Internet, a business
> model predicated on theft can't stand. The Groksters of the world are not
> innovators. Far from it. They are parasites who hide behind technology as
> they steal from the artists that create entertainment; they jeopardize the
> incentives to create new artistic works for society to enjoy. (RIAA 2005)

A lobbyist for the Motion Picture Association of America (MPAA)
adds that:

> I think that it's become pretty *obvious* today that if you don't attach the
> same kind of values to that which you do with real property in terms
> of people getting reasonably compensated for their works, you're not
> going to have those works. It's fairly *straightforward* and *simple*. (Emphasis
> added)

Downloads and other forms of unlicensed internet activities, according to
this perspective, not only harm the traditional market for cultural goods
but penalize the individual artists who lose out on royalty payments and
thus have no incentive to produce new works.

The problem is that this argument fails to do justice to the complexities
of cultural production. As argued in chapter 1, informational and cultural
products are not 'pure private' but 'public goods' with characteristics of
non-rivalry and non-excludability that make any easy equation between
the two rather misleading. Indeed, copyright is a deliberate strategy to
impose market disciplines on cultural goods in order that they may be
exchanged for a price. Moreover, the evidential basis of copyright as the
most effective incentivizing device is far from persuasive. The cultural
economist Ruth Towse (2006: 17) argues that the 'asymmetrical' relationship between author and publisher means that 'the case for copyright as
an economic incentive encouraging the creation of works of art by *artists*
[as opposed to the control of their products by corporations] is not strong'
(2006: 16). Yale law professor Yochai Benkler (2006: 38) concurs that the
'efficiency of regulating information, knowledge, and cultural production
through strong copyright and patent is not only theoretically ambiguous,
it also lacks empirical basis'.

For the industry, the fact that the benefits attributed to strong copyright
do not necessarily stand up to empirical analysis is less important than its
capacity to mobilize common-sense concerns about the dangers to private
property relations posed by activities like downloading and burning. In that
sense, the discourse of recording and film industry executives – that the
individuals behind P2P sites are 'parasites', that any unlicensed downloading is 'theft' and that IP is 'pretty obviously' like any other form of property
– serves to legitimize market-oriented structures and marginalize other

motivations for cultural production. According to Christopher May (2006: 35), this denotes a process of 'reification' that 'obscures certain avenues of reform and trajectories of socio-economic development by naturalizing the contemporary legal settlement that frames specific political economic issues'. The granting of intellectual property rights (IPRs) is therefore presented as a perennial, inevitable 'fact' that accompanies and facilitates the dissemination of communication and culture rather than a historically specific practice that originated with the emergence of capitalism. May focuses in particular on the 'anxieties' that surround IP in its most recent incarnation: the 'fears regarding theft, piracy and profitability of productive relations grounded on knowledge or informational resources . . . [that] has prompted a vigorous political campaign to establish (and perpetuate) IPRs' (2006: 44).

This refers to a campaign launched by rights holders that has, thus far, been eagerly supported by governments keen to re-establish both moral order and proprietary controls in the online world. In her reaction to the Supreme Court's ruling against Grokster for knowingly facilitating unlicensed downloads, Democratic Senator Barbara Boxer claimed that P2P services were 'affecting children's morality and well-being by giving them access to pornography and encouraging the everyday theft of music', a view shared by Republican commerce committee chair Ted Stevens (Green 2005). Interestingly, this is similar to the language used by RIAA CEO Mitch Bainwol in his reaction to the same ruling: that the 'legal and moral clarity provided by the *Grokster* decision is a shot of adrenaline for the legitimate marketplace. Capital will now naturally flow to technology companies that respect property and reward the future of music' (Bainwol 2005: 5) – an assertion that, as we shall see later, has not been borne out.

A more significant objective for the USA and the UK governments, however, is not to provide moral leadership but to ensure the smooth application of IPRs into the digital age by providing a strong legislative framework *for* rights holders *against* 'pirates'. This has been particularly true for the USA where a raft of copyright laws has been proposed since the mid-1990s, some of them falling at the last hurdle but many of them still making it on to the statute books. Perhaps most influential was the 1998 Digital Millennium Copyright Act (DMCA), which adopted the 1996 World Intellectual Property Organization (WIPO) treaties on copyright (WCT) and performances and phonograms (WPPT) which leveraged existing property rights into the online world, institutionalized corporate control through a new 'making available' right that favoured producers over consumers, and criminalized the use of technologies specifically designed to 'unlock' encrypted material (see Haynes 2005: 37–8). The DMCA included 'anti-circumvention' measures that were a direct response to the ability of digital tools to bypass the digital rights management (DRM) technologies employed by rights holders to protect their material and increased the penalties for copyright infringement on the internet.

The DMCA was followed by many other attempts at legislation, including the successful passage of the 1998 Copyright Right Term Extension Act (that increased copyright protection from seventy-five to ninety-five years), the 2002 Consumer Broadband and Digital Television Act (that required digital hardware to include government-approved copy protection systems), the 2004 Piracy Deterrence and Education (PIRATE) Act (that sought five-year prison sentences for people who make 1000 or more songs available for download on P2P sites), and the 2004 Inducing Infringements of Copyright (Induce) Act (that allowed rights holders to sue any company that 'induces' individuals to make unauthorized copies of protected works). While the latter three stalled in Congress, George W. Bush did manage to sign off the aptly named Family Entertainment and Copyright Act in 2005 that criminalizes the use of camcorders in cinemas and allows for the imprisonment for up to three years of those who distribute a single copy of any piece of film, music or software that has yet to be released.

While the British government has not matched these levels of enthusiasm for anti-piracy legislation, it has hardly been sluggish in its attempts to foster a culture of respect for IPRs in the digital age. It introduced the 2002 Copyright, etc. and Trade Marks (Offences and Enforcements) Act that increased the maximum prison sentence for copyright offences and gave the police more powers to search for pirated material, and was one of the first European member states to implement the 2001 EC Directive on Copyright. It set up a forum on intellectual property in 2004 on the basis that 'IP is at the heart of the economic value of the creative economy and the Government is determined to do all it can to ensure that IP is properly protected' (Patent Office et al. 2005: 3) and even promised, in its 2005 manifesto, further to 'modernise copyright and other forms of protection of intellectual property rights', warning that '[p]iracy is a growing threat and we will work with industry to protect against it' (Labour Party 2005: 99). More recently, the Treasury commissioned the former editor of the *Financial Times*, Andrew Gowers, to review the existing intellectual property regime and to suggest changes where necessary. While firmly rejecting industry demands for an extension of the copyright term to coincide with that in the USA and suggesting a degree of 'flexibility' in balancing the interests of individuals with the rights of companies, the Gowers Report nevertheless echoes the government's vision in calling for 'stronger enforcement of IP rights to ensure practical protection is provided for rights owners and effective deterrents to infringements' in order more effectively 'to compete in the global, knowledge-based economy' (Gowers 2006: 119).

In reality, these attempts to 'modernize' IPRs to meet digital challenges are further examples of the privatization of the cultural field – what Haynes (2005: 39) refers to as evidence of a 'gradual erosion of the public domain and the commons – the cultural pool of information which we can all draw from and work upon to create and innovate new ideas and new creations' – and of the intimacy of the relationship between policymakers and rights holders. Whereas government had, at times, to cajole sections of the industry into the switchover project, rights holders have played an often decisive role in pressing for, and winning, legislative support from government. The DMCA, for example, was 'the culmination of three years of lobbying' by the content industries that was eventually 'enough to tip the balance in favor of passage' (Benkler 2006: 413, 414); the 2004 PIRATE Act was 'the result of intense lobbying from large copyright holders over the last six months' (McCullagh 2004); while the Family Entertainment and Copyright Act has been described by one journalist as 'the entertainment industry's latest attempt to thwart rampant piracy on fileswapping networks' (McCullagh 2005). A senior lobbyist for the MPAA comments, perhaps somewhat disingenuously, that 'yeah, we get tremendous support from lawmakers [on copyright legislation] because they realize the importance [of IP] to the United States economy and to trade overseas, so absolutely'. In some cases, lobbyists have actually written documents that lawmakers have used against P2P services, as when the *New York Times* revealed that a letter sent out by the California Attorney General warning companies not to adopt file-sharing software was discovered to have been drafted by the senior vice-president for legislative affairs at the MPAA (Schwartz 2004).

European legislation – to which the British government is liable – has been equally subject to sustained industry pressure. According to a lobbyist for a music industry trade association who worked on the EC's copyright directive, 'we changed the face of that directive. If you look at the original directive that came out of the Commission and then look at was officially adopted and passed into law, there is very little resemblance between the two proposals' in terms of the protection afforded to rights holders. The head of government relations for one of the major UK internet portals argues that the British government set up its forum on intellectual property because 'they were put under a lot of pressure from the rights holder lobby to do something', and insists that the EC's IPR directive, agreed in 2004,

> was more or less written by the rights holders through contacts they had at the Commission. When it first came out it was absolutely appalling. I mean there was almost a strict liability for intermediaries for *anything* that went through the networks. We spent a year trying to deflect that and dilute it which we managed. But the result is still a pretty poor directive as far as consumers and intermediaries are concerned.

To the extent that the digital switchover process has been overwhelmingly government-led, it appears then to be the case that the initiative to strengthen corporate control of IP has come, above all, from content industries that are desperate to leverage their influence into the online world. The government's role, while hardly passive, is less about devising the precise strategies for the exploitation of copyright (as it was in imposing a timetable for switchover) than it is about ensuring that there is an adequate legislative environment that will assist the IP industries to maximize their revenue. As the British government argues in relation to IPRs:

> It's not the role of Government to pick winners but Government can help to create the climate for success. Part of that is leading and facilitating the debate to help industry itself identify the solutions to many of the problems it faces. (Patent Office et al. 2005: 2)

Indeed, the music industry has responded vigorously to the USA and the UK governments' encouragement to identify relevant solutions to the problem of digital piracy. It has pursued a range of strategies designed simultaneously to marginalize and emulate P2P culture (Freedman 2003b), including:

- the further deployment of copy protection technologies;
- the attempt to hack into unlicensed music files (what it calls 'spoofing');
- the purchase of selected P2P ventures;
- the launching of high-profile marketing and educational campaigns to teach young people in particular about the value of copyright and the dangers of P2P;
- the litigation of dozens of P2P companies and tens of thousands of individuals for facilitating or engaging in unlicensed downloading activities

(the *Wall Street Journal* described the Supreme Court's 2005 ruling that Grokster had knowingly contributed to illegal file-sharing as 'the Fourth of July for property rights in the hightech economy' (Hazlett 2005: A14));

- the launching of new, *legal* download services, including Apple's iTunes Music Store with a market share in the USA of some 70 per cent. According to the IFPI (2006: 6), they now constitute a 'fast-growing US $1.1 billion market' with more than 360 such services in 2005 operating in over forty countries across the world.

In sharing rights holders' identification of both the 'problem' (piracy and a growing lack of respect for IPRs), as well as the preferred solution (tougher IP legislation that criminalizes piratical behaviour and lays the basis for the development of legal markets), the USA and the UK governments have made significant, albeit highly partisan, contributions to the continuing prosperity of the entertainment industries. To what extent, however, has their approach been successful?

The consequences of the 'war on piracy'

The most obvious concern for both government and rights holders is that, despite the marketing campaigns and the threats of litigation, illegal file-sharing shows no signs of disappearing. According to one report, illegal downloads increased by 24 per cent in 2006, while another report estimated that more than one billion tracks are illegally traded *each month* in contrast to the two billion songs sold by market leader iTunes since its launch in 2003 (Adegoke 2007). Shutting down P2P sites and publicizing large fines awarded against file-sharers may have a short-term impact on downloading, but other sites soon emerge just as individual downloaders begin to regain their confidence and continue to engage in illegal P2P activity. Indeed, the evidence is that industry executives are aware that this is a losing battle: 'We've never stamped out piracy', argues one lobbyist for the MPAA, 'and we're never going to do that but I think the whole goal is to manage it to a level where we can continue to exploit our businesses and to sell more motion pictures and home videos.' 'Litigation', claims RIAA general counsel Cary Sherman, 'is an essential ingredient of a strategy – we need these court rulings that basically set limits on what peer-to-peer networks can do – but it can never be a strategy in and of itself. We obviously need to have complementary strategies' (quoted in Garrity 2002: 86).

The problem for the industry is that these 'complementary strategies' do not seem to be working either. Despite substantial growth of legal download services like iTunes, Rhapsody and Napster in 2005, their growth rate actually fell in 2006 leading *USA Today* to assert that 'online music has failed to interest the vast majority of the world's music consumers' and to dub the legal download services as 'failures' (Maney 2007). While illegal file-sharing continued to expand in 2006, just 3.2 per cent of online households in the USA bought a track from market leader iTunes over the course of the year; worse still, it was discovered that less than 3 per cent of all the songs stored on a typical iPod were bought from iTunes, with the other 97 per cent most likely downloaded from P2P sites or ripped from CDs (Maney 2007). Apple CEO Steve Jobs revealed these figures in a controversial statement in February 2007 where he floated the possibility of junking the use of copy protection technology that has long been at the heart of the entertainment industry's proprietary model for the internet. Jobs (2007) asserted that 'DRMs haven't worked and may never work, to halt music piracy' and called on consumers to lobby the major music companies 'to sell their music DRM-free'. Such a call was virtually blasphemous in relation to an industry that has lobbied so hard for ever-tighter controls on its intellectual property and was clearly against the spirit of the USA and the UK governments' determination to prevent the circumvention of DRMs. Desperate, however, to secure a return on their investment and a leading role in an online environment, the major labels are now 'moving closer to releasing music on the Internet with no copying restrictions – a step they once vowed never to take' (Shannon 2007). Some are even prepared to seek alliances with networking sites like MySpace and YouTube whose attitude to IPRs has, until recently, been less rigorous than their own (as witnessed by Viacom's one-billion dollar lawsuit against YouTube in 2007). One P2P advocate notes the ambiguity of the industry's argument, where the 'record labels are saying on the one hand it's piracy so we've got to provide protection. But on the other hand, it's their audience and they want to figure out ways to monetize that audience' (quoted in Adegoke 2007).

We are faced, therefore, with a situation in which the British and American governments have, at the behest of entertainment rights holders, established a legal environment that favours corporate conceptions of IP, but one that has demonstrably failed to 'monetize' music fans and induce them away from P2P sites. Indeed, a lobbyist for one of the largest commercial web portals suggests that the rights holders need to investigate their own role in undermining the market for legal downloads. Unlicensed P2P sites, he argues:

> wouldn't be a tenth as successful as they are if people had access to music at a reasonable price. And they don't. I don't understand it. There is no manufacturing cost, there is no distribution cost, there is no marketing cost. There is nothing. There are 0s and 1s and that's it. We have all the mechanisms in place for an accounting of who's listened to what music, how long for, and how many times. We can do the whole remuneration model. But the [record] companies aren't interested because what it does is challenge their existing primacy and monopoly.

Furthermore, the current privatized conception of IPRs means that, far from incentivizing creativity, copyright rules that veer too heavily towards rights owners and away from intermediaries and individual users actually threaten to undermine new and innovative applications of technology, in terms of the creation of new cultural forms (see Schumacher 1995 for an analysis of how copyright limitations have impacted on the development of hip hop), as well as the emergence of new digital services and business models. The same lobbyist quoted above argues that the current approach to IPRs is simply illogical:

> It is quite right that people want their rights protected. My company has a number of rights and we want to protect those. But we don't want to do it to the detriment of everybody else and the detriment of the market. The only people who benefit are the pirates because the use of IP has been so restricted that even we are struggling to get our hands on good IP that we can exploit in positive ways because there are such terrible licensing restrictions, or the terms aren't fair or the rates aren't fair. All that is grist for the mill for pirates.

This applies just as much to the creative possibilities facilitated by peer-to-peer technology. The campaign by rights holders to associate P2P sites with piratical behaviour has captured the attention of policymakers and contributed to a legislative environment that is more likely to penalize, rather than reward, innovation. In response to this, a range of voices – consisting of everything from advocates of a 'Creative Commons' (see Lessig 2004) to consumer electronics manufacturers to libertarian capitalists – have sought to highlight the potential benefits of P2P technologies. For example, *The Economist* (2005), keen to see a free market emerging for new digital services, warns that the current climate 'could dramatically set back the adoption of the many beneficial uses of P2P, from legitimate content distribution – such as individuals sharing their family photos or their home-recorded music online – to grid-computing'. In this context, the puzzle is less about why rights holders have vilified P2P and called for stronger copyright regimes than why policymakers appear to have been so willing to accommodate their interests at the expense of other voices in the sector.

A lobbyist for the largest P2P companies acknowledges the difficult task ahead ('I've described it as starting out being nine foot deep in a hole and now it's only about two foot deep') and attributes this partly to the effectiveness of the lobbying tactics of the rights holders.

> Politics is a human process and, far be it for me to suggest that even powerful members of Congress, who have healthy egos in their own right, are somehow above getting a charge from standing next to Bono or Shania Twain or Don Henley or any number of significant stars who can be brought in to engage in direct lobbying by these [entertainment] industries.
>
> Policymakers deal with, to be charitable, somewhere between a zillion and a gazillion issues a week if not a day and it's a very difficult job. So simplistic messages like 'peer-to-peer is theft' and 'peer-to-peer is piracy' have a visceral appeal, if not an intellectually rigorous one . . . The challenge is to get them [policymakers] to slow down just long enough to understand that it's a much more nuanced situation.

This is a process whose success is likely to ebb and flow – influenced, no doubt, by countervailing pressure from the powerful telecommunications and consumer electronics lobbies. In the end, however, it is more than likely that the existing rights holders will seek an accommodation with the P2P entrepreneurs, as the former look for more channels through which to distribute their material. It is also highly probable that the current 'outlaw' status of many P2P services will be somewhat diluted as the internet follows a pattern, witnessed in previous disruptive information and communication technologies, where innovation and 'creative anarchy' is quickly and firmly superseded by the re-establishment of rules and the securing of property rights (Spar 2001: 18–22).

Policymakers in the UK and the USA have already played a part in this 'structuring' (or taming) of a new technology through their imposition of corporate property rights as the key incentivizing principle for creative production. Both British and American governments have largely echoed the arguments of the major entertainment producers and distributors – that cultural goods need to be treated as private property and that private property is sacrosanct – and have sought to provide a legislative framework that, in turn, legitimizes these claims. However, in leaving the day-to-day implementation of copyright regimes to industry trade associations and assorted multinational media companies, assisted at times by the courts, 'the law has in effect delegated a lawmaking function to copyright owners' (Claude 2002: 250). The relentless lawsuits against file-sharers, the insistence on copy protection technologies, the public education campaigns urging respect for copyright and the very close contact with lawmakers themselves suggest that copyright holders have acted as leading policy actors in this area, with government effectively subcontracting the operation of intellectual property rights to the private sector. This is a kind of private 'policy laundering' that reveals, as Christopher May argues (2006: 54), 'the reified structures of governance for what they are: a system for benefiting certain segments of capital, constituted through *political bargaining*'.

Conclusion

Recent British and American governments have prioritized the deployment of digital technologies and the development of a digital infrastructure as a central part of their vision of an 'information society'. Both have assumed an activist position in relation to switching off analogue television and have employed a limited, economistic vocabulary about the benefits of digital television that has, thus far, failed to enthuse their populations about the prospect of switchover. Both governments have also sought to develop legislative environments that are aimed at the maximum exploitation of intellectual property rights in the digital age and have largely adopted the arguments of major rights holders in justifying harsher sanctions on violations of copyright. The USA has embarked on a particularly vigorous campaign to equate unlicensed digital downloads on P2P networks with acts of piracy and criminality – a campaign that has yielded little success up to this point in either warning the public away from file-sharing activities or producing a viable legal download industry. The case studies also demonstrate a deterministic approach to technological development on the part of government that paints market-led digital development as both desirable and inevitable. In relation to digital switchover and peer-to-peer services, this is a perspective that threatens to close off alternative models of technological development and media governance by naturalizing commercial orientations and privatized property rights as the most effective and dynamic principles of contemporary innovation.

9

Britain and America in the World

Insofar as the principal actors in this book are the British and American states, it is assumed that national frames of reference remain relevant in a world increasingly defined by the interdependence and interconnectedness of its economic and social relations. Despite theories about the 'end' (Ohmae 1995), 'retreat' (Strange 1996) and 'erosion' (Cerny 1995) of the nation-state, as its 'authority, legitimacy, policymaking capacity, and policy-implementing effectiveness' (1995: 625) is undermined by globalization developments, this book focuses on the enduring ability of the nation-state to shape major areas of contemporary life. Nations continue to be the key locations of military and economic power and, even in 'the case of the media, the development of new technologies, notably satellite television, does not abolish national boundaries, since states, businesses and audiences remain firmly rooted in terrestrial realities' (Sparks forthcoming). Our starting point, just as it is for Morris and Waisbord (2001: x), is that 'the state still matters as an analytic category' and as a key agent of social power.

This is not to suggest, however, that nothing has changed in the last 200 years. A huge increase in the mobility of capital, people and information is echoed in the media field by the emergence of transnational media corporations, increasing volumes of media exports, new centres of media production and shifting patterns of the international circulation of media artefacts (Herman and McChesney 1997; Sparks forthcoming). We have also seen, as was noted in chapter 4, the growing influence of supranational institutions of media governance with the rise of organizations like the World Trade Organization (WTO), World Intellectual Property Organization (WIPO) and the World Summit on the Information Society (WSIS). According to a recent study, the whole environment of media policymaking is changing under the influence of global pressures: 'What was still, even a short while ago, a field essentially defined by national legislative and regulatory frameworks and a minimum of international supervision, is now subject to a more complex ecology of interdependent structures'

(Raboy 2002: 6) that includes global organizations, multilateral clubs, regional groupings, national states, a transnational private sector and global civil society. While the nation-state remains as the central repository of power, it is therefore increasingly subject to external – notably supranational – pressures.

This chapter addresses two key media policy responses to globalization developments. First, it examines the attitudes of and roles played by recent US (and, to a lesser extent, UK) administrations in attempts to construct a multilateral trade framework for the audio-visual industries through the WTO's General Agreement on Trade in Services (GATS) process. It also considers US and UK involvement in a significant response to this process: the 2005 UNESCO Convention on Cultural Diversity (CCD). Second, it assesses contrasting motivations behind strategies to increase audio-visual exports to meet the challenge of global competition and, in the British case in particular, evaluates the consequences of an export-led policy on the domestic media environment.

'A world that trades in freedom'

One of George W. Bush's favourite visions (at least measured by the number of times he refers to it in speeches celebrating free-trade agreements) is of a 'world that trades in freedom'. He uses it to justify his pursuit of trade liberalization where open markets and the free movement of capital are, in his opinion, good not only for business but for the human spirit. Drawing on Bush's words, the US trade representative Robert Zoellick argues that this is a 'vision of a world in which free trade opens minds as it opens markets, encouraging democracy and greater tolerance' (USTR, 2004: 8). From the perspective of free-trade advocates, it is quite logical then that television programmes, movies and music – despite their cultural as well as economic significance – should increasingly feature in trade talks that are designed to bring about a less regulated trading environment and a more 'prosperous' way of life.

Indeed, the USA has long pursued the objective of the 'free flow of information' as part of a wider policy of free trade. Herbert Schiller, the American scholar who first identified the media's involvement in a 'powerful industrial-electronics complex working to extend the American socioeconomic system spatially and ideologically' (1971: 14), attributes this approach to America's hegemonic position following the Second World War. Schiller cites a key speech by President Truman in 1947, where he argued that securing 'freedom of enterprise', above even freedom of speech, was the main policy goal and an historic opportunity for the USA to be the world's major economic power. For Schiller:

> Freedom of speech, however, interpreted to signify the unrestrained opportunity for the dissemination of messages by the American mass media in the world arena, has developed in the years since Truman spoke as an equally significant support in the American imperial arch. (1971: 6)

Although the post-war trade framework, the General Agreement on Tariffs and Trades (GATT), did apply to some aspects of culture (GATT Article IV, for example, acknowledged the legitimacy of domestic screen quotas), it would be some years before the USA's more robust definition of the 'free flow of ideas' was formally or systematically applied to world trade talks concerning the media industries. When it was applied, during the Uruguay round of GATT negotiations in December 1993, it nearly caused the entire process to collapse. Confronted by heavy US pressure to give up its right to use domestic quotas, the French government refused and insisted on its right to maintain subsidies to protect its audio-visual industries. In the end, a compromise was reached between the desire of the USA to see full liberalization of the sector and the wish expressed by France, Canada and some other EU states to see the sector exempted from free-trade rules. Member states were allowed to make no commitments regarding liberalization of their audio-visual industries so that, in reality, the sector was formally excluded from the disciplines of the new world trade agreement.

Although this 'cultural exemption' has not prevented sections of the copyright industries from being affected by trade rules (see Grant and Wood 2004; Miller et al. 2005: 88), US trade officials decided that there would be no such compromise in any future negotiations. A confidential document circulating in government circles in early 1995 reveals the existence of an American 'Global Audiovisual Strategy', a plan designed to undermine the prospects of any future carve-out of the cultural sector from trade talks. The document suggested that negotiators consult closely with US entertainment industry trade associations like the MPAA and RIAA, and embark on a substantial process of lobbying foreign interests in order to:

- Exert a favourable influence on 'new markets' [named as China, Russia, Vietnam, South Africa] to ensure that they develop their audiovisual and intellectual property regimes in accordance with market-oriented principles;
- Discreetly enlist the support of domestic constituents adversely affected by programming restrictions;

- Explain to government officials in ministries of foreign affairs, economics, trade, telecommunications and private sector representatives why existing rules hinder the development of an advanced telecommunications network and a healthy audiovisual sector;
- Ensure that existing cultural restrictions are not included in future FTA [Free Trade Agreement] negotiations. (Quoted in Williams 2004)

The General Agreement on Trade in Services (GATS)

One of the central ways in which the USA has sought to stimulate the 'free flow of information' in recent years has been through multilateral negotiations concerning the General Agreement on Trade in Services (GATS), administered under the auspices of the WTO. The objective of the GATS is to ensure that markets for services, which now account for the majority of world trade, are progressively liberalized and privatized. Trade disciplines that have traditionally been applied to goods – measures that made it harder to justify domestic subsidies and tariffs – are now to be applied to industries, including those of water, health, education and audio-visual media. While member states have the right to opt in or out of agreements affecting particular sectors, the general understanding is that states will facilitate full market access and will not discriminate against foreign suppliers of services – very much in the spirit of current WTO agreements on 'mainstream' commodities like cars, steel and bananas. The point of the GATS, therefore, is to incorporate further 'awkward' service sectors into the logic of free trade and capital accumulation.

The negotiations were launched on the basis of a background note on audio-visual services produced by the WTO secretariat in June 1998 (WTO 1998). It is largely a descriptive document, containing quantitative statistics on the scale of the sector and details of state support mechanisms for audio-visual industries. On the question of regulation, however, it is more provocative. While acknowledging the cultural and political importance of the audio-visual industries and the consequential need for regulation and support, it leans very heavily on arguments proposed by the pro-liberalization Organisation for Economic Co-Operation and Development (OECD) that ownership restrictions are impediments to business expansion and corporate profitability, rather than instruments that are often necessary to prevent concentration and conglomeration and extend cultural diversity. While the background paper does not take an explicit position on regulation, both the general obligation in the GATS to minimize regulation and the specific assumption that existing regulatory regimes in the audio-visual sector impede technological development seem to reinforce the notion that negotiations on audio-visual issues would focus on deregulation as much as liberalization.

The USA was one of only three countries to respond to the WTO secretariat's paper with a submission that called for other countries to make firm liberalizing commitments in the sphere of audio-visual industries. The document opens by condemning an 'all or nothing' approach to audio-visual negotiations in which '[s]ome argue as if the only available options were to exclude culture from the WTO or to liberalize completely' (WTO 2000: 2) – a particularly ironic statement given that the USA played a major part in establishing an 'all or nothing' position in the Uruguay round with its clumsy and ultimately unsuccessful attempt to secure full liberalization of the audio-visual sector. The US position had now changed: it recognized the 'special cultural characteristics' of audiovisual media, acknowledged the validity of subsidies in promoting cultural diversity and simply requested more transparent rules for such subsidies. But the paper went on to argue that the best way to protect cultural diversity was precisely through further liberalization: 'in today's digital environment, it is quite possible to enhance one's cultural identity and to make trade in audiovisual service more transparent, predictable, and open. Indeed . . . the two objectives may reinforce each other' (2000: 3). The preservation of cultural diversity was directly connected, in the eyes of US negotiators, to the extent to which trade barriers were dissolved and free-trade flows accelerated.

Negotiations formally started in January 2000 with a timetable agreed at the Doha ministerial meeting in November 2001. Member states would make initial requests for commitments on market access by 30 June 2002 with initial offers, i.e. the response to the requests, tabled by the end of March 2003. Months of hard bargaining and trade-offs would follow, with the talks, it was hoped, concluded by January 2005. In reality, progress in the audio-visual sphere was excruciatingly slow. Only two countries out of the 147 WTO member states made preliminary commitments in all subcategories of the audio-visual sector: the USA and the Central African Republic. While few requests were made in the area of audio-visual industries, the USA was once again the exception. Indeed, despite the European Union's (EU) stated desire *not* to negotiate on issues concerning culture, American negotiators are reported to have requested of the EU 'binding commitments to liberalization . . . in areas such as motion picture and home video entertainment, production and distribution services, radio and television production services and sound recording services' (WDM 2003:

6). When the European trade commissioner Pascal Lamy refused to budge on making no commitments in the audio-visual sector, the assistant US trade representative replied that another audio-visual exemption for the EU was 'not something that we could agree to' (quoted in 2003: 6). Responses to requests were also very thin on the ground, with the USA one of only a handful of states to make any offers at all in the audio-visual sector, although its offer was limited to concessions on foreign ownership of cable television networks and satellite television companies (USTR 2003).

British involvement in these debates was constrained by its membership of the EU and its representation at the talks by a common European position. Conversations with UK trade officials at the time, however, reveal a strong pro-liberalization perspective tempered only by the obligation to reach a consensus with other EU states:

> It's pretty tough to get a liberalizing negotiating position developed in Brussels [home of the European Community] largely because of the opposition of the French and other like-minded countries who want to have a complete carve-out because they want to have absolute discretion to decide how to protect cultural diversity through any form of domestic regulation.

Negotiators were happy to align themselves with 'offensive', i.e. export-led, interests but complained that the prevalence of 'defensive' positions, together with the lack of involvement of British-based commercial interests, were undermining the possibility of further liberalization:

> We shouldn't be denying ourselves the possibility of export success just because this is a difficult sector. If there is a clear offensive interest for the UK that people can set out for us, we'll go out there and flog it to death. *That's basically what we're here for.* (Emphasis added)

Given this description of the official bargaining position as one that was representing specifically commercial interests, it is hardly surprising that British negotiators were very frustrated both by the domination of 'defensive' voices and the slow progress of the talks: 'We want to get this done as soon as we can because if it's a good thing to have then we want the benefits as quick as we can.'

It soon became clear that the January 2005 deadline would not be met and that for a variety of reasons (outlined by Freedman 2003c), notably the gap between the 'offensive interests' of the USA and the 'defensive' interests of most other WTO members, detailed negotiations on audio-visual liberalization were not going to come to fruition. In February 2006, more than six years after the talks had started, Alejandro Jara, the WTO's Deputy

Director-General, admitted that there had been 'almost no multilateral negotiations on the audiovisual sector between the WTO member countries' (BRCD 2006). One lobbyist at the MPAA agreed that:

> the negotiating partners have all staked out their turf and a lot of the positions cannot be reconciled: [in particular] the French position with the American position. So the multilateral form as a place to resolve market access issues [on audio-visual] is not really going any place at all.

Indeed, the wider GATS process stumbled in the face of determined opposition by developing countries to what they saw as proposals that would benefit the richest countries, and finally collapsed in July 2006 with the suspension by the WTO of all multilateral trade negotiations.

The American response to the breakdown of talks was to pursue trade agreements in bilateral, rather than multilateral, contexts. US trade representative Robert Zoellick had warned back in 2003 that if the WTO continued to be a 'forum for the politics of protest' then the US would have to look elsewhere: 'As WTO members ponder the future, the US will not wait: we will move towards free trade with can-do countries' (Zoellick 2003). The consequence of this threat has since become clear. By July 2006, the USA had concluded (or was in the process of concluding) bilateral free-trade agreements (FTAs) with twenty-nine countries, including Australia, Chile, Morocco and Singapore, on the basis that 'bilaterals tend to be more favourable to stronger negotiating parties than multilaterals, where exceptions and riders are less acceptable in final agreements' (Morgan 2006).

Crucially, these new FTAs now include liberalizing clauses that refer specifically to audio-visual industries. The US/Australia FTA, for example, allows the latter to maintain existing quotas for terrestrial television, pay-TV and commercial radio but prevents it from raising them. Australia will no longer have the ability to introduce screen quotas and its scope to determine the level of local content in new media services is even more limited. According to the executive director of the Australian film and television producers' association: 'US interests are now allowed to sit at our table before an Australian government can implement any increase in drama content regulations on Pay TV. We have to argue the merits of our case up against the interests of the US industry' (quoted in CCD 2004). It appears that the USA is willing to sanction the survival of existing subsidies and quotas (as long as they are not increased) but is ensuring that new media markets – particularly in relation to intellectual property and digital infrastructures – are kept free of such 'barriers'. According to one experienced commentator on trade policy, the USA has changed its approach to audio-visual negotiations in a shift that explains its *apparent* softening towards subsidies and quotas:

> The new strategy of the United States in the cultural sector rests quite clearly on the view that while measures that do not confirm to national treatment, most-favored-nation treatment and free market access can be tolerated as they presently exist in the traditional audiovisual sector because they are bound one way or another to disappear with time, no such toler- ance must be accepted for digitally delivered content which are at the hearth of the new communication economy and should therefore remain free of cultural protectionism. (Bernier 2004: 19–20)

The USA is, therefore, eagerly negotiating FTAs which limit co-signatories' ability to control existing media structures and completely deprive them of the ability independently to shape their audio-visual systems as they emerge in a digital age. These agreements are a crucial step towards the USA's ultimate objective in audio-visual trade negotiations: the end of the 'cultural exemption' and the imposition of free-market disciplines on key sectors of the cultural industries.

The UNESCO Convention on Cultural Diversity

The major international response to what was perceived by many coun- tries – apart from the USA and the UK – as the increasing commodification of culture facilitated through trade agreements was the attempt, under the auspices of UNESCO, to draw up an international convention on cultural diversity (CCD). This was designed to be a legal instrument that would act as a 'counterbalance' (Graber 2006) to the WTO and focus on issues of *cultural* rights that were marginalized in trade discussions. Negotiations started in September 2004 were completed in October 2005 and the CCD was finally ratified in March 2007. The convention is based on eight 'guiding principles' (including respect for sovereignty, solidarity, human rights and sustainable development) and allows each signatory to 'adopt measures aimed at protecting and promoting the diversity of cultural expressions within its territory' (UNESCO 2005: 6), including the use of subsidies, regulation and quotas.

US negotiators were suspicious of the CCD from the beginning, arguing that it represented a protectionist alternative to the values of free trade. They sought to shift the focus of debate away from the right to protect cultural diversity towards an emphasis on the means by which cultural expressions can be distributed: the market. 'The current draft conven- tion', claimed the State Department, 'would justify government-imposed restrictions on an individual's access to information as well as on the circulation and trade of some goods and services' (Department of State 2005: 4). While promising to support a convention that facilitated cultural diversity, negotiators insisted that it had to maximize the 'individual's freedom to access the culture of his or her own choice' (2005: 4). In other words, it was for consumers – and not foreign governments – to decide what material should be made available.

The key debate during the negotiations concerned the relationship of the CCD to 'other instruments', most obviously the GATS. Two options were proposed. Option A allowed signatories the ability to derogate from another agreement 'where the exercise of those rights and obligations would cause serious damage or threat to the diversity of cultural expressions'; Option B simply stated that 'nothing in this Convention shall affect the rights and obligations of the States Parties under any other existing international instruments' (UNESCO 2004: 10). Option A invited the wrath not just of American negotiators but of major entertainment industry groups who lobbied vociferously for the latter option to be accepted. According to lobbyists at the RIAA:

> What we raised at the UNESCO convention was to take out anything that interfered with WTO and GATS disciplines. In other words, the overall free movement in international free trade should not be hindered by cultural diversity . . . We are saying that it is good as a promotional instrument, but not if it interferes with the free trade spirit of the WTO.

Faced with substantial pressure from the USA (and an implicit threat to withdraw from the negotiations), it was a version of the latter formulation that was eventually incorporated into the final agreement, undermining the ability of the Convention to offer a meaningful counterweight to marketized forms of cultural exchange. While acknowledging that perhaps such a compromise was unavoidable in the context of consensus-led international bargaining, one informed commentator agrees that the final wording 'does not provide the clarity necessary to prevent further erosion of cultural sovereignty, let alone begin the difficult process of rolling back the extensive influence of the WTO and other bilateral and multilateral agreements' (Neil 2006: 260).

Despite the cautious language of the Treaty and its apparent inability to override trade agreements, the USA still continued to lead opposition to the Convention. In three procedural votes that preceded the final vote, the USA was defeated by 54 to 1, 53 to 1 and 158 to 1, leading to Secretary of State Condoleezza Rice writing to all member states, urging them to postpone any decision on the draft (Riding 2005: 3). Finally, when the CCD was put to delegates, 148 voted in favour with only the USA and Israel voting against. With even the *New York Times* acknowledging the 'relative weakness of the final draft' (2005: 3), US negotiators nevertheless sought to paint the Convention as a full-frontal assault on principles of individual choice and free trade. According to the American ambassador to UNESCO:

> This Convention as now drafted could be used by states to justify policies that could be used or abused to control the cultural lives of their citizens – policies that a state might use to control what its citizens can see; what they can read; what they can listen to and what they can do. We believe – in keeping with existing conventions – that the world must affirm the right of all people to make these decisions for themselves. (Oliver 2005)

Britain, part of a European delegation that was overwhelmingly supportive of the Convention, did not join the USA in her glorious isolation, but there is evidence to suggest that the British government was not desperately keen on the whole process. An early briefing paper from the DCMS (2004) is highly critical: it fails to make an argument for the need to take measures to protect diversity and instead complains that the 'scope of the convention seems to be extremely wide and the drafting of the text is imprecise', and insists that there would be 'major problems with implementing this convention into UK law in its current form'. It also notes the potential conflict with other existing international agreements and calls for Option B – the USA's favoured choice – to be implemented in order to respect the inviolability of WTO rules. Four months before the final vote, the UK was still resistant to the Convention but 'at the risk of being the only one of 24 European Community states not to vote in favour, and this during the year of the UK Presidency [of the European Union], the government signed up' (Aylett 2005: 2) – hardly a ringing endorsement of the government's commitment to cultural diversity. In its attitude towards both the CCD and the GATS, therefore, the British government has demonstrated more sympathy with the free-trade instincts of the USA than with the 'defensive' positions of its European partners with whom it was forced to reach a consensus.

The politics of television exports

The desire by the USA and the UK to seek fewer barriers to the international circulation of their cultural artefacts is guided primarily by economic motives and the recognition that the international activities of their copyright industries make an increasingly important contribution to GDP: some $110 billion to the USA (Siwek 2006: 5) and £11.6 billion to the UK (Nesta 2006: 2). Creative exports, however, also have significant ideological benefits that have helped both countries to increase their cultural and economic influence across the globe and, in the case of the UK in particular, to rebrand itself in order to meet the challenges posed by globalization.

Building up US exports

The USA has long viewed the international flow of American popular culture as a key strategic resource for exporting its values of freedom and democracy. It played a central role during the Cold War, where 'Western leaders relied on the apparently corrupting power of American popular culture to help win the hearts and minds of people inside the Communist bloc' (Crothers 2007: 3), and generally sought to legitimize the materialist and consumerist principles of American capitalism. This was precisely the damaging imperialist project that Herbert Schiller denounced in *Mass Communications and American Empire* as 'the global American electronic invasion' (1971: 79–92). However, since 2001 and George W. Bush's launching of a 'war on terror', the international performance of US media has taken on a new significance as policymakers urgently devise new ways of marketing American democracy. As a taskforce set up after 9/11 by the Council on Foreign Relations acknowledged:

> America has a serious image problem. World opinion of the United States has dangerously deteriorated. Around the world, from Western Europe to the Far East, many see the United States as arrogant, hypocritical, self-absorbed, self-indulgent and contemptuous of others. American culture, language and industry dominate the world stage in a way that many find discomfiting. (2003: 2)

This would suggest that a trade-led strategy to increase Hollywood exports might only exacerbate America's PR problem, but, as we have seen, the mere consideration of 'defensive' approaches to cultural trade would run up against the US government's firm commitment to trade liberalization. The taskforce's preferred solution, then, was to improve the communication, if not the direction, of American foreign policy by abandoning its 'hit and run style' (2003: 7) of top-down communication and implementing a more culturally sensitive, 'listening' (2003: 14) approach that would engage more fruitfully with foreign publics.

This call for the enhanced use of 'public diplomacy' and 'soft power' (Nye 2004) was echoed by the high-profile 9/11 Commission the following year. The Commission argued that the USA needed to engage in a 'struggle of ideas' (National Commission on Terrorist Attacks 2004: 375), and urged that more resources be made available for developing satellite broadcast initiatives that would 'defend our ideas abroad vigorously' (2004: 377). This was the idea behind the creation of US-backed broadcast initiatives such as Radio Sawa and Television Alhurra that were set up in 2002 and 2004 respectively to counter the hostile coverage of US policy in the Middle East. However, these ventures – seen by many Arabs as clear examples of propaganda and as extensions of US 'hard power' (see el-Nawawy 2006) – are even less likely to improve America's standing in the world than the traditional strategy of simply exporting huge volumes of US-originated film, television and music.

Building up UK exports

The UK has pursued a rather different approach to cultural exports that reflects a broader debate about (and perhaps lack of confidence in) Britain's role in the world in a globalized era. Tony Blair was one of the first world leaders to note the challenges posed by globalization to the continuing viability of the nation-state. Globalization, he argued, 'is changing the nature of the nation-state as power becomes more diffuse and borders become more porous. Technological change is reducing the power and capacity of government to control its domestic economy free from external influence' (Blair 1996: 204). Blair's solution, however, was to embrace globalization as a market-led consumer revolution and to position Britain as a country ideally placed to contribute to it, in particular through the dynamism and strength of its creative industries. This was the belief that underpinned Blair's 'Cool Britannia' project, the initiative in the first few years of his government to rebrand the UK as a 'cultural powerhouse whose television programmes, music, films, fashion and software programmes would triumphantly saturate world markets and make a significant impact on the UK's trade balance' (Freedman 2003a: 171). 'Cool Britannia' depended on a notion, actively fostered by New Labour ministers, that the British are somehow uniquely entrepreneurial and creative and therefore in the perfect position to profit from globalization.

> Change is in the blood and bones of the British – we are by our nature and tradition innovators, adventurers, pioneers . . . Britain today is an exciting, inspiring place to be. And it can be much more . . . If we face the challenge

of a world with its finger on the fast forward button; where every part of the picture of our life is changing. (Blair 1997b)

One of Blair's first actions was to launch a Creative Industries Taskforce in 1997 to examine ways of maximizing the export value of the creative sector. As part of this strategy, the government commissioned a piece of research to quantify the UK's share of the international television market and to consider if there was room for improvement. The report, *Building a Global Audience* (Graham 1999), was prepared by David Graham, a former member of the free-market think tank, the Institute of Economic Affairs, and backed by the sales arms of some of the UK's leading broadcasters such as Carlton, Pearson, Granada and the BBC. The survey appeared in April 1999 and made for some grim reading. Its first finding was that 'Britain is not perceived by people in other countries to produce "the best television in the world"' (1999: 8). It then identified a substantial trade deficit in television of some £272 million in 1997 when there had been a small trade surplus in 1989 (1999: 14). Even though sales had increased throughout the decade, this was more than offset by mainly American imports that were bought in to fill increased transmission times and new channels. Commercialization and expansion appeared to have made British television more, not less, dependent on US programmes. The problem was not to do with the poor performance of UK distributors but was more structural: that there were not enough programmes to sell with an international appeal. This was partly because while UK programmes 'are praised by international executives for their high production values, quirky sense of humour, and high standards of acting . . . our drama is too dark; too slow; unattractive; too gritty or socio-political' (1999: 24). The CEO of German channel RTL argued that there was 'too much darkness and a slow pace. We want to have fun watching television, we don't want to get depressed' (quoted in *Television* 1999: 15).

The report also found that the length of programmes and numbers of episodes in series that were designed for the UK market were often inappropriate for the international market and that the more popular genres abroad, such as TV movies and the mini-series, were not ones produced in any quantity in the UK. The logic for the authors of the report was that an emphasis on gritty dramas relevant to a UK audience should be replaced by output that is more internationally packageable: *Benny Hill*, *Mr. Bean*, *Teletubbies* and *Thomas the Tank Engine* were all mentioned as successful exports (Graham 1999: 18–19).

The recommendations of the report focused on one central issue: that 'Government and regulators should consider whether domestic regulation hinders export performance' (1999: 11). The report heartily suggested that any rights agreements with creative staff that might hinder the sale of programmes abroad should be renegotiated and that domestic scheduling patterns might be changed to suit international markets. The report was littered with hints that 'excessive regulation can leave catalogues of material that are incompatible with overseas audiences' (1999.: 32), and concluded that 'it is important to recognise that domestic regulation and export performance are in tension, if not in conflict . . . Another of our recommendations is that the Government and regulators consider this tension carefully. It may be constraining the UK's export potential' (1999: 40).

This invitation to consider whether domestic regulation was undermining international sales was eagerly received by a government engaged in its own discussions about whether to liberalize broadcasting regulation (see chapter 5). Indeed, according to Simon Blanchard (2006: 42), this was precisely the point of the exercise: 'What was required was the construction of an apparent [exports] "failure" which could serve as the rationale for a more fundamental restructuring of the industry towards exports' and, therefore, towards a more commercial orientation for broadcasting. Culture Secretary Chris Smith immediately set up a creative industries taskforce panel to take forward the recommendations made in *Building a Global Audience*. The panel consisted of leading representatives from the commercial broadcasting and independent production sectors as well as the commercial television regulator, the Independent Television Commission (ITC), and the industry trade body, the British Television Distributors' Association (BTDA). After only four months of discussion, the taskforce produced its own report in November 1999, *UK Television Exports Inquiry* (DCMS 1999a) that, much to the disappointment of the government, firmly rejected the line of thinking of the previous report and argued that there was no export 'problem'. Its key findings were that 'the UK is performing well in television exports' and that '[w]e are firmly in the number two position, as we would expect and hope' (1999a: 40). Britain's 9 per cent of global television exports was well below the USA's 68 per cent but was nevertheless three times as much as its nearest rivals, France and Australia (1999a: 39).

The report demonstrated that Britain's strongest export area lay in factual programming, one of the smallest export genres, while Britain was relatively weak in the rapidly growing export areas of children's programming and light entertainment. Not surprisingly, given that the panel was mainly composed of established figures in British terrestrial television production and regulation, it rejected the idea that domestic rules should be loosened to allow for increased sales abroad.

> Developing the international business is important for the industry, but serving the UK audience is essential. Dramatic modification to the style of UK programming is not, therefore, a realistic aim. It is not just the UK that prefers its own programmes – this is true across all territories. Local productions consistently attract the highest ratings. (1999a: 47)

Indeed, according to panel member Sarah Thane of the ITC, the whole discussion of regulation as an impediment to exports 'was the dog that didn't bark. It basically became very clear to people on the taskforce that it was a non-issue' (personal communication, 2000). For the panel, the strength of British television was precisely its orientation on domestic audiences and domestic issues, and it would simply not be possible to develop formats with a global appeal without undermining the domestic production base. For Thane, the whole government initiative of increasing exports resembled the worst elements of the 'Cool Britannia' strategy of rebranding the UK as a dynamic, cutting-edge creative economy more than an informed analysis of the complex nature of international broadcasting.

> One of the things I was curious about when I first joined [the taskforce] was whether he [Chris Smith] wanted an outcome of this to be more exports to export 'Britishness' abroad or more exports to help our trade balance. I think he probably wanted a bit of both . . . I don't want to sound pejorative about people who are highly intelligent . . . But what I got a sense of was that there was a lot of activity going on in all sorts of government, particularly the DTI and the Treasury, showing Britain as a very entrepreneurial, forward-looking sort of place and that the DCMS wanted a slice of that. I take my hat off to Chris Smith and others for engendering a sense of the economic power and importance of the creative industries . . . But I'm saying that all he needed to do was just test whether our television industry was batting as effectively as it could do. (Personal communication 2000)

The reluctance of the panel to endorse full-blooded regulatory change in the name of international sales failed to diminish the government's enthusiasm for increasing television exports. While noting the point about not disrupting the service to UK viewers, Chris Smith nevertheless argued that 'it is clear that the UK could do still better in exporting programmes and programme formats . . . quality is key to export success. Programmes made for UK audiences will sell abroad if they are good enough' (DCMS 1999b). Despite the resistance of the taskforce panel to precisely this line of argument, the government has not given up on its determination to see

Table 9.1 *International Television Transactions 1999–2005 (£million)*

	1999	2000	2001	2002	2003	2004	2005
Exports	440	551	673	684	677	664	740
Deficit	403	216	334	553	465	436	332

Source: ONS 2006

the UK share of the international television market grow and has continued to commission reports, publish statistics and launch initiatives to realize this objective.

To what extent has the government been successful in either increasing television exports or reversing the trade deficit in television? The most recently published figures suggest a mixed picture (table 9.1): that while exports have grown substantially (albeit with two consecutive years of decline), the deficit has continued to rise with only better sales in 2005 making the picture less bleak. The most recent government-commissioned report on British television's overseas performance, *Rights of Passage*, shows that the value of *finished* programme exports has actually fallen in real terms since 1998, a decline of some 2.5 per cent a year (TRP 2005: 4). The reason for this is that 'the international perception and characterisation of UK programming has not changed greatly since the publication of *Building a Global Audience*' [in 1999] (2005: 5), with many buyers still expressing their concern about the suitability of UK drama series for international audiences.

The falling value of completed programmes has been compensated for by the huge growth in merchandising (36 per cent), DVD and video sales (34.9 per cent), but most of all by the 41.5 per cent increase in format sales where, according to a proud Douglas Alexander, Minister for Trade and Investment, 'the UK has emerged as the world leader in TV format exports' (quoted in 2005: 1). The main reason for this is the unprecedented success of British formats like *Who Wants To Be a Millionaire, Survivor, Changing Rooms, The Weakest Link* and *Pop Idol*. The *Millionaire* format, for example, has been sold to over 100 countries, leading Paul Smith, the managing director of production company Celador, to employ a colonial analogy to describe the international success of the programme: 'It's a bit like the old days of the British empire. We've got a map of the world in the office colored in pink where we've placed the show. Most of the world is pink' (quoted in Carter 2000). Herbert Schiller and other exponents of the idea of 'cultural imperialism' could not have put it better.

At one level, the success of British formats is confirmation of Tony Blair's belief in the importance of creativity and his commitment to the export value of the copyright industries. This is the part of the television industry that the government likes to celebrate as particularly dynamic and innovative. For example, *Rights of Passage* notes that:

> a new entrepreneurial production and distribution culture has emerged alongside the traditional culture at an accelerating rate. The new culture is characterised by the growth of a cluster of outward-looking, more risk-positive companies with business models geared to production for the world market and to the maximisation of the global value of TV-driven intellectual property rights. (TRP 2005: 6)

This is the perfect neo-liberal vision of a television system dominated not by regulators, but by zealous entrepreneurs committed to seizing market opportunities and serving customers on a purely commercial basis.

At another level, however, formats – as the purest expression of a more commercial orientation – represent a highly problematic direction for the British television industry as the current enthusiasm for UK-originated formats relates mainly to light entertainment concepts that are universal and easily exportable, but not an area of programming in which Britain has traditionally been strong. A simple generic idea – put a group of people together on a desert island or in a house and see who survives – is more likely to be sold abroad and locally translated than quality drama or documentary programmes, the historic bedrock of British exports. If these often expensive domestic programmes do not have the same export potential as light entertainment formats, then UK broadcasters – encouraged by the government's emphasis on export sales – will increasingly be tempted to commission the latter and to marginalize the former.

This would reduce the space for programmes with a non-commercial focus and a remit to seek out distinctive parts of the domestic audience and would further undermine the unique structure of British broadcasting that earned Britain its reputation for quality programmes and innovation. The American broadcasting system, historically organized along commercial lines only, commissions long runs of programmes both because this is cheaper and because of the strong syndication market. Britain, traditionally with a more regulated public service system, commissions a relatively high number of series with shorter runs which means, according to *Variety*, that 'there's a lot to choose from' (Littleton 1999: 25). By following the government's advice to boost export sales, there is a danger that British producers will develop formats and programmes with a more commercially viable but less distinctive flavour. This is likely to prove unappealing to domestic viewers and to dilute the innovation and 'quirkiness' that attracted the interests of international broadcasters in the first place.

The government's aspiration to minimize regulation and to expand international sales is flawed in another way. According to Emily Bell (2001: 5), it has not been 'light-touch' but 'heavy-touch regulation' that has catapulted British programmes on to the world stage, through the creation of a strong funding base and a determination to provide a public service. Any attempt to loosen the regulatory framework and to commercialize the ethos of broadcasting is likely to undermine both programme quality and diversity. 'If we were less well funded', argues the experienced commercial broadcaster David Elstein, 'we might be driven into producing low-cost, high-volume series which might sell better overseas, but I'm rather pleased we aren't. Why damage our own TV industry to improve TV in Belgium?' (quoted in Waller 2001: 6).

The failure of the government's strategy to expand exports and overturn the deficit in the trade of television programmes is echoed in other parts of the creative industries. Yet another government-initiated report on the sector admits that 'export earnings [in design] have halved since 2001, while the value of exports in music, the visual and performing arts in 2003 was down 20 per cent from 2000' (Nesta 2006: 3). Even in the supposedly thriving area of computer games, foreign studios and publishers dominate the UK market, with spending on games development in the UK down by 18 per cent and the number of people employed in the sector down by 6 per cent since 2000 (2006: 23). Ironically, for all the government initiatives to increase exports, its attachment to a free-trade agenda means that its capacity to restrict imports, and therefore to start to tackle growing trade deficits, is extremely limited. According to Simon Blanchard (2006: 37), the government is trapped in a 'profoundly neo-liberal current of thinking' that leaves it with 'no viable space for public policy on imports – any shifts in the trade balance would have to work themselves out in the marketplace'.

The government's attempts to overturn its trade deficit in television may not have been successful thus far, but it has allowed liberalizers to raise an argument about the external environment in which British television is situated: in an increasingly competitive international market. Globalization, presented by Tony Blair as an inescapable and largely welcome fact, has provided government with the perfect opportunity to discuss ways of further commercializing broadcasting given the 'imperatives' of the global challenge. It justifies its focus on increasing television exports by repeating the mantra of neo-liberal globalization concerning the dynamism of global markets and transnational capital flows, together with the undesirability of trade barriers. However, the government's continuing determination to take advantage of a more globalized television market appears to be not only failing in its own terms but also unlikely to succeed without damaging programme quality and diversity for domestic viewers. Its enthusiasm for the reorientation of British television towards an export-led focus appears, therefore, to be both undiminished and unwarranted.

Conclusion

Recent US and UK governments have embraced globalization as an opportunity to secure increased economic benefits and cultural influence through the activities of their media industries. Both governments have been key agents behind the attempt to subject cultural goods to the disciplines of free-trade agreements, and both are committed to strategies to expand their share of the international television market despite, in the case of the UK, potentially negative consequences for its own domestic broadcast system. In pursuing these objectives, they have embraced neo-liberal globalization as an unassailable and novel phenomenon that *requires* the liberalization of domestic and international media markets as governments lose the ability to control the direction of domestic media systems. This illustrates Curran and Seaton's claim (2003: 311) that 'the idea that global communications are making national government irrelevant slips with deceptive ease from a description to a prescription'. In reality, far from seeing a terminal decline of state power, the British and American governments have been increasingly active in trying to reshape international systems of media regulation for the benefit of those countries with the largest 'offensive' interests. Indeed, even the authors of an account of the rise of 'global media governance' concur that 'governments remain at the center of the international system of governance' (Ó Siochrú et al 2002: 144). Globalization, therefore, has not led to the disappearance of the nation-state but, on the contrary, seems to provide contemporary states with a powerful narrative of why further commercialization and marketization (of media along with other goods and services) is not only necessary but ultimately beneficial for 'the national interest'.

10

Conclusion

The aim of this book has been to examine the underlying values and assumptions of key participants in the media policymaking field, and to restore a sense of agency and politics to a process often described in rather technical and administrative terms. It has argued for an expanded definition of media policy that recognizes the importance of informal as well as formal modes of policy behaviour, and that acknowledges the role played by lobbyists, industry 'experts', pressure groups and consumer watchdogs together with that of politicians, regulators, judges and civil servants. Finally, the rival narratives of liberal pluralism and neo-liberalism have been used as the main explanatory frameworks for making sense of recent policy developments concerning the British and American media. To what extent have these aims and arguments been borne out by the examples and analysis provided in the book?

First, it is clear that there are significant differences between the British and American approaches to media policy that reflect the enduring differences between their respective media and political systems. As long as the most powerful sections of the US media continue to be driven by the overarching need to maximize ratings, to enhance profitability and to reward shareholders, its corporate strategy and public policy dynamics are likely to differ from those of a media system that features a more heterogeneous pattern of public/private ownership and is subject to frequent and multiple forms of government intervention. Such is the scale and influence of the US communications industry that it has been able to demand legislative reforms and economic benefits in a way that the smaller and more mixed British media sector has been less equipped to press for.

For example, we saw in chapter 5 how many American regulators and politicians largely adopted the arguments for loosening media ownership rules that were proposed by the country's leading media corporations. Anti-liberalization arguments only emerged in Congress as a result of the grass-roots campaign in 2003–4 that mobilized millions of Americans in protest at what they saw as the anti-democratic corporate takeover of the nation's airwaves and columns. Through their trade associations and legions of lobbyists, US corporations have repeatedly pressed for tighter intellectual property restrictions and for further trade liberalization that would benefit those with the greatest 'offensive' export interests. Constrained by continuing parliamentary reluctance fully to embrace media ownership liberalization, and by its membership of a European Community that is populated by countries antagonistic to US proposals for the liberalization of audio-visual trade, the UK has been less vigorous in its pursuit of radical deregulatory media reforms. Indeed, the eventual agreement by the government in 2003 to a public interest test in the case of major media mergers appears to signal an interventionist approach to media ownership that has been sorely lacking in the upper echelons of the FCC and the White House.

Furthermore, while the Bush administration has regularly pushed for cuts in the funding of public broadcasting, New Labour has now twice agreed to licence fee increases and has only recently presided over a Charter review that maintains the BBC at the heart of British broadcasting and sustains the licence fee as the main source of BBC funding for the foreseeable future. Despite increasing pressure to place the governance of the BBC under the control of the competition regulator Ofcom, the government has instead introduced a BBC Trust that is designed to oversee the interests of licence fee payers and to ensure the independence of the BBC in its dealing with government and the commercial sector. Even the instruction in its 2006 White Paper, that the BBC should play a key role in delivering analogue switch-off, is a sign of confidence by the government in the corporation's ability to play a decisive role in the future of British broadcasting.

There are, however, a growing number of similarities between the media policy approaches of recent US and UK governments that threaten to eclipse the points of contrast between them. Most fundamentally, both American neo-conservatives and British supporters of the 'third way' share a devotion to the market (whether they describe it as a 'free' or as a 'social' one) as the key mechanism for guaranteeing the dynamism, efficiency and diversity of their media environments. There may be different starting points but the values and objectives applied by both governments to their respective media systems are leading them in similar directions. While the USA has adopted a particularly robust stance in relation to the ability of market forces to cater for corporate need and consumer choice, New Labour has demonstrated an equal fervour in using the market to meet the requirements of private capital, public service and individual consumers. In its determination decisively to implant market disciplines throughout the British media, New Labour has been as eager as anyone to extol the ability of capitalist entrepreneurs and captains of industry to deliver not just private profit but also public *value*, creativity, innovation and competition (to name just a few attributes that are seen as desirable in Britain today). Market principles have therefore been applied to the pursuit of a range of media policy instruments and objectives, including the extended use of self- and co-regulation, the promotion of digital channels and content, the creation of 'national champions' and the expansion of exports.

These objectives are based on the highly restricted definition of key policy principles where pluralism and diversity, for example, are measured in quantitative terms that emphasize the number of media outlets rather than the different content they provide or the rival perspectives they publicize (best exemplified by the FCC's Diversity Index produced for the 2002 review of ownership rules); where the public interest is reduced to a consumerist index of whatever individuals choose to purchase (or not to purchase) in the market; and where an expansive commitment to freedom is replaced by an interpretation that favours the rights of corporations to operate without fear of government regulation, rather the rights of individuals to be able to speak and be heard and to air the conflicts that permeate twenty-first-century societies. Policy principles designed to facilitate the emergence and maintenance of meaningful democratic arrangements are instead being used – or rather redefined – to justify a much narrower and more consumer-oriented role for the media.

This re-imagining of media policy takes it further away from the 'common concern with collective subjectivity' (Hesmondhalgh 2005: 95) that typifies one way of conceptualizing media policy and towards a focus on the largely economic benefits that may accrue from the exploitation of the media industries. The recent rhetoric concerning the significance of the 'copyright industries' in the USA and the 'creative industries' in the UK is a tilt towards the value of intellectual property in contemporary 'knowledge societies', as well as a confirmation that media policy, as a Downing Street policy adviser suggests, is 'industrial policy with a strange tinge of social policy thrown in'. The increasing involvement in the formulation of media policy by the Department for Trade and Industry and by Ofcom, a regulator set up specifically to promote market competition in the communications sector, is further evidence of the industrial basis of much of Britain's media policy; the long-established economic basis of the FCC's regulatory and policy work only confirms the strategic industrial perspective of US communications policy.

In assisting market forces to operate 'freely' and to extend their reach, the influence of the state has been crucial in both the USA and the UK. From their decisions on what constitutes an acceptable level of concentration to their determination to secure analogue switch-off, from their unyielding support for domestic rights holders to increase market opportunities in export ventures, to their commitment to leverage existing copyright protections on to emerging distribution platforms, the British and American states have played a decisive role on behalf of key sections of their media industries. This level of state activity throws up an important contradiction. For all the claims of free markets to function with only the minimal intrusion of 'big government', the media in both countries share the paradoxical situation of having to face, at certain times, quite decisive government intervention and regulation. In a situation, for example, in which the FCC has sought to dictate what content is 'obscene', 'indecent' or 'profane' (and has severely punished broadcasters for infringing their regulations), it makes little sense to talk, as influential News International lobbyist Irwin Stelzer does, of a clear difference between the willingness in Britain 'to have Government regulate content' and the existence of a 'completely unregulated American culture' (quoted in House of Commons 2002: paras. 553, 556).

Indeed, the administrations of George W. Bush and Tony Blair have used the premise of the 'war on terror' to introduce a series of measures that curtail the freedom of journalists to hold government to account and to monitor the activities of the rich and powerful. The US Patriot Act and the UK Terrorism Acts, together with an increased willingness to control the release of official information and to restrict the use of Freedom of Information legislation, have affected the ability of reporters to gather information and produce content free from the threat of official sanctions and punitive measures. Both administrations have been equally keen to use a range of public relations and news management techniques further to influence media content and to minimize unfavourable reports and critical coverage. When this has failed, they have attempted to marginalize major media outlets by refusing them access to privileged sources, or by favouring news outlets more likely to reproduce official statements and voices. The impact of these various state-sponsored initiatives has been the potential 'chilling' of independent and inquisitive content – precisely the type of media the market is supposed to facilitate.

Both administrations have also knowingly contributed to a culture of lobbying, partly by accepting the legitimacy of the millions of dollars and pounds donated and spent by major corporations in order to influence key policymakers, and partly by granting special access to corporate actors on a regular basis. This has led to accusations, particularly in the case of Tony Blair, that his administration has been willing to tailor controversial policies in order not to antagonize powerful media proprietors such as Rupert Murdoch. This in turn feeds into perceptions that the media policy process in both countries is skewed towards corporate voices and industry data, despite repeated claims of its transparency and evidential rigour.

Taken together, these various developments – increasingly common to the policy environments of both countries – suggest that media policy emerges as the result of informal pressures as well as formal procedures. It is hard to sustain an argument that the development of media policy is a bounded, rational process that is open to multiple voices representing disparate interests. Instead, media policy appears to be a rather slippery process that favours those who share an ideological disposition towards markets and free enterprise, rather than a commitment to public service and a conception of communicative activity in which profits and economic value are *not* the decisive factors.

These are all indices of a firmly neo-liberal approach to public policy, based on the systematic embedding of market mechanisms, private property and trade disciplines into the media field. While this is most obvious in relation to the commercial orientation of the American media system, it is no less relevant to the mixed economy of the British media. Reforms have been proposed that not only intensify the profit-seeking instincts of the existing commercial sector, but also seek further to force public service enterprises to abide by the logic of free markets and economic values. We saw in chapter 7 how the government's 2006 White Paper on the future of the BBC conceptualizes the corporation in terms of its impact on the rest of the media market, rather than by seeing it as a cultural institution in its own right. The fact that New Labour has chosen not to privatize the BBC or substantially to cut its funding does not indicate in any way that, as a publicly owned body, it is outside the scope of neo-liberalizing reforms. As Wendy Brown puts it (2003: para. 9), neo-liberalism 'does not simply assume that all aspects of social, cultural and political life can be reduced to such a calculus [of utility, benefit or satisfaction], rather it develops institutional practices and rewards for enacting this vision'. Neo-liberalism aims to impose this narrow 'vision' of the freedom and efficiency enabled through private, economic activity on all parts of contemporary life – private and public, economic and social, material and symbolic.

This is, quite clearly, an account of media policy in which the main characteristics of a pluralist perspective seem to be mostly absent. The case studies in this book point to a concentration and not a 'dispersion' of political resources, where decisions taken about a range of issues – from the level of the BBC licence fee to the date of analogue switch-off and from the setting of ownership limits to the definition of piracy – are made by a small number of insiders in often opaque circumstances. In the majority of key media policy issues, well-resourced industry groups are able to mobilize their influence and disseminate their data to eager policymakers in a way that makes a mockery of the notion of open 'sub-governments' and genuinely competitive bargaining arrangements.

Those conflicts that do arise between industry and government provide little evidence of meaningful autonomy and instead demonstrate the need for governments to arbitrate between the rival private interests that are seeking to stake their claims on new and emerging areas of activity. For example, the fierce turf wars that were identified in chapter 8, between rights holders and intermediaries over the question of intellectual property rights and peer-to-peer networks, presented the US and UK governments with a tactical dilemma concerning how best to stimulate a viable digital media industry. Lobbied hard by the largest entertainment corporations, both governments sought to extend existing proprietorial arrangements into the digital universe, in a move that was aimed more at defending the sanctity of private property than it was at penalizing intermediaries or asserting some sort of political independence from them. While it is true that governments are not mechanically 'captured' by industry interests – particularly given the range of interests to which they have to respond – neither is it true that media policymakers are willing to insulate themselves from private interests in general.

Where there is a more profound disagreement – for example, concerning depictions of nudity or critical coverage in the context of the 'war on terror' – governments *have* been willing to stand up to industry pressure. The Bush administration has antagonized many powerful press and broadcast executives with its support for increased fines for indecent programming and its attempt to bypass newspapers like the *New York Times* and *Washington Post*. Tony Blair's government was, at times, on a virtual war footing with the country's most influential broadcaster, the BBC, for its reluctance to toe the official line. However, this does not equate to a mature exercise of power and a robust demonstration of governmental autonomy, given that it is motivated by narrow ideological and partisan interests and is aimed at short-term political gain: to silence critics or, in the case of indecency legislation, to firm up conservative electoral support for George W. Bush.

Finally, the idea that the policymaking process is marked by its transparency and 'multiple access points' is countered by the lack of systematic opportunities for public engagement and participation. Policymakers repeatedly highlight the ability of the internet to democratize decision-making and to act as a communication channel between the public and policymakers. However, the mere existence of websites publicizing consultations, facilitating citizens' access to official information and carrying public comment back to policymakers, does little to challenge the control over the policymaking process exercised by senior civil servants, government ministers and well-resourced private interests. While the number of people involved in the policymaking process is increasing along with the size of the industry, entry into and control over this process remains highly restricted. When over two million people objected to the FCC's plans to liberalize media ownership rules in 2003, their views were initially rejected by regulators as being ill-informed and biased. It took a vigorous campaign of public mobilization and lobbying before their views were eventually allowed on to the policy agenda and the FCC's proposals were then suspended. This was not a sign of pluralism but of its opposite: a process largely closed to the public and determined by a small group of politically motivated actors in government, civil service and industry.

If pluralism is therefore an inadequate descriptor, to what extent can all these characteristics of US and UK media policy be contained within a coherent definition of neo-liberalism? One response to the tendency to treat neo-liberalism as an undifferentiated 'bogeyman' of contemporary capitalism is to stress its multiple characteristics and warn of the dangers of reducing complex systems to unproblematically singular phenomena. This sensitivity to local adaptations of a broader theory is best expressed by the claim, first raised in chapter 2, that we are now witnessing 'the emergence of *varieties of neoliberalism*' (Cerny et al. 2005: 21 – emphasis in original). Rather than working to a general model, states are experimenting with and internalizing different aspects of the neo-liberal agenda, contributing to the emergence of 'diversity within convergence' (2005: 21). Neo-conservatism and third way politics could be said, in this context, to be two different variations of neo-liberalism.

This is a useful area of research in its ability to identify specific and unique characteristics of neo-liberal governance, but it is nevertheless limited. What is in danger of being lost is a sense of what links together different neo-liberal strategies and practices and their deployment as a purposeful political project, albeit in different political contexts. David Coates (2000) addresses this argument in his assessment of three different variations or 'models' of capitalism (market-led, state-led and negotiated capitalisms). Coates concludes that identification of a particular model is difficult to sustain, not only because they are all volatile but also because 'the problem seems to lie not with modelling but with capitalism' (2000: 233). Despite the distinctive features of their development, 'what is actually more striking about all three models is the commonality of the difficulties into which they are now running' (2000: 250) in terms of declining profitability, problems with productivity, pressure on welfare budgets and so on.

We can apply this approach to our assessment of neo-liberalism in relation to media policy. While there are distinct nuances to their media policy approaches that reflect important differences between their respective media and political cultures, there is nevertheless an overarching commitment to the intensification of market disciplines in the British and American media that threatens to minimize these differences and to cement the victory of private over public interests. This is likely to put pressure on those remaining spaces in the USA where there is an opportunity to explore new creative possibilities, to address difficult or controversial issues, or to cater for unprofitable minorities. It is also likely to accelerate the commercialization of the British media and, in particular, to limit the scope of public service broadcasting and reduce it to a ghettoized corner of the broadcast market where private operators have no desire (and no compulsion) to go. The neo-liberalization of media policy, like its impact on the wider social forces, is designed to transform the existing balance of power inside the US and UK media systems: to assist the expansion of private accumulation and to undermine the legitimacy and existence of non-profit and public service media provision. It will do this in different ways and at different speeds in Britain and America but, if left unchecked, it will further damage the ability of the media to provide 'the widest possible dissemination of information from diverse and antagonistic sources' that pluralists long ago argued was the essential role of a democratic media.

The continuing hegemony of neo-liberal forces, however, is far from assured. We have already identified a significant gap between the governmental and corporate policy communities and the public they are supposed to serve. Millions of Americans opposed their government's support for liberalizing media ownership rules; tens of millions continue to defy the instructions of their government to avoid illegal internet downloads; the majority of British people continue to trust the BBC more than their own government and support the idea of an expansive and subsidized public broadcasting system against neo-liberal plans to diminish this space; tens of millions in both countries are simply frustrated by the fostering of unaccountable concentrations of media power. These views express some of the broader contradictions that are inherent to the neo-liberal project, as the appeal of its language of 'free' markets, open competition and individual liberty starts to wilt given popular experiences of growing inequality, insecurity and global instability. As David Harvey puts it (2005: 203), the 'widening gap between rhetoric (for the benefit of all) and realization (the benefit of a small ruling class) is now all too visible.' The distance between what neo-liberal reforms of the media are promised to deliver and what neo-liberalization actually turns out to provide may well be one of the issues that connects to the 'resurgence of mass movements, voicing egalitarian political demands and seeking economic justice, fair trade and greater economic security' (2005: 203–4). The voices that have dominated this book have belonged largely to neo-liberal elites; let us hope that it is not these voices that dominate the future.

References

Please note that all unattributed quotes in the text are taken from anonymous interviews carried out for this research (see preface for more details).

Abrams vs. United States 1919: 250 US 616.

Abramson, B. D. 2001: 'Media policy after regulation?' In *International Journal of Cultural Studies* 4(3), 301–26.

ACT (Association of Commercial Television in Europe), AER (Association Europeene des Radios, EPC (European Publishers Council) 2004: *Safeguarding the Future of the European Audiovisual Market. A White Paper on the Financing and Regulation of Publicly Funded Broadcasters.* Brussels: ACT/AER/EPC.

Adda, J. and Ottaviani, M. 2005: 'The transition to digital television'. In *Economic Policy*, January, 159–209.

Adegoke, Y. 2007: 'Despite lawsuits, digital music downloads grow', Reuters, 6 February. Available at <http://today.reuters.com/news/articlenews.aspx?type=technologyNews&storyid=2007-02-08T003759Z_01_N26295384_RTRUKOC_0_US-PIRACY.xml> (15 February 2007).

Advisory Committee on Public Interest Obligations of Digital Television Broadcasters 1998: *Charting the Digital Broadcasting Future*. Washington, DC: NTIA. Available at <http://www.ntia.doc.gov/pubintadvcom/piacreport.pdf> (5 January 2007).

AEJMC (Association for Education in Journalism and Mass Communication) 2006: 'A motion to object to the Bush administration's anti-press policies and practices'. Available at <http://www.aejmc.org/_events/convention/resolutions/06resolutions/antipress_1.pdf> (15 December 2006).

Albiniak, P. 2000: 'Straight telecom talk'. *Broadcasting & Cable*, 24 July.

Albiniak, P. 2001: 'The new D.C.: friend or foe?' *Broadcasting & Cable*, 19 February.

Alterman, E. 2005: 'Bush's war on the press'. *The Nation*, 21 April.

Anderson, P. and Mann, N. 1997: *Safety First: The Making of New Labour*. London: Granta.

Annan, Lord. (chair) 1977: *Report on the Committee of the Future of Broadcasting*, Cmnd. 6753. London: HMSO.

Arestis, P. and Sawyer, M. 2001: 'The economic analysis underlying the "Third Way"'. In *New Political Economy* 6(2), 255–78.

Armstrong, D. 2002: 'Dick Cheney's song for America'. *Harpers* 305 (1829), October.

Aroldo, P., Goodwin, P. and Vittadini, N. 2006: 'Digital TV in UK and Italy: two national cases'. In F. Colombo and N. Vittadini (eds), 2006: *Digitising TV: Theoretical Issues and Comparative Studies across Europe*. Milan: Vita e Pensiero, 205–37.

Article 19 2000: *Secrets, Spies and Whistleblowers: Freedom of Expression and National Security in the United Kingdom*. Article 19 and Liberty, November.

Ashley, J. 2003: 'Spinning out of control'. The *Guardian*, 21 July.

Associated Press vs. United States 1945: 326 US 1.

Associated Press 2006: 'FCC chair orders probe into why media ownership studies were destroyed', 19 September. Available at <http://www.foxnews.com/printer_friendly_story/0,3566,214392,00.html> (22 September 2006).

Atkinson, C. 2006: 'Privatization "tsunami" sweeps old media'. *Advertising Age*, 8 November.

Aufderheide, P. 1999: *Communications Policy and the Public Interest*. New York: Guilford.

Auletta, K. 2004: 'Fortress Bush: how the White House keeps the press under control'. *New Yorker*, 19 January.

Aylett, H. 2005: 'Transatlantic drift: Britain and the UNESCO Convention for Cultural Diversity'. *Vertigo*, autumn/winter.

Bachrach, P. and Baratz, M. 1962: 'Two faces of power'. In *American Political Science Review*, 56(4), 947–52.

Bainwol, M. 2005: Statement to Senate Committee on Commerce, Science and Transportation hearing on *MGM V. Grokster*, 28 July. Available at <http://commerce.senate.gov/pdf/bainwol.pdf> (18 December 2006).

Baker, C. E. 2002: *Media, Markets and Democracy*. Cambridge: Cambridge University Press.

Baker, P. 2006: 'Bush signs legislation on broadcast indecency'. *Washington Post*, 16 June.

Barnett, S. 2006a: 'Can the BBC invigorate our political culture?' In J. Lloyd and J. Seaton (eds), *What Can Be Done? Making the Media and Politics Better*. Oxford: Blackwell Publishing, 58–69.

Barnett, S. 2006b: Comments in Westminster Media Forum Seminar on the BBC White Paper. London: Westminster Media Forum, 23–5.

Barnouw, E. 1990: *Tune of Plenty: The Evolution of American Television*, 2nd revised edn. Oxford: Oxford University Press.

BBC 1999: 'UK digital TV turn-on outlined', 17 September. Available at <http://news.bbc.co.uk/1/hi/uk/449849.stm> (28 February 2007).

BBC 2001: 'Smith defends digital TV plans', 22 March. Available at <http://news.bbc.co.uk/1/hi/uk/1234772.stm> (20 March 2003).

BBC 2004: *Building Public Value: Renewing the BBC for a Digital World*. London: BBC.

BBC 2005: *Editorial Guidelines*. Available at <http://www.bbc.co.uk/guidelines/editorialguidelines/edguide/privacy/publicinterest.shtml> (17 November 2006).

BBC 2006: 'Reactions in quotes: ad ban', 17 November. Available at http://news.bbc.co.uk/1/hi/health/6157956.stm (10 January 2007).

BBG (Broadcasting Board of Governors) 2007: 'Broadcasting budget strengthens targeted programming', press release, 5 February. Available at <http://www.bbg.gov/_bbg_news.cfm?articleID=142&mode=general> (16 February 2007).

Bell, E. 2001: 'Dumb luck or good planning?' The *Guardian*, 28 May.

Bell, E. 2005a: 'Opinion'. *Media Guardian*, 31 January.

Bell, E. 2005b: 'Birt's BBC role burns out hope of independence'. *Media Guardian*, 21 February: 5.

Bell, E. 2005c: 'Opinion'. *Media Guardian*, 24 January.

Bell, E. 2007: 'After finally learning about Dyke, we want the floodgates open'. *Media Guardian*, 15 January.

Bell, W. 2005: 'My Conservative beef'. *National Review Online*, 11 May. Available at <http://www.nationalreview.com/bell/bell200505110754.asp> (9 February 2007).

Benkler, Y, 2006: *The Wealth of Networks: How Social Production Transforms Markets and Freedom*. New Haven: Yale University Press.

Bennett, W. L. and Entman, R. (eds) 2001: *Mediated Politics: Communication in the Future of Democracy*. Cambridge: Cambridge University Press.

Bernier, I. 2004: 'The recent free trade agreements of the United States as illustration of their new strategy regarding the audiovisual sector'. *Media Trade Monitor*. Available at <http://www.mediatrademonitor.org/node/view/146> (18 June 2005).

BIPA (British Internet Publishers Alliance) 2003: BIPA submission to Graf review of BBC Online, 24 November. Available at <http://www.bipa.co.uk/getArticle.php?ID=322> (18 October 2006).

Birnbaum, J. 2004: 'Lawmakers, lobbyists keep in constant contact'. *Washington Post*, 28 June.

Blair, T. 1996: *New Britain: My Vision of a Young Country*. London: Basic Books.

Blair, T. 1997a: Interview with Tony Blair. *New Statesman*, 21 March.

Blair, T. 1997b: Speech to Labour Party Conference, Brighton, 30 September.

Blair, T. 1998: *The Third Way: New Politics for a New Century*. Fabian pamphlet 588. London: Fabian Society.

Blair, T. 2003: Speech to US Congress, 17 July. Available at <http://www.cnn.com/2003/US/07/17/blair.transcript/> (13 November 2006).

Blair, T. 2007: Lecture on 'public life', Reuters, London, 12 June. Available at <http://www.number-10.gov.uk/output/Page11923.asp> (13 June 2007).

Blanchard, S. 2006: 'The "wrong type" of television: New Labour, British broad-casting and the rise and fall of an exports "problem"'. In S. Harvey (ed.), *Trading Culture: Global Traffic and Local Cultures in Film and Television*. Eastleigh: John Libbey, 33–46.

Blumler, J. (ed.) 1991: *Television and the Public Interest*. London: Sage.

Boehlert, E. 2003: 'The big blackout'. *Salon.com*, 22 May. Available at <http://dir.salon.com/story/tech/feature/2003/05/22/fcc_blackout/index.html> (1 December 2006).

Boehlert, E. 2005a: 'Indecency wars'. *Salon*, 14 April.

Boehlert, E. 2005b: 'Third columnist caught with hands in the Bush till'. *Salon*, 27 January.

Boliek, B. 2005: 'Key lawmaker calls for criminalizing TV indecency'. *Hollywood Reporter*, 5 April.

Born, G. 2004: *Uncertain Vision: Birt, Dyke and the Reinvention of the BBC*. London: Secker & Warburg.

Born, G. 2006: 'Public service communications in the digital era: communicative democracy, pluralism and the politics of presence'. In F. Colombo and N. Vittadini (eds): *Digitising TV: Theoretical Issues and Comparative Studies across Europe*. Milan: Vita e Pensiero, 37–68.

Bourdieu, P. 1998: *Acts of Resistance: Against the New Myths of Our Time*. Cambridge: Polity.

Bourdieu, P. and Wacquant, L. 2001: 'NewLiberalSpeak: notes on the new planetary vulgate'. In *Radical Philosophy* 105, January/February, 2–5.

Boyle, D. 2002: *The Tyranny of Numbers*. London: Flamingo.

Braman, S. 2004: 'Where has media policy gone? Defining the field in the twenty-first century'. In *Communication Law and Policy*, 9(2), 153–82.

BRCD (Broadcasting Regulation & Cultural Diversity) 2006: 'The audiovisual sector at the WTO: conference led by Alejandro Jara', 22 February. Available at <http://www.brcd.net/cac_brcd/AppPHP/modules/publications/files/050306_summary_jara_conference.pdf> (18 February 2007).

Brenner, N. and Theodore, N. 2002: 'Cities and the geographies of "actually existing neoliberalism"'. In N. Brenner and N. Theodore (eds), *Spaces of Neoliberalism: Urban Restructuring in North American and Western Europe*. Oxford: Blackwell, 2002, 2–32.

Broache, A. 2005: 'Digital TV Switch Set for Early 2009', CNet News, 21 December. Available at <http://news.com.com/Digital+TV+switch+set+for+early+2009/2100-1028_3-6004429.html> (18 December 2006).

Broadcasting and Cable 2006: Editorial – 'Tell the people', 29 May.

Brown, A. and Picard, R. (eds) 2004: *Digital Terrestrial Television in Europe*. Mahwah, NJ: Lawrence Erlbaum.

Brown, M. 2007: 'Something has got to go'. *Media Guardian*, 22 January.

Brown, W. 2003: 'Neo-liberalism and the end of liberal democracy'. In *Theory and Event* 7(1). Available at <http://muse.jhu.edu/journals/tae/toc/archive.html#7.1> (26 March 2006).

Burns, T. (chair) 2004: Report of the Independent Panel on BBC Charter Review – 'Emerging themes'. 1 December. Available at <www.bbccharterreview.org.uk/pdf_documents/041130_emerging_themes.rtf> (1 August 2006).

Bush, B. 2005: Speech at symposium on 'Media policy-making and power', 23 September, Goldsmiths College, London. Available at <http://www.goldsmiths.ac.uk/departments/media–communications/session2.pdf> (18 December 2005).

Bush, G. W. 2005: 'Excerpts from President Bush's comments to Radio-Television News Directors Association (RTNDA) Board of Directors', 1 June. Available at <http://www.rtnda.org/news/2005/050602b.shtml> (11 October 2006).

Cabinet Office 2003: *Digital Television: A Policy Framework for Accessing e-Government Services.* London: Office of the e-Envoy.

Calabrese, A. 2005: 'Casus Belli: U.S. media and the justification of the Iraq War'. In *Television and New Media* 6(2) May, 153–75.

Callinicos, A. 2001: *Against the Third Way.* Cambridge: Polity.

Callinicos, A. 2003: *An Anti-Capitalist Manifesto.* Cambridge: Polity.

Carey, J. 1978: 'The ambiguity of policy research'. In S. Braman (ed.), 2003, *Communication Researchers and Policy-Making.* Cambridge: MIT Press, 437–44.

Carr, D. 2006: 'The Pulitzer: now a badge of controversy'. *New York Times,* 24 April.

Carter, B. 2000: 'Britons revamp American TV'. *New York Times,* 18 July.

Cassidy, J. 2006: 'Murdoch's game: will he move left in 2008?' *New Yorker,* 16 October.

Castells, M. 1996: *The Rise of the Network Society.* Cambridge: Polity.

Cater, D. 1965: *Power in Washington: A Critical Look at Today's Struggle to Govern in the U.S.A.* London: Collins.

CBS 2006: Comments of CBS Corporation in the matter of the 2006 Quadrennial Review, FCC 06–121, 23 October.

CCD (Coalition for Cultural Diversity) 2004: *Coalition Currents* 2(2), March. Available at <http://www.cdc-ccd.org/coalition_currents/Mars04/coalition_currents_en.html> (18 June 2005).

Central Hudson Gas vs. Public Service Commission of New York 1980: 447 US 557.

Centre for Public Integrity 2004: *Networks of Influence: The Political Power of the Communications Industry,* 28 October. Available at <http://www.publicintegrity.org/telecom/report.aspx?aid=405> (8 July 2006).

Cerny, P. 1995: 'Globalization and the changing logic of collective action'. In *International Organization* 49 (4), autumn, 595–625.

Cerny, P. 2004: 'Mapping varieties of neoliberalism'. IPEG Papers in *Global Political Economy,* no. 12, May. Available at <http://www.bisa.ac.uk/groups/ipeg/papers/12%20Philip%20Cerny.pdf> (26 March 2006).

Cerny, P., Menz, G. and Soederberg, S. 2005: 'Different roads to globalization: neoliberalism, the competition state, and politics in a more open world'. In S. Soederberg, G. Menz and P. Cerny (eds), *Internalizing Globalization: The Rise of Neoliberalism and the Decline of National Varieties of Capitalism*. Houndmills: Palgrave Macmillan, 1–30.

CFOI (Campaign for Freedom of Information) 2006: 'Government agrees to consult over plans to "scythe" freedom of information act. Press release, 14 December. Available at <http://www.cfoi.org.uk/foi141206pr.html> (9 January 2007).

Chakravartty, P. and Sarikakis, K. 2006: *Media Policy and Globalization*. Edinburgh: Edinburgh University Press.

Cheney, D. 1993: *Defense Strategy for the 1990s: The Regional Defense Strategy*. Available at <http://stinet.dtic.mil/cgibin/GetTRDoc?AD=ADA268979& Location=U2&doc=GetTRDoc.pdf> (10 August 2006).

Clarke, S. 2001: 'Jackson to TV toppers: quality over ratings'. *Variety.com*, 31 October.

Claude, G. 2002: 'After digitopia: The Internet, copyright and information control'. In D. McClean and K. Schubert (eds), *Dear Images: Art, Copyright and Culture*. London: ICA/Ridinghouse. 241–52.

CNN (2004) National exit poll, 4 November. Available at <http://edition.cnn. com/ELECTION/2004/ pages/results/states/US/P/00/epolls.0.html> (18 October 2006).

Coates, D. 2000: *Models of Capitalism: Growth and Stagnation in the Modern Era*. Cambridge: Polity.

Colebatch, H. 1998: *Policy*. Buckingham: Open University Press.

Collins, R. 1993: *Broadcasting and Audio-visual policy in the European Single Market*. Luton: John Libbey.

Collins, R. 2006: *The BBC and Public Value*. CRESC working paper series, No. 19, June. Milton Keynes: Centre for Research on Socio-Cultural Change.

Collins, R. and Murroni, C. 1996: *New Media, New Policies*. Cambridge: Polity.

Colombo, F. and Vittadini, N. (eds) 2006: *Digitising TV: Theoretical Issues and Comparative Studies across Europe*. Milan: Vita e Pensiero.

Committee on Government Reform Minority Office 2004: *Secrecy in the Bush Administration*, 14 September.

Compaine, B. 2001: 'The myths of encroaching global media ownership', *Open Democracy*, 6 November. Available at <http://www.opendemocracy.net/ content/articles/PDF/87.pdf> (8 July 2006).

Compaine, B. and Gomery, D. 2000: *Who Owns the Media? Competition and Concentration in the Mass Media Industry*. Mahwah, NJ: Lawrence Erlbaum.

Congdon, T., Graham, A., Green, D. and Robinson, B. 1995: *The Cross Media Revolution: Ownership and Control*. Luton: John Libbey.

Consumers Union 2005: 'House bill would leave most consumers in the dark during digital TV transition', press release, 25 October. Available at <http://

www.consumersunion.org/pub/core_telecom_and_utilities/002788.html> (31 October 2005).

Cooper, C. and Steinberg, B. 2005: 'Bush draws fire over fee paid to columnist to promote policy'. *Wall Street Journal*, 10 January.

Copps, M. 2004: 'Corporate media and local interests: downsizing the monster'. *San Francisco Chronicle*, 19 July.

Corcoran, F. 2006: 'Refocusing on the question of power in new media research'. In F. Colombo and N. Vittadini (eds), *Digitising TV: Theoretical Issues and Comparative Studies across Europe*. Milan: Vita e Pensiero, 3–19.

Couldry, N. 2006: 'Reality TV, or the secret theatre of neoliberalism'. Article commissioned for special edition of *Hermes on Economy and Communication*. Available at <http://www.goldsmiths.ac.uk/departments/media-communications/staff/realitytv.pdf> (10 August 2006).

Council on Foreign Relations 2003: *Finding America's Voice: A Strategy for Reinvigorating U.S. Public Diplomacy*. New York: Council on Foreign Relations.

Cox, B. 2004: *Free For All: Public Service Television in the Digital Age*. London: Demos.

Cox, M. 2004: 'Empire? The Bush doctrine and the lessons of history'. In D. Held and M. Koenig-Archibugi (eds), *American Power in the 21st Century*. Cambridge: Polity, 21–51.

Creech, K. 2000: *Electronic Media Law and Regulation*, 3rd edn. Boston: Focal Press.

Croteau, D. and Hoynes, W. 2001: *The Business of Media: Corporate Media and the Public Interest*. London: Sage.

Crothers, L. 2007: *Globalization and American Popular Culture*. Lanham: Rowman & Littlefield.

Curran, J. 2000: 'Rethinking media and democracy'. In J. Curran and M. Gurevitch (eds), *Mass Media and Society*, 3rd edn. London: Arnold, 120–54).

Curran, J. 2002: *Media and Power*. London: Routledge.

Curran, J. and Park, M-J. 2000: *De-Westernizing Media Studies*. London: Routledge.

Curran, J. and Seaton, J. 1991: *Power without Responsibility*, 4th edn. London: Routledge.

Curran, J. and Seaton, J. 2003: *Power without Responsibility*, 6th edn. London: Routledge.

Curtis, L. 1984: *Ireland: The Propaganda War*. London: Pluto Press.

Dahl, R. 1961: *Who Governs?: Democracy and Power in an American City*. New Haven: Yale University Press.

Daly, M. 2003: 'Governance and social policy'. In *Journal of Social Policy* 32(1), 113–28.

Dana, R. 2006: '@$#&*% Ken Burns! PBS Scrubbing G.I. Mouths With Soap', *New York Observer*, 1 October.

ınkard, J. 2005: 'Report: PR spending doubled under Bush'. *USA Today*, 26 January.

ГI (Department for Trade and Industry)/DCMS 2000: *A New Future for Communications*, white paper, Cm 5010. Norwich: HMSO.

ГI/DCMS 2003: *Communications Act 2003*. Norwich: TSO.

ГI 2004: *Enterprise Act 2002: Public Interest Intervention in Media Mergers*. Guidance document. London: DTI. Available at <http://www.dti.gov.uk/files/file14331.pdf (16 November 2006).

ınbar, J. 2005: '2004 broke all records on indecent broadcasting', Centre for Public Integrity, 30 June. Available at <http://www.publicintegrity.org/telecom/report.aspx?aid=717> (20 September 2006).

ınbar, J., and Pilhofer, A. 2003: *Big Radio Rules in Small Markets*. Centre for Public Integrity. Available at <http://www.publicintegrity.org/telecom/report.aspx?aid=63> (April 22, 2004).

ʳke, G. 2005a: *Inside Story*. London: Harper Perennial.

ʳke, G. 2005b: 'Some of us simply don't want to embrace the digital age'. *The Independent*, 19 September.

Ɔ (European Commission) 1989: *Television without Frontiers*, Council Directive 89/552/EEC, 3 October. Available at <http://eurlex.europa.eu/LexUriServ/LexUriServ.do?uri=CELEX:31989L0552:EN:HTML> (3 November 2006).

Ɔ 1994: *Europe and the Global Information Society*, the Bangemann Report. Available at <http://europa.eu.int/ISPO/infosoc/backg/bangeman.html> (24 March 2006).

ɔnomist 2005: 'Face the music'. *The Economist*, 31 March.

ˌgerton, J. 2005a: 'Attorney General will fight obscenity'. *Broadcasting & Cable*, 28 February.

ˌgerton, J. 2005b: 'Bush backs pay indecency regs'. *Broadcasting & Cable*, 14 April.

ˌgerton, J. 2006: 'Redstone to regulators: stay out of our homes'. *Broadcasting & Cable*, 17 October.

-Nawawy, M. 2006: 'US public diplomacy in the Arab world: the news credibility of Radio Sawa and Television Alhurra in five countries'. In *Global Media and Communication* 2(2), 183–203.

ˌstein, D. 2002: 'The politics of digital TV in the UK'. *Open Democracy*, 17 July. Available at <http://www.opendemocracy.net/content/articles/PDF/21.pdf> (27 November 2006).

ˌstein, D. 2004: *Building Public Value: A New Definition of Public Service Broadcasting?* London: Institute of Economic Affairs.

ıtman, R. 2003 [1993]: 'Putting the First Amendment in its place: enhancing American democracy through the press'. In S. Braman (ed.), *Communication Researchers and Policy-Making*. Cambridge, MA: MIT Press, 461–84.

ʸre, R. 1999: MacTaggart lecture, Edinburgh, 27 August. Available at <http://www.observerunlimited.co.uk/BBC/Story/0,,200890,00.html> (11 September 2006).

Davies, W. 2005: 'Evidence-based policy and democrac'
23 November. Available at <http://www.opendemo
articles/PDF/3056.pdf> (18 December 2006).

Davis, A. 2002: *Public Relations Democracy*. Manchester: Ma
Press.

Davis, A. 2003: 'Whither mass media and power? Evidenc
theory alternative'. In *Media, Culture and Society* 25(5), 66

DCA (Department for Constitutional Affairs) 2006: *Draft Fre
and Data Protection (Appropriate Limit and Fees) Regulations*
Paper 28.06. 14 December.

DCMS (Department for Culture, Media and Sport) 1999a: U
Inquiry: The Report of the Creative Industries Task Force In
Exports. London: DCMS.

DCMS 1999b: 'More than a tenth of global TV exports show
British', press release, 26 November, 287/99.

DCMS 2000: *Consumers Call the Tune: The Impact of New Techn*
Industry. London: DCMS.

DCMS 2003: *Privacy and Media Intrusion. The Government's F*
Report of the Culture, Media and Sport Select Committee on
Intrusion'. Cm 5985. Norwich: TSO.

DCMS 2004: 'Background to UNESCO Consultation on the
on the protection of the diversity of cultural contents and ar
Available at <http://www.culture.gov.uk/NR/rdonlyres/
4672-890A-11FD37B803FD/0/BACKGROUND.pdf> (10 N

DCMS 2006: *A Public Service for All: The BBC in the Digital Age.*
6763. Norwich: TSO.

DCMS/DTI 2001: *Consultation on Media Ownership Rules*. Lon

Department of State (International Organizations Bureau) 2(
Commission for UNESCO Monthly Update. February.

Digital UK 2005: *A Guide to Digital Television and D*
London: Digital UK. Available at <http://www.digitalt
pdf_documents/publications/guide_dtvswitchover_june05
ber 2006).

Digital UK 2006: *Get Set: The Newsletter about the Digital TV S*
spring. London: Digital UK.

DNH (Department for National Heritage) 1995a: *Media Owner*
ment's Proposals, white paper, CM 2872. London: HMSO.

DNH 1995b: *Digital Terrestrial Broadcasting: The Government's*
paper, CM 2946. London: HMSO.

Domhoff, W. 1967: *Who Rules America?* Englewood Cliffs: Prer

Domhoff, W. 1983: *Who Rules America Now? A View for the 1*
Simon & Schuster.

Doyle, G. 2002: *Media Ownership*. London: Sage.

Farrell, M. 2003: 'Karmazin: attacks cost Viacom $200m'. *Multichannel News*, available at <http://www.multichannel.com/article/CA170525. html?display=Finance> (10 December 2006).

Faulkner, S., Leaver, A., Vis, F. and Williams, K. 2006: 'Art for art's sake or selling up?', unpublished paper, University of Manchester.

FCC vs. Pottsville Broadcasting 1940: 309 US 134.

FCC vs. Pacifica 1978: 438 US 726.

FCC vs. Syracuse Peace Council 1987: 2 F.C.C.R. 5043.

FCC 1999: *Report and Order*, 5 August, FCC 99–209. Available at <http://www. fcc.gov/Bureaus/Mass_Media/Orders/1999/fcc99209.pdf> (10 October 2006).

FCC 2003a: *Report and Order and Notice of Proposed Rulemaking*, 2 June, FCC 03–127. Available at <http://hraunfoss.fcc.gov/edocs_public/attachmatch/ FCC–03–127A1.pdf> (5 June 2003).

FCC 2003b: 'FCC sets limits on media concentration', press release, 2 June. Available at <http://hraunfoss.fcc.gov/edocs_public/attachmatch/ DOC–235047A1.pdf> (5 June 2003).

FCC 2003c: Memorandum Opinion and Order, FCC 03-3045, 3 October. Available at <http://fjallfoss.fcc.gov/edocs_public/attachmatch/DA-03-3045A1. pdf> (18 October 2006).

FCC 2004a: 'Memorandum opinion and order', FCC 04–43, 18 March. Available at <http://hraunfoss.fcc.gov/edocs_public/attachmatch/FCC-04-43A1. pdf> (10 October 2006).

FCC 2004b: 'Notice of Apparent Liability for Forfeiture', FCC 04-209, 22 September. Available at <http://www.fcc.gov/eb/Orders/2004/FCC-04-209A1.html> (10 October 2006).

FCC 2005: 'Obscenity, indecency and profanity: frequently asked questions'. Available at <http://www.fcc.gov/eb/oip/FAQ.html> (31 October 2005).

FCC 2006a: 'Further notice of proposed rule-making', 24 July. Available at <http://hraunfoss.fcc.gov/edocs_public/attachmatch/FCC-06-93A1.pdf> (2 November 2006).

FCC 2006b: 'Notices of apparent liability and memorandum opinion and order' ('Omnibus Order'), FCC 06–17, 15 March. Available at <http:// hraunfoss.fcc.gov/edocs_public/attachmatch/FCC-06-18A1.pdf> (2 November 2006).

FCC 2006c: 'Forfeiture order', FCC 06–19, 15 March. Available at <http:// hraunfoss.fcc.gov/edocs_public/attachmatch/FCC-06-19A1.pdf> (2 November 2006).

FCC 2006d: *Digital Television (DTV) – FCC Consumer Facts*. Available at <http:// www.fcc.gov/cgb/consumerfacts/DTVShoppersGuide.pdf> (18 December 2006).

Feintuck, M. 2004: *'The Public Interest' in Regulation*. Oxford: Oxford University Press.

Feree, K. 2004: Testimony to 'completing the digital television transition' hearing, Senate Committee on Commerce, Science and Transportation, 9 June. Available at <http://commerce.senate.gov/hearings/testimony.cfm?id=1220&wit_id=3513> (5 March 2007).

Flew, T. 2002: 'Broadcasting and the social contract'. In M. Raboy (ed.), *Global Media Policy in the New Millennium*. Luton: University of Luton Press, 113–29.

Folkenflik, D. 2005: 'E-mails Link White House to CPB's Tomlinson', npr.org, 22 February. Available at <http://www.npr.org/templates/story/story.php?storyId=4711997> (22 February 2007).

Fortune 500 2007: Annual ranking of America's largest corporations. Available at <http://money.cnn.com/magazines/fortune/fortune500/2007/snapshots/1529.html> (15 March 2007).

Fowler, M. and Brenner, D. 1982: 'A marketplace approach to broadcast regulation'. In *Texas Law Review* 60(2), 1–51.

Frank, T. 2006: *What's the Matter with America?* London: Vintage.

Free Press 2007: 'Attack on federal funding'. Available at <http://freepress.net/publicbroadcasting/=funding> (16 February 2007).

Freedman, D. 2003a: *The Television Policies of the Labour Party, 1951–2001*. London: Frank Cass.

Freedman, D. 2003b: 'Managing pirate culture: corporate responses to peer-to-peer networking'. In *International Journal on Media Management* 5(3), 173–9.

Freedman, D. 2003c: 'Cultural policy-making in the free trade era: an evaluation of the impact of current World Trade Organization negotiations on audio-visual industries'. In *International Journal of Cultural Policy* 9(3), 285–98.

Freedman, D. 2006: 'Dynamics of power in contemporary media policy-making'. In *Media, Culture and Society* 28(6), 907–23.

Freeman, J. L. 1965: *The Political Process: Executive Bureau-Legislative Committee Relations*. New York: Random House.

Fritz, B., Keefer, B. and Nyhe, B. 2004: *All the President's Spin: George W. Bush, the Media, and the Truth*. New York: Touchstone.

Galperin, H. 2004: *New Television, Old Politics. The Transition to Digital TV in the United States and Britain*. Cambridge: Cambridge University Press.

Galston, W. 2005: *The Practice of Liberal Pluralism*. Cambridge: Cambridge University Press.

Gamble, A. 2001: 'Neo-liberalism'. In *Capital & Class* 75, 127–34.

GAO (Government Accountability Office) 2007: *Telecommunications – Issues Related to the Structure and Funding of Public Television*. GAO-07-150. Washington DC: GAO.

Garnham, N. 1994: 'The broadcasting market and the future of the BBC'. In *Political Quarterly* 65(1), 11–19.

Garnham, N. 1998: 'Policy'. In A. Briggs and P. Cobley (eds), *The Media: An Introduction*. London: Longman, 210–23.

Garnham, N. 2000: *Emancipation, the Media, and Modernity: Arguments about the Media and Social Theory*. Oxford: Oxford University Press.

Garnham, N. 2005: 'From cultural to creative industries: an analysis of the creative industries' approach to arts and media policy making in the United Kingdom. In *International Journal of Cultural Policy* 11(1) 2005, 15–29.

Garrity, B. 2002: 'Victory eludes legal fight over file swapping'. *Billboard*, 13 April.

Gibbons, T. 1998: *Regulating the Media*. London: Sweet & Maxwell.

Gibbons, T. 2000: 'Pluralism, guidance and the new media'. In C. Marsden (ed.), *Regulating the Global Information Society*. London: Routledge, 304–15.

Gibson, O. 2006: 'Watchdog puts ban on celebrities advertising junk food to under-10s'. The *Guardian*, 29 March.

Gibson, O. 2007: 'Code breaker'. *Media Guardian*, 29 January.

Giddens, A. 1998: 'After the left's paralysis'. *New Statesman*, 1 May, 18–21.

Giddens, A. 2000: *The Third Way and its Critics*. Cambridge: Polity.

Glasgow University Media Group (1976): *Bad News*. London: Routledge and Kegan Paul.

Gold, M. 2006a: 'A Feud over Bush's Pick'. *Los Angeles Times*, 22 December.

Gold, M. 2006b: 'Is the PBS happy meal a future menu item?' *Los Angeles Times*, 23 October.

Goodman, P. 2001: 'Powell plans fewer FCC rules'. *Washington Post*, 30 March.

Goodman, T. 2004: 'PBS watches its mouth rather than pay big fines'. *San Francisco Chronicle*, 12 July 2004.

Goodwin, P. 1998: *Television under the Tories: Broadcasting Policy 1979–1997*. London: BFI.

Gore, A. 1994: Speech to the International Telecommunications Union, Buenos Aires, 24 March. Available at <http://www.goelzer.net/telecom/al–gore.html> (24 March 2006).

Gore, A. 1997: Comments to Presidential Advisory Committee on Public Interest Obligations for Digital TV, 22 October. Available at <http://www.ntia.doc.gov/pubintadvcom/octmtg/vp102297.htm> (28 February 2007).

Gowers, A. 2006: *Gowers Review of Intellectual Property*. Norwich: TSO.

Graber, C. B. 2006: 'The new UNESCO Convention on Cultural Diversity: a counterbalance to the WTO?'. In *Journal of International Economic Law* 9(3), 553–74.

Graber, D. 2002: *Mass Media and American Politics*, 6th edn. Washington, DC: CQ Press.

Graham, A. and Davies, G. 1997: *Broadcasting, Society and Policy in the Multimedia Age*. Luton: John Libbey.

Graham, D. 1999: *Building a Global Audience: British Television in Overseas Markets*. London: DCMS.

Grant, P. and Wood, C. 2004: *Blockbusters and Trade Wars: Popular Culture in a Globalized World*. Vancouver: Douglas & MacIntyre.

Green, K. 2005: 'Downloading music affects children's morality, Senators say', *infoZine.com*, 4 August. Available at <http://www.infozine.com/news/stories/op/storiesView/sid/9389/> (5 August 2005).

Greenslade, R. 2003: 'Their master's voice'. The *Guardian*, 17 February.

Greenslade, R. 2004: 'Is the Telegraph's fate in this woman's hands?' *Media Guardian*, 8 March.

Gunter, B. 2004: 'The prospects for e-government on digital television'. In *Aslib Proceedings* 56(4), 222–33.

Habermas, J. 1989 [1962]: *The Structural Transformation of the Public Sphere: An Inquiry into a Category of Bourgeois Society*. Cambridge: Polity.

Hackett, R. and Carroll, W. 2006: *Remaking Media: The Struggle to Democratize Public Communication*. London: Routledge.

Hallin, D. and Mancini, P. 2004: *Comparing Media Systems: Three Models of Media and Politics*. Cambridge: Cambridge University Press.

Ham, C. and Hill, M. 1993: *The Policy Process in the Modern Capitalist State*. Hemel Hempstead: Harvester Wheatsheaf.

Hamelink, C. 2002: 'The civil society challenge to global media policy'. In M. Raboy (ed.), *Global Media Policy in the New Millennium*. Luton: University of Luton Press, 251–60.

Hardy, J. 2004: 'Safe in their hands: New Labour and public service broadcasting'. In *Soundings* 27, July, 100–13.

Harkin, S. 2005: 'Big idea: public value judgments'. The *Guardian*, 22 October.

Hart, J. 2004: *Technology, Television and Competition: The Politics of Digital TV*. Cambridge: Cambridge University Press.

Harvey, D. 2005: *A Brief History of Neoliberalism*. Oxford: Oxford University Press.

Harvey, S. 2006: 'Ofcom's first year and neoliberalism's blind spot'. In *Screen* 47(1), Spring, 91–105.

Hay, C. (2004) 'The normalizing role of rationalist assumptions in the institutional embedding of neoliberalism'. In *Economy and Society* 33(4), November, 500–27.

Haynes, R. 2005: *Media Rights and Intellectual Property*. Edinburgh: Edinburgh University Press.

Hazlett, T. 2005: 'Grokster's loss is America's gain'. *Wall Street Journal*, 29 June.

Hearn, T. 2007: 'Don't panic. Yet'. *Multichannel News*, 19 February. Available at <http://www.multichannel.com/article/CA6417227.html> (21 February 2007).

Heclo, H. 1978: 'Issue networks and the executive establishment'. In A. King (ed.), *The New American Political System*. Washington, DC: American Enterprise Institute, 87–124.

Herman, E. and McChesney, R. 1997: *The Global Media: The New Missionaries of Global Capitalism*. London: Cassell.

Hesmondhalgh, D. 2002: *The Cultural Industries*. London: Sage.

Hesmondhalgh, D. 2005: 'Media and cultural policy as public policy: the case of the British Labour Government'. In *International Journal of Cultural Policy* 11(1), 1–13.

Hewitt, P. and Jowell, T. 2002: 'A summary of our proposals'. Available at <http://www.archive2.official-documents.co.uk/document/cm55/5508-iii/550800.html> (10 October 2006).

Hewlett, S. 2006: 'The devil in the detail'. *MediaGuardian.co.uk*, 15 March Available at <http://www.guardian.co.uk/uk_news/story/0,,1731278,00.html> (16 March 2006).

Hewlett, S. 2007: 'Media FAQ'. *Media Guardian*, 22 January.

Hoekstra, P. 2006: 'Roles and responsibilities of the media with respect to unauthorized disclosures of classified information', House Permanent Select Committee on Intelligence, 26 May. Available at <http://www.fas.org>.

Hoppe, R. 1999: 'Policy analysis, science and politics: from "speaking truth to power" to "making sense together"'. In *Sci Public Policy* 26(3), 201–10.

Horwitz, R. 1989: *The Irony of Regulatory Reform: The Deregulation of American Telecommunications*. Oxford: Oxford University Press.

Horwitz, R. 2004: 'On media concentration and the diversity question'. Available at <http://communication.ucsd.edu/people/HORWITZ/onmedia.pdf> (27 October 2006).

House of Commons Culture, Media and Sport Committee 2002: Examination of Witnesses, 5 March. Available at <http://www.publications.parliament.uk/pa/cm200102/cmselect/ cmcumeds/539/2020501. Htm> (12 December 2004).

House of Commons Culture, Media and Sport Committee 2006a: *Analogue Switch-Off*, second report of 2005–6, Vol. 1. HC 650–I. London: TSO.

House of Commons Culture, Media and Sport Committee 2006b: *Analogue Switch-Off*, second report of 2005–6, Vol. 2. HC 650–II. London: TSO.

Hoynes, W. 1994: *Public Television for Sale: Media, the Market and the Public Sphere*. Boulder: Westview Press.

Huck, P. 2006: 'US tries to break the language barrier'. *Media Guardian*, 8 May.

Humphreys, P. 1996: *Mass Media and Media Policy in Western Europe*. Manchester: Manchester University Press.

Hundt, R. 1996: 'Statement of Chairman Reed Hundt regarding agreement on DTV standard', 25 November. Available at <http://www.fcc.gov/Speeches/Hundt/spreh652.txt> (28 February 2007).

Hutchison, D. 1999: *Media Policy*. Oxford: Blackwell.

IFPI 2006: *The Recording Industry 2006: Piracy Report*. London: IFPI.

Iosifidis, P. 2006: 'Digital switchover in Europe'. In *International Communication Gazette* 68(3), 249–68.

Ireland, D. 2005: 'The man who would destroy PBS'. *LA Weekly*, 1 July.

Jaenicke, D. 2000: 'New Labour and the Clinton Presidency'. In D. Coates and P. Lawler (eds), *New Labour in Power*. Manchester: Manchester University Press, 32–48.

Jakubowicz, K. 2004: 'Another threat to public service broadcasting'. In *Intermedia* 32(1), April, 20–3.

Jarvis, J. 2004: 'The shocking truth about the FCC: censorship by the tyranny of the few'. *BuzzMachine*, 15 November. Available at <http://www.buzzmachine.com/archives/2004_11_15.html> (18 December 2006).

Jessop, B. 2004: Comments on 'New Labour's double-shuffle'. Available at <eprints.lancs.ac.uk/236/01/E-2004e_Hall-Shuffle.doc> (10 May 2007).

Jobs, S. 2007: 'Thoughts on music'. Apple.com, 6 February. Available at <http://www.apple.com/hotnews/thoughtsonmusic/> (12 March 2007).

Joint Commenters 2003: Comments of Fox, NBC and Viacom in the matter of the 2002 Biennial Regulatory Review, FCC 02–277, 2 January.

Joint Committee on the Draft Communications Bill 2002: *Draft Communications Bill, Vol. I – Report*. HL Paper 169–I, HC 876–I. London: TSO.

Jones, N. 2000: *Sultan of Spin: Media and the New Labour Government*. London: Orion.

Jordan, G. 1990: 'Sub-Governments, Policy Communities and Networks: Refilling the Old Bottles?' In *Journal of Theoretical Politics* 2(3), 319–38.

Jordan, G. and Richardson, J. 1982: 'The British policy style or the logic of negotiation?' In J. Richardson (ed.), *Policy Styles in Western Europe*. London: George Allen & Unwin, 80–110.

Jowell, T. 2003: Speech to IPPR Convention on Public Service Communications, 15 January. Available at <http://www.culture.gov.uk/NR/rdonlyres/A482D2E9–C6E5–4097–8E24–3930F34194EF/0/TJowellspeechIPPR15103.pdf> (21 November 2006).

Jowell, T. 2005: Keynote speech to the Royal Television Society, 15 September. Available at <http://www.culture.gov.uk/Reference_library/Minister_Speeches/Tessa_Jowell/tessa_jowell_rts_speech.htm> (3 February 2007).

Jowell, T. 2006: 'The politics and economics of digital'. Speech to the Royal Television Society, 14 September. Available at <http://www.culture.gov.uk/Reference_library/ Minister_Speeches/Tessa_Jowell/dcms_jowell_rts_speech.htm> (27 October 2006).

Keay, D. 1987: 'Aids, education and the year 2000 – An interview with Margaret Thatcher'. *Woman's Own*, 31 October, 8–10.

Kelly, G., Mulgan, G and Muers, S. 2002: *Creating Public Value: An Analytical Framework for Public Service Reform*. London: Strategy Unit, Cabinet Office.

Kincaid, C. 2005: 'Paying for PBS with poor people's money', 22 July, *AIM Media Monitor*. Available at <http://www.aim.org/media_monitor/A3860_0_2_0_C/> (22 February 2007).

Kiss, J. 2006: 'UK internet body applauds BBC licence fee decision'. *MediaGuardian.co.uk*, 22 December. Available at <http://media.guardian.co.uk/bbc/story/0,,1977767,00.html> (13 February 2007).

Klinenberg, E. 2007: *Fighting for Air: The Battle to Control America's Media*. New York: Metropolitan Books.

Klontzas, M. 2006: 'Digitalisation and the BBC: the net effect'. Paper presented to the COST A20 Conference on 'The Impact of the Internet on the Mass Media in Europe', 26–28 April 2006, Delphi.

Konz, K. 2005: *Report of Review of Alleged Actions Violating The Public Broadcasting Act of 1967, as Amended*. Report No. EPB503–602. Washington, DC: Office of Inspector General.

Krasnow, E. and Longley, L. 1978: *The Politics of Broadcast Regulation*, 2nd edn. New York: St Martin's Press.

Kristol, I. 2003: 'The neoconservative persuasion'. *Weekly Standard*, 25 August 8(47).

Labaton, S., Manly, L. and Jensen, E. 2005: 'Republican chairman exerts pressure on PBS, alleging biases'. *New York Times*, 2 May.

Labour Party 1995: *Communicating Britain's Future*. London: Labour Party.

Labour Party 2001: *Ambitions for Britain*. Labour's manifesto 2001. London: Labour Party.

Labour Party 2005: *Britain: Forward Not Back*. London: Labour Party 2005.

Larner, W. 2003: 'Guest editorial'. In *Environment and Planning D: Society and Space* Vol. 21, 509–12.

Lasswell, H. 2003 [1951]: 'The policy orientation'. In S. Braman (ed.), *Communication Researchers and Policy-Making*. Cambridge: MIT Press, 85–104.

Leahy, P. 2001: Statement to Senate Judiciary Committee hearing on 'Online Entertainment and Copyright Law', 3 April. Available at <http://judiciary.senate.gov/member_statement.cfm?id=198&wit_id=50> (18 February 2007).

Leigh, D. and Evans, R. 2005: 'Files show extent of Murdoch lobbying'. The *Guardian*, 3 January.

Lessig, L. 2004: *Free Culture: The Nature and Future of Creativity*. New York: Penguin.

Lewis, J. 2003: 'Facts in the line of fire'. The *Guardian*, 6 November.

Leys, C. 2001: *Market-Driven Politics: Neoliberal Democracy and the Public Interest*. London: Verso.

Lichtenberg, J. 1990: 'Foundations and limits of freedom of the press'. In J. Lichtenberg (ed.), *Democracy and the Mass Media*. Cambridge: Cambridge University Press, 102–35.

Liebling, A. J. 1964 [1961]: *The Press*. New York: Ballantine.

Lindblom, C. 1980: *The Policy-Making Process*, 2nd edn. Englewood Cliffs: Prentice Hall.

Liptak, A. 2006: 'Gonzales says prosecutions of journalists are possible'. *New York Times*, 22 May.

Littleton, C. 1999: 'Blighty yucks save mighty bucks'. *Variety*, 12–18 April.

Livingstone, S., Lunt, P. and Miller, L. 2006: *Citizens and Consumers: Discursive Debates during and after the Communications Act 2003*. SCARR Working Paper 2006/10. Available at <http://www.kent.ac.uk/scarr/papers/Livingstone%20Wk%20Paper10.(2).pdf> (20 December 2006).

Lloyd, J. 2004: *What the Media are Doing to our Politics*. London: Constable & Robinson.

Lowi, T. 1979: *The End of Liberalism: The Second Republic of the United States*, 2nd edn. New York: Norton.

Luckhurst, T. 2007: 'Licence to kill: how No 11 nobbled the BBC'. *The Independent*, 21 January.

Machet, E. and Robillard, S. 1998: *Television and Culture: Policies and Regulation in Europe*. Dusseldorf: European Institute for the Media.

Majone, G. 1996: *Regulating Europe*. London: Sage.

Majure, R. 2001: Comments to FCC roundtable discussion on media ownership policies, 29 October. Available at <http://www.fcc.gov/realaudio/tr102901.pdf> (10 October 2006).

Maney, K. 2007: 'Download biz has to change or sing a swan song'. *USA Today*, 14 February.

Marsh, D. 2002: 'Pluralism in the study of British politics: it is always the Happy Hour for men with money, knowledge and power'. In C. Hay (ed.), *British Politics Today*. Cambridge: Polity, 14–37.

Marsh, D. and Rhodes, R. (eds) 1992: *Policy Networks in British Government*. Oxford: Oxford University Press.

Martin, K. 2005: Comments to the Open Forum on Decency, Senate Committee on Commerce, Science and Transportation, 29 November. Washington, DC: US Government Printing Office.

Martin, K. 2006: Written statement to Senate Committee on Commerce, Science & Transportation, 12 September. Available at <http://commerce.senate.gov/public/_files/MartinStatement.pdf> (15 December 2006).

May, C. 2006: 'The denial of history: reification, intellectual property rights and the lessons of the past. In *Capital & Class* 88, spring, 33–56.

McCain, J. 1998: Comments to the 'Transition to HDTV' hearing, Senate Committee on Commerce, Science and Transportation, 8 July. Available at <http://commerce.senate.gov/hearings/0708mcc.pdf> (5 January 2007).

McCain, J. 2004: Comments to the 'Completing the digital television transition' hearing, Senate Committee on Commerce, Science and Transportation, 9 June. Available at <http://commerce.senate.gov/hearings/testimony.cfm?id=1220&wit_id=2546> (5 March 2007).

McCain, J. 2005: 'Introduction of the Save Lives Act of 2005', 14 June. Available at <http://mccain.senate.gov/press_office/view_article.cfm?ID=163> (3 March 2005).

McCallister, M. no date: 'The financial interest and syndication rules'. New York: Museum of Broadcast Communications. Available at <http://www.museum.tv/archives/etv/F/htmlF/financialint/financialint.htm> (2 November 2006).

McChesney, R. 1999: 'Noam Chomsky and the struggle against neoliberalism'. *Monthly Review* 50, 1 April.

McChesney, R. 2000: *Rich Media, Poor Democracy*. New York: The New Press.

McChesney, R. 2003: 'Theses on media deregulation'. In *Media, Culture and Society* 25(1), 125–33.

McChesney, R. 2004: *The Problem of the Media*. New York: Monthly Review Press.

McChesney, R. and Scott, B. 2005: 'Cleaning up TV'. *Detroit Free Press*, 27 March.

McCleary, P. 2005: 'Swearing by free speech'. *Columbia Journalism Review*, 18 February.

McConnell, B. 2000: 'Chairman in waiting'. *Broadcasting & Cable*, 18 December.

McCullagh, D. 2004: 'House panel approves copyright bill', CNet News.com, 31 March. Available at <http://news.com.com/2100-1028-5182898.html> (5 April 2004).

McCullagh, D. 2005: 'New law cracks down on P2P pirates', CNet News.com, 27 April. Available at <http://news.com.com/2100-1028_3-5687495.html> (10 January 2007).

McGuigan, J. 2005: 'Neo-liberalism, culture and policy'. In *International Journal of Cultural Policy* 11(3), 229–41.

McQuail, D. 1992: *Media Performance*. London: Sage.

McQuail, D. 2000: *Mass Communication Theory*, 4th edn. London: Sage.

McQuail, D. 2005: *Mass Communication Theory*, 5th edn. London: Sage.

Messerlin, P. 2000: 'Regulating culture: has it "Gone with the Wind"?' Conference proceedings, *Achieving Better Regulation of Services*. Canberra: 26–7 June. Available at <http://www.pc.gov.au/research/confproc/abros/abros.pdf> (3 November 2006), 287–318.

Meyer, C. 2006: 'We know better than the courts'. In *British Journalism Review* 17(3), September, 27–32.

Miami Herald vs. Tornillo 1974: 418 US 241.

Milbank, D. 2003: 'Curtains ordered for media coverage of returning coffins'. *Washington Post*, 21 October.

Miliband, R. 1973: *The State in Capitalist Society*. London: Quartet.

Mill, J. S. 1989 [1851]: *On Liberty*. Cambridge: Cambridge University Press.

Miller, T., Govil, N., McMurria, J., Maxwell, R., Wang, T. 2005: *Global Hollywood 2*. London: British Film Institute.

Mills, C. W. 1956: *The Power Elite*. London: Oxford University Press.

Mitchell, N. 1997: *The Conspicuous Corporation: Business, Public Policy, and Representative Democracy*. Ann Arbour: University of Michigan Press.

Moore, M. 1995: *Creating Public Value: Strategic Management in Government*. Cambridge, MA: Harvard University Press.

Moran, M. 2003: *The British Regulatory State: High Modernism and Hyper-Innovation*. Oxford: Oxford University Press.

Morgan, O. 1999: 'Did Blair order Byers' block?'. *Observer*, 21 November.

Morgan, O. 2006: 'Uncle Sam faces a world trade backlash'. *Observer*, 30 July.

Morris, N. and Waisbord, S. 2001: 'Introduction: rethinking media globalization and state power'. In N. Morris and S. Waisbord (eds), *Media and Globalization: Why the State Matters*. Lanham: Rowman and Littlefield, vii–xvi.

Morrison, D. and Svennevig, M. 2002: 'From "public interest" to "social importance": the public's view of the public interest'. In D. Tambini and C. Heyward (eds), *Ruled by Recluses? Privacy, Journalism and the Media after the Human Rights Act*. London: IPPR, 65–79.

Mosco, V. 2004: *The Digital Sublime*. London: MIT Press.

Mundy, A. 2003: 'Put The Blame on Peggy, Boys'. *Cable World*, 30 June.

Murdoch, J. 2005: Speech to the 2005 European Audio Visual Conference, Liverpool, 21 September. Available at <http://www.culture.gov.uk/about_dcms/eupresidency2005/broadcasting.htm#documents> (18 October 2005).

Murdoch, R. 1998: Presentation by Rupert Murdoch to the European Audiovisual Conference, 6 April. Available at <http://europa.eu.int/eac/speeches/murdoch_en.html> (April 22, 2004).

Murdock, G. 1990: 'Redrawing the map of the communications industries: concentration and ownership in the era of privatization'. In M. Ferguson (ed.), *Public Communication: The New Imperatives*. London: Sage, 1–15.

Murdock, G. and Golding, P. 1999: 'Common markets: corporate ambitions and communication trends in the UK and Europe'. In *Journal of Media Economics* 12(2): 117–32.

Napoli, P. 1999: 'Deconstructing the diversity principle'. In *Journal of Communication* 49(4), 7–34.

Napoli, P. 2001: *Foundations of Communications Policy*. Cresskill: Hampton Press.

National Commission on Terrorist Attacks 2004: *Final Report of the National Commission on Terrorist Attacks Upon the United States*. Available at <http://a257.g.akamaitech.net/7/257/2422/05aug20041050/www.gpoaccess.gov/911/pdf/fullreport.pdf> (15 January 2005).

Neil, G. 2006: 'Assessing the effectiveness of UNESCO's new Convention on Cultural Diversity'. In *Global Media and Communication* 2(2), 257–62.

Nesta (National Endowment for Science, Technology and the Arts) 2006: *Creating Growth: The State of the UK's Creative Industries*. London: Nesta.

New America Foundation 2004: *The Decline of Broadcasters' Public Interest Obligations*, 29 March. Washington, DC: New America Foundation.

News International 2002: Response to the Draft Communication Bill, August. Available at <http://www.communicationsact.gov.uk/responses_organisations.html> (18 December 2006).

Newspaper Society 2006: 'Blair bows to pressure over FOI consultation', news release, 27 November. Available at <http://www.newspapersoc.org.uk/Default.aspx?page+2101> (11 January 2007).

New York Times vs. Sullivan 1964: 376 US 254.

New York Times vs. United States 1971: 403 US 713.

New York Times 2005: 'Politicizing public broadcasting'. *New York Times*, 4 May.

Novak, R. 2005: 'War waged over public broadcasting'. *Chicago Sun Times*, 21 July.

NUJ (National Union of Journalists) 2004: 'The public interest'. Available at <http://www.nuj.org.uk/inner.php?docid=224> (27 January 2005).

Nye, J. 2004: *Soft Power: The Means to Success in World Politics*. New York: Public Affairs.

Ofcom 2004: *Ofcom Review of Public Service Television Broadcasting. Phase 2 – Meeting the Digital Challenge*. London: Ofcom.

Ofcom 2005: *Ofcom Broadcasting Code*. London: Ofcom. Available at http://www.ofcom.org.uk/tv/ifi/codes/bcode/ofcom-broadcasting-code.pdf (4 November 2006).

Ofcom 2006a: *Review of Media Ownership Rules*, 14 November. London: Ofcom.

Ofcom 2006b: *The International Communications Market 2006*. London: Ofcom.

Ofcom 2007: *A New Approach to Public Service Content in the Digital Media Age*. London: Ofcom.

Ohmae, K. 1995: *The End of the Nation State*. London: Harper Collins.

Oliver, L. 2005: 'Explanation of Vote of the United States on the Convention on the Protection and Promotion of the Diversity of Cultural Expressions', 20 October. Available at <http://usinfo.state.gov/xarchives/display.html?p=washfile-english&y=2005&m=October&x=20051020170821GLnesnoM3.670901e-02&t=gi/gi-latest.html> (19 March 2007).

O'Malley, T. 2006: 'Keep broadcasting public'. Speech to Campaign for Press and Broadcasting conference on the BBC White Paper, 1 April. Available at http://keywords.dsvr.co.uk/freepress/body.phtml?category=&id=1269 (10 June 2006).

O'Neill, O. 2002: 'Licence to Deceive', Reith Lecture 5. Available at <http://www.bbc.co.uk/radio4/reith2002/> (8 November 2006).

O'Neill, O. 2004: *Rethinking Freedom of the Press*. Dublin: Royal Irish Academy. Available at <http://www.ria.ie/reports/pdf/pressfreedom.pdf> (13 November 2006).

ONS (Office for National Statistics) 2006: 'International transactions of the UK film and television industries, 2005', 10 November. Available at <http://www.statistics.gov.uk/pdfdir/ukft1106.pdf> (2 February 2007).

OSI (Open Society Institute) 2005: *Television across Europe: Regulation, Policy and Independence*. Budapest: OSI.

Ó Siochrú, S., Girard, B., Mahan, A. 2002: *Global Media Governance: A Beginner's Guide*. Lanham: Rowman & Littlefield.

Panitch, L. and Leys, C. 1997: *The End of Parliamentary Socialism: From New Left to New Labour*. London: Verso.

Papathanassopoulos, S. 2002: *European Television in the Digital Age*. Cambridge: Polity.

Parry, R. 2006: 'Bush and the limits of debate'. *Consortium News*, 16 January.

Patent Office, DTI and DCMS 2005: 'Government response to the recommendations of the Creative Industries Forum on Intellectual Property'. Available at <http://www.culture.gov.uk/NR/rdonlyres/12017917-F8D5-4CEB-B898-D839BFC90DA7/0/GovernmentResponse_CIF.pdf> (18 February 2007).

PBS 2005: 'Public broadcasting hearings'. *News Hour with Jim Lehrer*, 11 July. Available at <http://www.pbs.org/newshour/bb/congress/july-dec05/cpb_7-11.html> (4 October 2006).

PCC (Press Complaints Commission) 2006: *Editors' Code of Practice*. London: PCC. Available at <http://www.pcc.org.uk/assets/111/Code_aug_06.pdf> (15 October 2006).

Peck, J. and Tickell, A. 2002: 'Neoliberalizing space'. In N. Brenner and N. Theodore (eds), *Spaces of Neoliberalism: Urban Restructuring in North American and Western Europe*. Oxford: Blackwell, 2002, 33–57.

Peters, B. G. 1986: *American Public Policy: Promise and Performance*, 2nd edn. Basingstoke: Macmillan.

Peters, J. D. 2004: 'The "Marketplace of Ideas": A History of the Concept'. In A. Calabrese and C. Sparks (eds), *Toward a Political Economy of Culture: Capitalism and Communication in the Twenty-first Century*. Lanham: Rowman & Littlefield, 65–82.

Petley, J. 1999: 'The regulation of media content'. In J. Stokes and A. Reading (eds), *The Media in Britain: Current Debates and Developments*. Basingstoke: Palgrave, 143–57.

PMOS (Prime Minister's Official Spokesperson) 2004: Press Briefing, 26 February. Available at <http://www.number-10.gov.uk> (10 January 2007).

Powell, M. 1998a: 'The public interest standard: a new regulator's search for enlightenment'. Speech to the American Bar Association, 5 April. Available at <http://www.fcc.gov/Speeches/Powell/spmkp806.html> (22 February 2005).

Powell, M. 1998b: Statement of Commissioner Powell in relation to 1998 Biennial Regulatory Review, 12 March. Available at <http://www.fcc.gov/Speeches/Powell/Statements/stmkp805.html> (18 December 2006).

Powell, M. 2000: Statement of Commissioner Powell in relation to 1998 Biennial Regulatory Review, 20 June. Available at <http://www.fcc.gov/Speeches/Powell/Statements/2000/stmkp013.html> (18 December 2006).

Powell, M. 2002: 'Digital television: the time is now', speech to Association for Maximum Television DTV Update Conference, Washington, DC, 22 October. Available at <http://www.fcc.gov/Speeches/Powell/2002/spmkp211.html> (28 February 2007).

Powell, M. 2003a: 'Statement of Chairman Michael K. Powell', 2 June, available at <http://hraunfoss.fcc.gov/edocs_public/attachmatch/FCC-03-127A3.doc> (10 December 2006).

Powell, M. 2003b: 'Should limits on broadcast ownership change?' *USA Today*, 21 January.

Powell, M. 2004a: 'The reluctant planner'. *Reason*, December. Available at <http://www.reason.com/news/show/36417.html> (18 December 2006).

Powell, M. 2004b: 'FCC takes next steps to promote digital TV transition', statement by Michael Powell, 7 September 2004. Available at <http://hraunfoss.fcc.gov/edocs_public/attachmatch/DOC-250542A2.pdf> (18 December 2006).

Prescott, M. and Hellen, N. 1996: 'Blair to oppose tighter rules on media ownership'. *Sunday Times*, 7 April.

Press Complaints Commission (PCC) 2006: *Editors' Code of Practice*, ratified 7 August. Available at <http://www.pcc.org.uk/cop/practice.html> (17 November 2006).

Price, L. 2006: 'Rupert Murdoch is effectively a member of Blair's cabinet'. The *Guardian*, 1 July.

Price, M. and Verhulst, S. 2000: 'In search of the self: charting the course of self-regulation on the Internet in a global environment'. In C. Marsden (ed.), *Regulating the Global Information Society*. London: Routledge, 57–78.

Prometheus Radio Project vs. FCC 2004: US Court of Appeals for the Third Circuit, 24 June. Available at <http://www.ca3.uscourts.gov/opinarch/033388p.pdf> (10 September 2006).

Puttnam, D. 2006: 'Nation of fools'. *New Statesman*, 4 December.

Raboy, M. 2002: 'Media policy in the new communications environment'. In M. Raboy (ed.), *Global Media Policy in the New Millennium*. Luton: University of Luton Press, 3–16.

Rayment, S. 2006: 'Ministers seeking tougher sanctions on whistleblowers'. *Daily Telegraph*, 4 July.

RCFP (Reporters Committee for Freedom of the Press) 2005: *Homefront Confidential*, 6th edn. Arlington, VA: RCFP.

Red Lion Broadcasting Co. vs. Federal Communications Commission 1969: 395 U.S. 367.

Rhodes, R. 1990: 'Policy networks: a British perspective'. In *Journal of Theoretical Politics* 2(3), 293–317.

Rhodes, R. 1994: 'The hollowing out of the state: the changing nature of the state in Britain'. In *Political Quarterly*, 65(2), 138–51.

RIAA (Recording Industry of America) 2005: Motion Picture and Music Companies File Brief for U.S. Supreme Court Review of Grokster, Morpheus Case, press release, 25 January. Available at <http://www.riaa.com/news/newsletter/012505.asp> (28 June 2005).

Rich, F. 2004a: 'The great indecency hoax'. *New York Times*, 28 November.

Rich, F. 2004b: 'Bono's new casualty: "Private Ryan"'. *New York Times*, 21 November.

Richards, E. 2005: 'Ofcom annual lecture – trends in television, radio and telecoms', 20 July. Available at <http://www.ofcom.org.uk/media/speeches/2005/07/nr_20050720> (18 December 2006).

Riding, A. 2005: 'U.S. stands alone on UNESCO cultural issue'. *New York Times*, 13 October.

Rintouls, J. 2006: 'Big chill: how the FCC's indecency decisions stifle free expression, threaten quality television and harm America's children', 23 September. Washington, DC: Center for Creative Voices in Media. Available at <http://www.creativevoices.us> (15 December 2006).

Rosen, J. 2004: 'Bush to press: "You're assuming you represent the public. I don't accept that"'. *Pressthink*, 25 April. Available at <http://journalism.nyu.edu/pubzone/weblogs/pressthink/2004/04/25/bush_muscle.html> (5 January 2007).

Rosen, J. 2005: 'In the press room of the White House that is post press'. *Pressthink*, 25 February. Available at <http://journalism.nyu.edu/pubzone/weblogs/pressthink/2005/02/25/wht_prss.html> (5 January 2007).

Rumsfeld, D. 2006: 'War in the information age'. *Los Angeles Times*, 23 February.

Sabbagh, D. 2005: 'Switchover to digital television doesn't add up'. *The Times*, 23 September.

Sarasohn, J. 2004: 'Time Warner lobbyist's pay turns heads'. *Washington Post*, 15 April.

Scannell, P. 1989: 'Public service broadcasting and modern public life'. In *Media, Culture and Society* 11, 135–66.

Scannell, P. and Cardiff, D. 1990: *A Social History of British Broadcasting: Volume One 1922–1939 Serving the Nation*. Oxford: Blackwell.

Schatz, A. 2005: 'Why indecency, once hot at FCC, cooled'. *Wall Street Journal*, 16 November.

Scherer, M. 2005: 'The FCC's cable crackdown', salon.com, 30 August. Available at <http://dir.salon.com/story/news/feature/2005/08/30/fcc_indecency/> (30 October 2006).

Schiller, D. 2000: *Digital Capitalism: Networking the Global Market System*. London: MIT Press.

Schiller, H. 1971: *Mass Communications and American Empire*. Boston: Beacon Press.

Schumacher, T. 1995: ' "This is a sampling sport": digital sampling, rap music and the law in cultural production'. In *Media, Culture and Society* 17(2), 253–73.

Schwartz, J. 2004: 'States may be aiming at web file sharing'. *New York Times*, 17 March.

Seaton, J. 1998: 'A fresh look at freedom of speech'. In *Political Quarterly* 69(b), 117–29.

Seymour-Ure, C. 1987: 'Media policy in Britain: now you see it, now you don't'. In *European Journal of Communication* 2, 269–88.

Seymour-Ure, C. 1991: *The British Press and Broadcasting since 1945*. Oxford: Blackwell.

Shane, S. 2006: 'U.S. reclassifies many documents in secret review'. *New York Times*, 21 February.

Shannon, V. 2007: 'Record labels contemplate unrestricted digital music'. *New York Times*, 23 January.

Silverstone, R. 2005: 'The sociology of mediation and communication'. In C. Calhoun, C. Rojek and B. Turner (eds), *The Sage Handbook of Sociology*. London: Sage, 188–207.

Simpson, J. 2006: 'Here's the news . . . we won't be broadcasting'. *Telegraph. co.uk*, 15 January. Available at <http://www.telegraph.co.uk/opinion/main. jhtml?xml=/opinion/2006/01/15/do1501.xml&sSheet=/opinion/2006/01/15/ixopinion.html> (8 January 2007).

Siwek, S. 2006: *Copyright Industries in the U.S. Economy: The 2006 Report*, prepared for the International Intellectual Property Alliance, November. Available at <http://www. iipa.com/pdf/2006_siwek_full.pdf> (15 January 2007).

Smith, M. 2004: 'Conclusion: defining New Labour'. In S. Ludlam and M. Smith (eds), *Governing as New Labour: Policy and Politics under Blair*. Houndmills: Palgrave Macmillan, 211–25.

Spar, D. 2001: *Ruling the Waves: Cycles of Discovery, Chaos, and Wealth from the Compass to the Internet*. New York: Harcourt.

Sparks, C. 1998: *Communism, Capitalism and the Mass Media*. London: Sage.

Sparks, C. forthcoming: *Development, Globalization and the Media*. London: Sage.

Spitzer, R. 1993: 'Introduction' to R. Spitzer (ed.), *The Media and Public Policy*. Westport: Praeger, 1–18.

Stanyer, J. 2002: 'Politics and the media: a loss of political appetite?' In *Parliamentary Affairs* 55(2), 377–88.

Stanyer, J. 2003: 'Politics and the media: a breakdown in relations for New Labour'. In *Parliamentary Affairs* 56(2), 309–21.

Starr, P. 2004: *The Creation of the Media: Political Origins of Modern Communications*. New York: Basic Books.

Stein, L. 2004: 'Understanding speech rights: defensive and empowering approaches to the First Amendment'. In *Media, Culture and Society* 26(1), 103–20.

Strange, S. 1996: *The Retreat of the State: The Diffusion of Power in the World Economy*. Cambridge: Cambridge University Press.

Streeter, T. 1996: *Selling the Air: A Critique of the Policy of Commercial Broadcasting in the United States*. Chicago: University of Chicago Press.

Sunstein, C. 2001: 'The future of free speech'. In *The Little Magazine* 2(2), April.

Tabb, W. 2003: 'After neoliberalism?'. In *Monthly Review Online*, June. Available at <http://www.monthlyreview.org/0603tabb.htm> (10 August 2006).

Tambini, D. 2001: 'Through with ownership rules? Media pluralism in the transition to digital'. In D. Tambini (ed.), *Communications: Revolution and reform*. London: IPPR, 21–44.

Teinowitz, I. 2007: 'Bush proposes steep cut to PBS funding'. *TV Week*, 5 February.

Television 1999: 'Export or die', journal of the Royal Television Society, October.

Thompson, J. 1995: *The Media and Modernity: A Social Theory of the Media*. Cambridge: Polity.

Towse, R. 2006: *Copyright and Creativity: Cultural Economics for the 21st Century*, inaugural lecture, 30 May, Erasmus University, Rotterdam.

Tracey, M. 1998: *The Decline and Fall of Public Service Broadcasting*. Oxford: Oxford University Press.

Trinity Mirror 2002: Response to the consultation on media ownership rules. Available at <http://www.culture.gov.uk/PDF/media_own_trinity_mirror. PDF> (15 December 2006).

TRP (Television Research Partnership) 2005: *Rights of Passage: British Television in the Global Market*. London: TRP.

Truman, D. 1951: *The Governmental Process: Political Interests and Public Opinion*. New York: Knopf.

Tryhorn, C. 2005: 'Public broadcast funding "may breach EU rules"'. *MediaGuardian.co.uk*, 3 March. Available at <http://media.guardian.co.uk/broadcast/story/0,,1429820,00.html> (7 July 2006).

Tunstall, J. and Machin, D. 1999: *The Anglo-American Media Connection*. Oxford: Oxford University Press.

Turner, T. 2004: 'My big beef with big media'. *Washington Monthly*, July/August.

Turow, J. 1999: *Media Today: an Introduction to Mass Communication*. Boston: Houghton Mifflin.

UNESCO 2004: *Preliminary Draft on a Convention of the Protection of the Diversity of Cultural Contents and Artistic Expressions*. Paris: UNESCO. Available at <http://portal.unesco.org/culture/en/file_download.php/382d

532908a5a5258ffe1465d5a15c2aEng-PreliminaryDraftConv-conf201-2.pdf>
(15 January 2005).

UNESCO 2005: *Convention on the Protection and Promotion of the Diversity of Cultural Expressions 2005*. Paris: UNESCO. Available at <http://unesdoc.unesco.org/images/0014/001429/142919e.pdf> (18 December 2005).

USTR (United States Trade Representative) 2003: 'Free trade in services: opening dynamic new markets, supporting good jobs', 31 March. Available at <http://www.ustr.gov/assets/Document_Library/Fact_Sheets/2003/asset_upload_file40_4138.pdf> (4 May 2004).

USTR 2004: *The President's Trade Policy Agenda*, March. Available at <http://www.ustr.gov/assets/Document_Library/Reports_Publications/2004/2004_Trade_Policy_Agenda/asset_upload_file931_4751.pdf> (4 May 2004).

Venturelli, S. 1998: *Liberalizing the European Media: Politics, Regulation and the Public Sphere*. Oxford: Clarendon.

Vogel, S. 1996: *Freer Markets, More Rules: Regulatory Reform in Advanced Industrial Countries*. Ithaca: Cornell University Press.

Waller, E. 2001: 'Free speaker'. *PACT magazine*, July.

Watt, N. 2004: 'New poll reveals public mistrust'. The *Guardian*, 30 January.

Watts, R. 2006: 'Advertising regulator caves in to industry'. *Food Magazine*, 22 May.

WDM (World Development Movement) 2003: 'GATS: from Doha to Cancun', 25 August. Available at <http://www.wdm.org.uk/resources/reports/trade/GATSfromdohatocancun20092003.pdf> (18 January 2004).

Webster, F. 2006: *Theories of the Information Society*, 3rd edn. London: Routledge.

Wells, M. and Cassy, J. 2002: 'TV stations up for grabs'. The *Guardian*, 8 May.

Wells, M. and Wray, R. 2002: 'Easing the reigns on media moguls'. The *Guardian*, 8 May.

Wells, M., Cassy, J. and White, M. 2001: 'Murdoch TV hopes put on hold'. *The Guardian*, 27 November.

White, J. and Graham, B. 2005: 'Military says it paid Iraq papers for news'. *Washington Post*, 3 December.

Wilby, P. 2006: 'A predatory capitalist who stifles competition and delivers mediocrity'. The *Guardian*, 22 November.

Wilkinson, R. 2000: 'New Labour and the global economy'. In D. Coates and P. Lawler (eds), *New Labour in Power*. Manchester: Manchester University Press, 136–48.

Williams, G. 2004: 'US government global audio-visual strategy document leaked'. *SpinWatch*, 15 December. Available at <http://www.spinwatch.org/content/view/14/8/> (28 January 2005).

Williams, G. 2005a: 'Lobbying government: is Sky the limit?' *SpinWatch*, 17 January. Available at <http://www.spinwatch.org/content/view/123/8/> (10 July 2005).

Williams, G. 2005b: 'What is the "Television without Frontiers" directive?' *Free Press*, October.

Williams, K., Floud, J., Johal, S., Leaver, A. and Phillips, R. 2006: 'Stressed by choice: a business model analysis of the BBC'. CRESC working paper series, No. 22. Milton Keynes: Centre for Research on Socio-Cultural Change.

Williams, R. 1974: *Television: Technology and Cultural Form*. London: Fontana.

Winship, M. 2007: 'Back to the future of public broadcasting', *BuzzFlash*, 30 January. Available at <http://www.buzzflash.com/articles/contributors/755> (7 February 2007).

Woodward, S. 2006: Comments in *From TV without Frontiers to the Audiovisual Media Services Directive*. London: Westminster Media Forum.

WTO (World Trade Organization) 1998: *Audiovisual Services: Background Note by the Secretariat*, 15 June, S/C/W/40. Available via <http://www.wto.org/English/tratop_e/serv_e/audiovisual_e/audiovisual_e.htm> (16 January 2003).

WTO 2000: *Communication from the United States: Audiovisual and Related Services*, 18 December, S/CSS/W/21. Available via <http://www.wto.org/English/tratop_e/serv_e/audiovisual_e/audiovisual_e.htm> (16 January 2003).

Yang, C. 2004: 'Oh Janet, what hast thou wrought'. *Business Week*, 22 March.

Zeff, J. 2005: Comments in *Analogue Switch-off and New Digital Services*. Westminster Media Forum Seminar Series. London: Westminster Media Forum, 8–10.

Zoellick, R. 2003: 'America will not wait for the won't-do countries'. *Financial Times*, 22 September.

Index